An Arbor Cookin'!

Over 600 recipes
including 70 from
Ann Arbor restaurants

Proceeds to benefit the Ronald McDonald House

All proceeds of this special cookbook are given to the Ann Arbor Ronald McDonald House®. For additional copies of the cookbook, use the order blank in the back of the book or write directly to:

Cookbook
c/o Ronald McDonald House®
1600 Washington Heights
Ann Arbor, MI 48104
(313-994-4442)

The price of each book is $12.00. If ordering the cookbook, add $2.00 for postage and handling. Checks should be made payable to Arbor House.

FIRST PRINTING	5,000 copies	November, 1985
SECOND PRINTING	5,000 copies	April, 1986
THIRD PRINTING	5,000 copies	May, 1987

ISBN 0-9618208-0-2

Printed by
Mitchell-Shear, Inc.
Ann Arbor, Michigan

COOKBOOK COMMITTEE

Editor .... Ann Betz
Assistant Editor .... Susan Hurwitz
Marketing .... Leo Carey
                                                    Karen Feldenzer
                                                    Nancy Schuon
                                                    Nancy Schleicher
                                                    Janet Shatusky
                                                    Susan Wall
Cover Design and Artwork .... Carol Salter
                                                    (Blixt & Assoc.)
Consultant .... Linda Kelleher
Members .... Carol Colby
                                                    Susan Custer
                                                    Sue Henderson
                                                    Sally Johnston
                                                    Kay Moler
                                                    Mary Waskerwitz

Acknowledgement . . .
We extend grateful appreciation to all who helped in the production of this cookbook and especially Blixt and Associates for donating the cover, advertising and marketing services; The University of Michigan Hospitals Pediatric Neurology Section for Apple Macintosh Computer use; and John Van Roekel and The University of Michigan College of Engineering for use of an Apple LaserWriter printer. We also wish to thank McDonald's for their continued support. A warm thank you, too, to all of the busy Ann Arbor cooks (many affiliated with Mott Hospital) who submitted their prized recipes. We apologize that some had to be omitted because of space and duplications. We also thank the area restaurants and shops for freely sharing some of their kitchen secrets.

FORWARD

Ann Arbor's Cookin'! is a unique collection of treasured recipes that reflect both the casual lifestyle and stimulating atmosphere of Ann Arbor.

Start your football Saturday with a tailgate picnic of Maize 'N Blueberry Bread, Beer Cheese Soup and Hot Cajun Sausage Calzone. Later that evening (after a victory, of course), test your culinary skills with Herbed Duckling With Strawberry Sauce and Royal Marble Cheesecake for dessert. For a quick and easy Sunday brunch, enjoy Pumpkin Pancakes or Ham and Cheese Strata, each of which requires only minutes of preparation. And, for your convenience, we have included valuable tips and comments provided by many of our talented cooks for whom these recipes are tried and tested favorites.

One of the highlights of *Ann Arbor's Cookin'!* is an extensive selection of recipes from popular area restaurants and shops. This unprecedented collection will undoubtedly enhance any cook's repertoire and reputation. In addition, we have also included a chapter just for children, featuring recipes meant to foster a child's creativity as well as be both fun to prepare and good to eat. While most of these recipes are "kid-proof", they do require some adult help and supervision during their preparation. We're certain, though, that the kids won't need any help when these treats are ready to be eaten.

So cook, eat and enjoy! We're sure that *Ann Arbor's Cookin'!* will prove to be a valuable addition to your kitchen library.

TABLE OF CONTENTS

Appetizers and Beverages

APPETIZERS

Gouda Bread Appetizer

1 package refrigerator crescent rolls
Dijon mustard
1 package Gouda cheese
1 egg white, slightly beaten
Sesame seeds

Preheat oven to 350 degrees. Lay out crescent rolls pinching edges together to prevent cheese from escaping. Brush a layer of Dijon mustard over dough. Place Gouda in center. Pull up edges of dough and pinch together. Brush egg whites all around and sprinkle with sesame seeds. Bake until brown, about 20 minutes. (8+ servings)

DEE CORNISH

Olive-Cheese Snacks

1-1/2 cups grated sharp cheddar cheese
1/2 cup mayonnaise
1 cup sliced pitted ripe olives
1/2 cup thinly sliced green onions
1/2 to 1 teaspoon curry powder
1 loaf sliced party rye bread

In a medium bowl combine all ingredients except bread. Spread on bread and place on a cookie sheet. Broil until bubbly. Serve hot. Stores in refrigerator for 2 weeks or freezer for 1 month. Flavor improves with age. (30-40 servings) *"Easy to fix ahead; these are always a hit!"*

DIANE AR

The Babe's Rarebit

1 pound cheddar cheese (cut into chunks)
2 egg whites, slightly beaten
1 cup milk
1/2 teaspoon salt
1/2 teaspoon pepper
1/2 teaspoon dry mustard
1 tablespoon cornstarch, dissolved in 2 tablespoons water
Toast or crackers
Paprika

Melt the cheese either in a double boiler or in the microwave. Stir frequently or use electric beater frequently during the entire time. Add egg whites and stir. Add milk and stir. Add salt and pepper, dry mustard and cornstarch mixture. Stir frequently until bubbly. Serve warm on toast or crackers. Sprinkle with paprika. May be served for breakfast or as an appetizer. *"Recipe from Dr. Paul Ertel's mother who was nicknamed 'The Babe'."*

INTA ERTEL

3

Sausage Bread

1 loaf frozen bread dough
1 pound bulk Italian sausage
2 cups grated mozzarella cheese

Let dough rise and spread into square on cookie sheet with buttered hands as if making a square pizza. Preheat oven to 350 degrees. Remove casing from sausage if not bulk; brown and crumble. Drain grease. Spread on dough. Sprinkle cheese over dough. Roll like a jelly roll and let set about 30 minutes. Bake for 25-30 minutes until golden brown. Slice and enjoy. (10 pieces per loaf)   SANDY EILER

Bacon Roll-Ups

1/2 pound bacon
1 package refrigerated crescent rolls
1/2 cup sour cream
1/2 teaspoon garlic powder

Heat bacon in a skillet until limp. Spread rolls on board and cut each into thirds. Spread mixture of sour cream and garlic on rolls. Put small piece of bacon in middle and wrap roll over to seal. Bake at 350 degrees until golden. May be baked ahead and rewarmed, but best served out of oven.
                                                   SANDY EILER

Scallop Ceviche

1 pound bay scallops, uncooked
Juice of 12 limes (fresh if possible)
3 bay leaves
1/4 teaspoon white pepper
1/3 cup chopped green onion
Crushed red pepper to taste
Salt to taste
2 tomatoes, chopped
1/2 cup sliced stuffed olives
1 (4-ounce) can chopped green chilies
Lettuce

Put scallops in a glass jar, cover with lime juice and refrigerate overnight. Drain lime juice and add remainder of ingredients. Cover and refrigerate for at least 1 hour. Remove bay leaves and liquid and serve on lettuce. Ceviche will keep several days in refrigerator. Serve as a salad as written or serve as an appetizer on corn tortillas, quartered and fried in lard.
                                                  JANET GILSDORF

Hot Asparagus Canapes

20 slices bread (cut off edges)
2 ounces Danish bleu cheese
1 (8-ounce) package cream cheese, softened
1 egg
20 spears asparagus (blanched and cooled)
1/2 cup margarine

Flatten bread with a rolling pin. Blend cheeses and egg in a mixing bowl and spread onto bread. Roll a spear of asparagus on each slice. Brush roll with margarine. Freeze on cookie sheet with seam down. When slightly frozen, cut each roll in thirds, then freeze in bag until needed. Bake 15-20 minutes at 400 degrees.

MARY WASKERWITZ

Caponata on Crackers

4 tablespoons olive oil
1 small eggplant, cut in 1-inch cubes (not peeled)
1 medium yellow onion, chopped fine
1/3 cup chopped celery
1 cup tomato puree
1/3 cup chopped, pitted green (and/or ripe) olives
4 anchovy fillets, minced
2 tablespoons capers
1 tablespoon sugar
2 tablespoons red wine vinegar
1/2 teaspoon salt
Freshly ground pepper
1 tablespoon minced parsley

Heat 3 tablespoons oil in a large heavy saucepan for 1 minute over moderately high heat. Add eggplant and saute, stirring occasionally for about 10 minutes or until golden and slightly translucent. Add remaining oil, onion and celery and stir-fry for 5-8 minutes or until pale golden. Add remaining ingredients except for parsley. Cover and simmer for 1-1/4 to 1-1/2 hours or until quite thick, stirring occasionally. Mix in parsley, cool to room temperature. Taste for salt and adjust as needed. Serve at room temperature as a spread for crackers. Will keep in refrigerator for a week.

CAROLIN DICK

Eggplant Appetizer

1 large or 2 medium eggplants
3-4 tablespoons olive oil
2-3 green peppers
1 (28-ounce) can tomatoes (use juice)
1 tablespoon vinegar
2-3 cloves garlic, minced
Salt and pepper to taste
Pita bread

Peel and chop eggplant into 1/4-inch pieces. Soak 2-3 hours at room
temperature or overnight in refrigerator in salted water (weighted down with
heavy plate). Squeeze out water. Heat oil and saute in a skillet. Chop green
pepper. Fry with above. Remove from oil to cool. Chop tomatoes, fry with
juice in above oil until it forms a paste. In a bowl combine vinegar, garlic, salt
and pepper to taste. Pour over eggplant. Serve cold with Pita bread triangles as
a dip or spread. Flavor improves with age.

DIANE AR

Pita Spinach Triangles

1 (16-ounce) container sour cream
1 package Knorr vegetable soup mix
4 Pita breads, cut into 4 triangles
1 (10-ounce) package fresh spinach, washed and crisped

Combine sour cream and soup mix in a bowl. Refrigerate several hours.
Spread inside of Pita bread with sour cream and soup mixture. Stuff with
spinach.

JERI KELCH

Cheese Ball or Spread

1 (8-ounce) package cream cheese
1/2 cup butter
1 (4-ounce) package Treasure Cove bleu cheese
1 small onion, grated with juice
1 teaspoon prepared mustard
1-3 teaspoons paprika (for color)

Soften cream cheese and butter in a mixing bowl. Blend in other ingredients
until smooth. Let harden in refrigerator; then shape into a ball or use as a
spread. Serve at room temperature.

PHYLLIS ASKEW

Hawaiian Cheeseball

2 (8-ounce) packages cream cheese, softened
1 tablespoon minced onion (dehydrated)
1 tablespoon Lawrey's seasoned salt
1/2 green pepper, chopped small
1 (13-ounce) can drained crushed pineapple
1/4 cup ground pecans (optional)

In a large mixing bowl combine all ingredients together except pecans. (It will be very stiff at first.) May add pecans into mixture or sprinkle over ball. Refrigerate overnight.

CATHERINE ANDREA

Mock Boursin
(Herb Cream Cheese)

1 cup unsalted butter
2 (8-ounce) packages cream cheese
1 clove garlic, minced
1 tablespoon parsley, chopped
1 teaspoon chives
1 teaspoon thyme
1 teaspoon dill
1/2 teaspoon pepper
1/2 teaspoon marjoram

Whip butter and cream cheese together in a mixing bowl. Put all ingredients in food processor and mix thoroughly. Should be made at least 12 hours ahead. Serve with crackers.

PRUE ROSENTHAL

Herb Curry Veggie Dip

1 cup mayonnaise
1/2 cup sour cream
1 teaspoon crushed mixed Herbes from Provence
1/4 teaspoon salt
1/8 teaspoon curry powder
1 tablespoon parsley, chopped
1 tablespoon grated onion
1-1/2 teaspoons lemon juice
1/2 teaspoon Worcestershire sauce
Assorted vegetables

Mix all dip ingredients in a bowl and chill well, preferably at least 2 hours. Suggested veggies for dip: Carrot sticks, mushrooms, zucchini sticks, celery. (4-10 servings)

CAROLINE BLANE

7

Chicken Liver Pate

1/2 cup butter
1 pound chicken livers
1/4 pound mushrooms, chopped
1/4 cup chopped parsley
1/4 cup chopped shallots
1/2 teaspoon thyme leaves
1/2 teaspoon salt
2 tablespoons brandy or Madeira
1/2 cup red wine
1 cup butter (cut into chunks)
Condiments: Crackers, toast or French bread

Melt butter in a skillet over medium heat. Add chicken livers, mushrooms, parsley, shallots, thyme and salt. Cook, stirring often until livers are browned on all sides but still slightly pink in the middle. In a small pan over low heat, warm brandy and set aflame; pour over livers and shake pan until flame dies. Add wine and heat to simmering. Remove from heat and let mixture cool to room temperature. Puree livers and cooking juices in food processor. Add butter blending until smooth. Pour into decorative mold (4-5 cups size) if desired. Cover and refrigerate until firm. Serve with crackers, toast or French bread baguettes. (Makes 1-1/2 pounds)

JANET GILSDORF

Humus

2-3 cloves garlic, minced
1 (20-ounce) can chick-peas (rinsed and drained)
Juice of 1 lemon
1/4 cup imported tahini
Water
Olive oil (optional)
Garnish: Parsley, tomatoes or onions
Pita bread

Add minced garlic to blender or food processor. Mash chick-peas with fork and add in small quantities to blender. Blend after each amount. Add lemon juice as more chick-peas are added. Add tahini; keep blending. Depending on texture, add water and/or olive oil. Garnish with chopped parsley, tomatoes or onions. Serve with torn Pita bread for dipping. (8-10 servings)

DIANE BAKER
GINA ARANKI

Quick and Easy Vegetable Dip

1 cup small curd cottage cheese
1 cup mayonnaise
1 cup sour cream
1 (1-ounce) package Hidden Valley original recipe dressing mix

Put all ingredients into a mixing bowl. Blend with mixer and chill before serving. (Makes 3 cups of dip)

Note: Other flavors of Hidden Valley dressing mix may be used for a different flavor.

MARY KAY BARRY

Skinny Dilly Dip

1/2 cup sour cream
1/2 cup mayonnaise
1 tablespoon chopped green onions
1 tablespoon dried parsley
1 teaspoon Lawrey's seasoned salt
2 teaspoons dried dill weed (not seed)
1/2 teaspoon Worcestershire sauce
1 teaspoon Accent
2 drops Tabasco sauce
Raw vegetables

Mix all ingredients in a bowl except veggies. Chill. Serve with raw veggies. Will keep refrigerated several days.

SUSAN LIPTON

Spinach Dip

1 cup mayonnaise
1 pint sour cream
1 tablespoon chopped onion (dehydrated)
1 package Knorr vegetable soup mix
1 (10-ounce) package frozen chopped spinach (thawed, drained well and squeezed)

Blend all ingredients together in a bowl the day before. Serve in a hollowed-out round loaf of bread.

CATHERINE ANDREA

Vegetable Dip I

1 cup mayonnaise
1 cup sour cream
1 teaspoon dill weed
1 tablespoon dried green onion
1 tablespoon Beau Monde seasoning
1 tablespoon dry parsley flakes

Mix all ingredients well in a medium-sized bowl and refrigerate, preferably overnight. *"Wonderful with any kind of vegetable, especially carrots, cauliflower and broccoli."*

RIE HARDING

Vegetable Dip II

1 (10-ounce) package frozen chopped spinach
1-1/2 cups mayonnaise
1/2 cup sour cream
1/2 cup chopped green onions
1/4 cup dried parsley flakes
1 teaspoon lemon juice

Drain and squeeze spinach. Place in a mixing bowl and blend in other ingredients. Serve with crackers or bread.

SALLY WHITE

Mustard Dip

1/3 cup water
1/3 cup white vinegar
1/4 cup vegetable oil
3 tablespoons light soy sauce
2-3 tablespoons dry mustard
2 tablespoons sesame oil
2 tablespoons dry sherry
1 tablespoon sugar
Salt to taste

Combine all ingredients and use as dipping sauce for artichokes, pea pods or cooked shrimp.

RUTH LUM

Avocado and Crabmeat Dip

2 large avocadoes (mushy green ones)
1 (8-ounce) package cream cheese, softened
1 teaspoon Worcestershire sauce
1/4 cup sour cream
1 tablespoon grated onion
1/4 teaspoon MSG
1 tablespoon lemon juice
1/4 teaspoon salt
1 (6-ounce) can crabmeat

Combine all above ingredients in a mixing bowl. Serve with corn chips.

MARY CORNILS

Crabmeat Spread With Cocktail Sauce

SPREAD:
1 (8-ounce) package cream cheese
1 (6 to 8-ounce) can crabmeat
1 tablespoon mayonnaise

Allow cream cheese to soften. Drain crabmeat. Mix cream cheese, crabmeat and mayonnaise in a bowl. Form into a ball. Make a thumbprint or indentation in the middle.

COCKTAIL SAUCE:
1/2 cup ketchup
Horseradish to taste

Mix ketchup and horseradish. Pour cocktail sauce over top of ball. Serve spread on wheat crackers.

MARY KAY BARRY

Salmon Cheeseball

1 (16-ounce) can salmon
1 (8-ounce) package cream cheese, softened
1 tablespoon lemon juice
2 teaspoons grated onion
1 teaspoon horseradish
1/4 teaspoon salt
1/4 teaspoon liquid smoke
1/2 cup chopped nuts
1 tablespoon parsley flakes

Drain and flake salmon. Remove bones. Combine salmon with all ingredients except nuts and parsley in a large bowl. Chill 8 hours. Roll on foil in nuts/parsley. Serve with Old London Bacon Rounds.

DEBBIE ARTHURS

Shrimp Mold

1-1/2 envelopes Knox gelatin dissolved in 1/2 cup cold water
1 (10-ounce) can hot tomato soup, undiluted
1 (8-ounce) package cream cheese (at room temperature)
1 cup mayonnaise
2 (4-1/4 ounce) cans shrimp
1-1/2 cups (total) onion and celery, chopped fine

Mix all of the above ingredients together in a bowl and put in an oiled mold or Pyrex dish. Refrigerate. Serve with crackers.

CATHY MARTINEZ

Shrimp and Crab Dip

1 (4-1/4 ounce) can shrimp
1 (6-ounce) can crabmeat
6 ounces cream cheese
1 tablespoon mayonnaise
1/2 teaspoon paprika
1/4 teaspoon salt
1/8 teaspoon pepper
1 teaspoon Worcestershire sauce
2 teaspoons lemon juice
1 teaspoon prepared mustard
Sour cream to taste

Rinse and pick over shrimp and crabmeat. Set aside. Mix all other ingredients thoroughly. Add shrimp and crabmeat and more salt and pepper if desired. *"Good with raw veggies or crackers."*

SUSAN HURWITZ

Bagna Cauda

3/4 cup olive oil (good quality extra virgin)
3 tablespoons butter
2 teaspoons garlic, minced
8-10 flat anchovy fillets, chopped
1 teaspoon salt
Assorted raw vegetables (artichokes, asparagus, broccoli, cauliflower, zucchini) and/or cubes of French bread

Heat the oil and butter in a saucepan till the butter is liquified and barely begins to foam. Add garlic and saute very briefly. Add the anchovies and cook over very low heat, stirring frequently, till anchovies dissolve into a paste. Add the salt, stir and use as dip for vegetables and/or bread.

JANET GILSDORF

Hot Clam Dip

1/4 pound butter
1 pound Velveeta cheese
4 tablespoons sherry
1 cup ketchup
1 green pepper, chopped
1 onion, chopped
2 cups minced clams, drained
1/8 teaspoon cayenne pepper
Bread cubes

In a large saucepan melt the butter and cheese. Add sherry. Add remaining ingredients. Cook 10 minutes. Serve hot in a fondue dish and dip large dried bread cubes into it.

MARY WASKERWITZ

Crab Fondue

5-6 ounces cheddar cheese
1 (8-ounce) package cream cheese
1/4 cup half-and-half cream
1/2 teaspoon Worcestershire sauce
1/4 teaspoon garlic salt
1/2 teaspoon cayenne pepper
2 packages Wakefield crab (thawed) or Wakefield artificial crab

Melt cheddar and cream cheese together in a fondue pot. Stir in rest of ingredients.

AILEEN SEDMAN

Hot Crab Dip

1 (8-ounce) package cream cheese, softened
1 (6-ounce) can crabmeat
1 teaspoon prepared horseradish
2 tablespoons milk
1/4 teaspoon salt
1/8 teaspoon pepper
2 tablespoons minced onion
1/3 cup toasted slivered almonds

Preheat oven to 375 degrees. Combine all ingredients except almonds. Spread in a small baking/serving dish or glass pie pan. Sprinkle with slivered almonds. Bake for about 15 minutes. Serve with crackers.

SHELLY ROBBINS

Brook Lodge Hors D'Oeuvre Teri-Yaki

1 pound boneless chicken breast meat*
2/3 cup soy sauce (preferably a good Japanese brand)
1/4 cup dry sherry or dry white wine
3 tablespoons sugar
1/2 teaspoon freshly grated gingerroot
Juice of 1/2 lemon
1 finely minced garlic clove
Fresh pineapple chunks (or canned)
Melted butter

Cut chicken in pieces 1 x 2 x 1/4-inch thick. Mix all ingredients together except pineapple and butter and marinate meat in the sauce several hours or overnight. Can be frozen in the marinade. Thread meat on bamboo picks with a pineapple chunk on one or both ends. Can refrigerate at this point until use. Brush lightly with melted butter. Broil under medium heat, just heating them through and until lightly browned. (8-12 servings) *Preparing double amount needed and freezing remainder in marinade gives you a great appetizer for unexpected guests.*

*Can use beef instead of chicken.

NANCY FEKETY

Sesame-Curry Chicken Wings

1 pound chicken wings, halved
SAUCE:
2 tablespoons soy sauce
2 tablespoons sherry
3 tablespoons sesame oil
2 tablespoons brown sugar
2 packets Sweet N' Low (or 1 tablespoon honey)
1-2 tablespoons curry powder
1 tablespoon sesame seeds
1 tablespoon finely chopped peanuts

Preheat oven to 400 degrees. Mix all sauce ingredients well in a bowl and coat wings. Bake the wings for 30 minutes basting every 8 minutes. Broil 3-4 minutes before serving. (1-4 servings)

KAREN EPSTEIN
JOHN TOWNSEND

14

Sweet-Sour Meatballs

6 slices dry bread (or 3/4 cup bread crumbs)
2 pounds ground beef
1/2 cup onion, finely chopped
1/2 teaspoon garlic salt
1/4 teaspoon pepper
1 teaspoon salt
2 eggs, slightly beaten

In a large mixing bowl, combine all meatball ingredients and make into balls. Fry in a skillet or bake at 350 degrees in a large roasting pan for 20 minutes, until browned and nearly cooked through. (Makes about 50 meatballs) Make sauce.

SAUCE:
1 (28-ounce) can tomatoes, drained
1 cup brown sugar
1/4 cup vinegar
1/2 teaspoon salt
1 teaspoon grated onion, chopped
10 gingersnaps, crushed

In a large saucepan heat sauce ingredients to boiling. Mix with meatballs and bake in covered casserole at 325 degrees for 45 minutes. Best when reheated and served the next day. *"I serve in a crockpot as an appetizer."*

LYNN HUTZEL

Sausage-Cheese Balls

3 cups Bisquick
1 pound bulk pork sausage
4 cups grated cheddar cheese (about 1 pound)
2/3 cup grated Parmesan cheese
3/4 teaspoon rosemary leaves (do NOT omit)
3/4 teaspoon parsley flakes

Preheat oven to 350 degrees. Mix all ingredients in a large bowl and shape into 1-inch balls. Place on ungreased 15 x 10-inch jelly roll pan (if not, the grease makes a mess in the oven!). Bake until brown, about 20-25 minutes. (Makes 6 dozen)

COOK'S TIP: I prefer hot spicy sausage and I find this is not good made in the microwave. They freeze well and can be reheated in the microwave if you are willing to serve them a bit chewy.

NIKKI WOODROW-RUTH
SISTER CAROLE FEDDERS

15

Cheese and Spinach Puffs

1 (10-ounce) package thawed chopped spinach
1/2 cup chopped onion
2 slightly beaten eggs
1/2 cup grated Parmesan cheese
1/2 cup grated cheddar cheese
1/2 cup bleu cheese salad dressing
1/4 cup butter or margarine, melted
1/8 teaspoon garlic powder
1 (8-1/2 ounce) package corn muffin mix

In a saucepan, combine spinach and onion; cook according to spinach package directions. Drain well, pressing out excess liquid. Combine eggs, cheeses, salad dressing, butter or margarine and garlic powder. Add spinach mixture and muffin mix; mix well. Cover and chill. Shape dough into 1-inch balls. Cover and chill till serving time. (Or, place in a freezer container; seal, label, and freeze.) Preheat oven to 350 degrees. Place chilled or frozen puffs on a baking sheet. Bake till light brown; chilled puffs for 10-12 minutes, frozen puffs for 12-15 minutes. Serve warm. (Makes about 60 puffs)

KAY BRABEC

Hot Cheese Balls

1 cup freshly grated Monterey Jack cheese plus 1 cup freshly grated cheddar or longhorn cheese (or 2 cups any combination)
2 tablespoons all-purpose flour
1 cup fresh cracker crumbs (made from pulverized saltines)
3 egg whites
1-1/2 teaspoons prepared mustard
Vegetable oil for deep frying
Salt to taste

Combine the grated cheeses and flour in a deep mixing bowl. Spread the cracker crumbs on a piece of wax paper . Beat the egg whites until stiff. Scoop the egg whites over the cheese mixture with a rubber spatula, add the mustard, and fold the ingredients together. To make each cheese ball, scoop up a heaping tablespoon of the cheese mixture and mold into a ball. Slide the cheese ball off the spoon onto the cracker crumbs and coat evenly. Transfer the cheese ball to a piece of wax paper and set it aside. Shape and coat the remaining balls. At this stage, the cheese balls can be draped with wax paper and refrigerated for up to 12 hours or overnight. Pour vegetable oil into a deep fryer or large heavy saucepan to a depth of about 3 inches. Heat the oil to 375 degrees. Deep fry the cheese balls, 4-5 at a time, about 3 minutes or till they are crisp and golden brown. Transfer to a paper towel to drain. (Makes 2 dozen 1-inch balls)
"Arrange the cheese balls on a heated platter, season with salt and serve while warm with drinks."

KAY BRABEC

Artichoke Pie

2 (8-ounce) cans unmarinated artichoke hearts
2 cups mayonnaise
2 cups grated Parmesan cheese
1-2 cloves garlic, minced
1 round sourdough bread

Preheat oven to 350 degrees. In a food processor blend artichoke hearts, mayonnaise, Parmesan and garlic. Hollow out bread and set aside pieces. Fill middle of bread with artichoke mixture. Bake for 20 minutes. Use pieces of bread for dipping.

GRACE BRAND

Artichoke Nibbles

1 (14-ounce) can artichoke hearts
1 tablespoon butter
1 small onion, chopped
1 clove garlic, minced
4 eggs
1/4 cup fine bread crumbs
Salt and pepper to taste
1/8 teaspoon oregano
1/8 teaspoon Tabasco sauce
2 tablespoons minced parsley
1/2 pound grated cheddar cheese (approximately 2 cups)
1 tablespoon Italian salad dressing (or plain oil)

Preheat oven to 325 degrees. Chop artichoke hearts and set aside. In a small skillet saute onions and garlic over medium heat about 5 minutes or until limp. Set aside. Beat eggs. Add crumbs, salt and pepper, oregano, Tabasco and remainder of ingredients. Spread evenly in a greased 7 x 11-inch pan. Bake for 30 minutes or until slightly browned and set. Let cool and then cut into squares. (Makes 30-40 squares) *Mild but delicious tidbits one cannot stop nibbling."*

STEFANIE O'TOOLE

Stuffed Mushrooms I

1 pound large mushrooms (about 16)
1/2 cup part-skim ricotta cheese
1/2 cup fresh white bread crumbs (about 1 slice)
1 tablespoon minced parsley
1/2 teaspoon salt
1/2 teaspoon oregano leaves
1/8 teaspoon pepper
1 egg
1 tablespoon grated Parmesan cheese

Preheat oven to 350 degrees. Trim ends of mushroom stems; remove stems and mince. Reserve mushroom caps. In a medium bowl, combine minced stems, ricotta cheese and remaining ingredients, except Parmesan cheese. Spoon mixture into caps. In a 12 x 8-inch baking dish, arrange stuffed mushrooms, stuffing side up. Sprinkle mushrooms with Parmesan cheese. Bake in oven 20 minutes or until golden. Serve hot or chilled. (Makes 16 hors d'oeuvres; 30 calories each)

JOYCE LONDON

Stuffed Mushrooms II

1 pound large fresh mushrooms
2 tablespoons chopped shallots
6 tablespoons butter
1 cup Pepperidge Farm herb seasoned stuffing mix
1/2 cup chicken broth
1/4 teaspoon garlic salt

Preheat oven to 350 degrees. Clean mushrooms and remove stems. Saute chopped stems and shallots in 4 tablespoons butter. Stir in stuffing mix, chicken broth and garlic salt. Stuff mushrooms with mixture and place in a glass pie plate with 2 tablespoons butter. Bake for 20 minutes or until done. May be prepared ahead and refrigerated or frozen. (4-6 servings)

CAROL MESZAROS

Zucchini Appetizers

1 cup Bisquick
4 cups zucchini, thinly sliced
1/4 cup grated Parmesan cheese
2 tablespoons parsley
1/2 teaspoon salt
1/2 cup chopped onion
1/2 cup salad oil
1 teaspoon oregano
Dash of pepper
1/4 teaspoon garlic powder
4 eggs, beaten

Preheat oven to 350 degrees. Mix all ingredients in a large bowl. Spread into a greased 9 x 11-inch pan. Bake for 45 minutes. Serve hot or cold.

MARY WASKERWITZ

Bourbon Slush

1 (6-ounce) can frozen orange juice
1 (6-ounce) can frozen lemonade
2 juice cans water
2 juice cans bourbon
7-Up

Mix all ingredients together except 7-Up and pour into a covered refrigerator container. Place in freezer. (Alcohol prevents total freezing.) When ready to serve, scoop out 1/2 glass of slush and fill remainder of glass with 7-Up.

NANCY MORIN

Brandy Slush

7 cups water
2 cups sugar
4 green tea bags
1 (12-ounce) can frozen orange juice, undiluted
1 (12-ounce) can frozen lemonade, undiluted
1 quart brandy
7-Up, Squirt or Fresca

Mix water and sugar together in a saucepan; bring to a boil. Steep green tea bags in sugar mixture for 5 minutes. Let cool. Then add the orange juice, lemonade and brandy. Place and store in freezer. (This does not freeze hard.) To serve add one part slush to one part 7-Up, Squirt or Fresca.

CAROL COLBY

Slush

1 cup sugar
7 cups water
1 (12-ounce) can orange juice
1 (6-ounce) can limeade
2 cups vodka
7-Up

Boil sugar and water in a large pot. Add concentrated orange juice and limeade. Cool. Add vodka. Put in freezer. Will develop icy/slushy consistency. Combine with 7-Up in individual glasses at serving time, stirring a bit before serving.

STEPHANIE MINERATH

Mulled Cider With Calvados

16 cups apple cider (4 quarts)
1/2 cup dark brown sugar
16 cardamom pods (crushed)
24 allspice (whole)
2 teaspoons nutmeg
3 (1-inch) slices peeled fresh ginger
1 orange cut into 8 slices (not wedges)
32 whole cloves
4 whole sticks of cinnamon
2 cups calvados or applejack brandy

In a large stainless steel or enamaled saucepan or stockpot, combine cider, brown sugar, cardamom pods, allspice, nutmeg and ginger. In each orange slice insert 4 whole cloves in the peel, and insert half a cinnamon stick in the center of the slice. Add slices to cider and simmer uncovered for 15 minutes. Add calvados or applejack and heat for 3 minutes more or until hot enough. *"This makes alot, and recipe can be cut in half. It is wonderful on a cold day."*

SUSAN HURWITZ

Sangria

1 ounce lime juice
1 ounce lemon juice
2 tablespoons sugar
1-1/2 ounces brandy
1-1/2 ounces Cointreau
13 ounces red wine
8 ounces soda water
Fruit slices (such as oranges, pineapple, strawberries)

Combine everything together except soda water and fruit slices. Refrigerate overnight. Add soda water and fruit just before serving. (4 servings)

CAROLINE BLANE

White Punch

2 quarts white wine
1 quart vodka
2 quarts gingerale
2 (46-ounce) cans pineapple grapefruit juice

Combine all chilled ingredients in a punch bowl.

MARY WASKERWITZ

Strawberry Daiquiris

1 (6-ounce) can frozen lime juice
1-1/4 cups light rum
3 cups fresh strawberries (hulled)
1/2 cup sugar
Finely crushed ice, about 4 cups
Whole strawberries for garnish

Place lime juice, rum, strawberries and sugar in food processor. Cover and blend until smooth. Place crushed ice in pitcher and stir in pureed mixture. Serve in stemmed glasses garnished with whole strawberries. May be prepared in advance and kept in freezer until 20 minutes before serving. (6 servings)

ANN BETZ

Christmas Cheer

3 quarts cranberry juice cocktail
1 fifth Southern Comfort
6 ounces fresh or frozen lime juice
1-2 sliced limes

Combine all chilled ingredients in a large punch bowl. Float a large ice mold with lime slices on top. (Serves 40) *This makes a very seasonally attractive punch with punch!"*

DIANE AR

Christmas Punch

1 (46-ounce) can pineapple juice
4 (6-ounce) cans frozen limeade concentrate
2 quarts 7-Up
1 fifth vodka
1 pint frozen strawberries

In a punch bowl mix all ingredients together. *"A red ice mold looks nice in this."*

BARBARA LANESE

Holiday Punch

1 (6-ounce) can frozen orange juice
1 (6-ounce) can lemonade
3/4 cup lemon juice
1 fifth Southern Comfort
3 (32-ounce) bottles 7-Up
Slices of oranges
Red food coloring (optional)

Combine all chilled ingredients together in a punch bowl.

MARY WASKERWITZ

Pineapple, Banana and Orange Slush

6 cups water
4 cups sugar
1 (46-ounce) can pineapple juice
1 (12-ounce) can concentrated orange juice
7 bananas, mashed

Boil water and sugar together for 3 minutes. Cool. Mix together with the pineapple juice, orange juice concentrate and bananas. Freeze in flat pan.

TONIE LEEDS

Russian Tea

1/2 cup instant tea
2 cups Tang
1 cup sugar
1 (13-ounce) can dry lemonade mix
1/2 teaspoon cinnamon
1/2 teaspoon cloves

Mix all ingredients together. Add 1 tablespoon to 1 cup of hot water, depending on the tartness you like.

SUE HENDERSON

23

BEVERAGES

Soups

SOUPS

Gazpacho

1 medium onion, chopped
1 medium cucumber, peeled and chopped
1 green pepper, chopped
1 clove garlic, minced
1/8 teaspoon basil
1/8 teaspoon oregano
1/8 teaspoon thyme
1/4 cup olive oil
1/4 cup wine vinegar
Sugar to taste
1 teaspoon salt
4-5 fresh tomatoes, chopped
1 cup tomato juice
Garnish: Cucumber, avocado, croutons
Sour cream

Blend all ingredients together in a blender or food processor. Allow to sit one hour. Garnish with a spear of cucumber, slice of avocado, seasoned croutons and top with a dab of sour cream. (2-4 servings)

ANN BETZ

White Gazpacho Soup

3 medium cucumbers
1 clove garlic, minced
3 cups chicken broth
2 cups sour cream
1 cup yogurt
3 tablespoons white wine vinegar
2 teaspoons salt
2 teaspoons pepper
4 medium tomatoes, peeled and chopped
1/2 cup chopped scallions, tops included
1/2 cup chopped parsley
3/4 cup toasted almonds or sunflower seeds

Peel and dice cucumbers. Blend with garlic and a small amount of chicken broth. Puree the mixture in food processor. Add remaining broth and blend thoroughly. Mix the sour cream and yogurt in a medium bowl and thin with 1/3 of the cucumber mixture. Season with vinegar, salt and pepper. Chill 6-8 hours. Serve in bowls garnished with tomatoes, scallions, parsley and nuts. (6 servings)

JANET GILSDORF

Carrot-Thyme Soup

6 cups chicken stock, canned
1-1/2 pounds carrots, peeled and sliced into 1-inch pieces
1 medium onion, chopped
3 tablespoons butter or margarine
1/2 cup heavy cream
1-1/2 tablespoons fresh thyme, minced (or 3/4 teaspoon dried)
Pinch of nutmeg
Salt and pepper to taste

Bring chicken stock to boil in a stockpot and add carrots. Simmer 20 minutes. Cool slightly and puree. Place back in pot. In another pan, cook onion in butter for 3 minutes. Add to stockpot. Add cream, thyme, nutmeg, salt and pepper. Simmer 5 minutes. *"This is wonderful hot or cold. It has a velvety texture that is great."*

SUSAN HURWITZ

Cold Broccoli Soup

2 tablespoons butter
1 large onion, chopped
1 (14-1/2 ounce) can chicken broth
2-1/2 cups potatoes, peeled and diced
Freshly ground pepper
2-1/2 cups broccoli, cut into pieces
Milk or cream
Freshly chopped parsley for garnish

In a large saucepan heat butter and cook onion until translucent. Add chicken broth, potatoes and pepper to taste. Cook over moderate heat 15 minutes. Add broccoli and continue cooking 15 more minutes. At this point broccoli and potatoes should be soft. Puree in food processor. Store in refrigerator until needed. Will keep 5 days in closed container. To serve, mix with equal amounts of milk and serve (for richer soup use 1/2 milk and 1/2 cream mixture). Garnish with parsley. (4 servings)

CAROLINE BLANE

Cream of Zucchini Soup

2 tablespoons butter
2 tablespoons chopped shallots
1 clove garlic, minced
1 pound sliced or grated zucchini
1 teaspoon curry powder
1/2 teaspoon salt
1/2 cup heavy cream
1-3/4 cups chicken broth
Chopped almonds (optional)
Sour cream (optional)

Place butter, shallots and garlic in a skillet. Add zucchini, cover and simmer 10 minutes. Place curry powder, salt, heavy cream and chicken broth in blender and blend 1/2 minute. Pour into zucchini mixture. Chill. Garnish top with toasted almonds or dollop of sour cream if desired.

NANCY HOPWOOD

Black Bean Soup

1 quart chicken or beef stock
1 cup dried black beans
1 ham hock (optional)
2 cloves garlic, minced
2 stalks celery, chopped
2 small onions, chopped
Salt and pepper to taste
1 bay leaf
Sour cream

In a soup pot combine the stock and dried beans; bring to a boil, cover and set aside for 1 hour. Add ham (optional), garlic, celery, onions, salt, pepper and bay leaf. Cover and simmer 2-3 hours (until beans are soft). Remove ham bone and bay leaf. Serve in soup bowls and garnish with a dollop of sour cream. (6 servings)

JANET GILSDORF

Chicken Soup

3-4 pounds chicken
Chicken feet
Gizzard and heart
3 quarts water
Salt to taste
1 onion, browned
1 carrot, sliced
1 stalk celery, diced
2 sprigs parsley

Cut chicken at joints. Scald and skin the feet and remove the nails. Extra chicken feet will enhance the flavor of the soup. If the flavor of the meat is to be retained, cover chicken with hot water. If you would rather save the flavor in the soup, cover chicken with cold water. Bring to a boil and do not skim. Simmer for an hour, then add rest of ingredients. When chicken is tender, remove the meat from soup. Strain soup and remove the fat. Chicken may be cooked the day before. Cool soup after straining and set in refrigerator. Before serving, lift off the hard layer of fat from top and serve soup hot.

BLANCHE EHRENKREUTZ

Meat Stock

3 pounds beef
Beef bone with marrow
3 quarts cold water
1 tablespoon salt
1 onion, diced
1 cabbage leaf
1 celery stalk, diced
2 sprigs parsley (or small parsnip)
2 carrots, diced
1 bay leaf

Bring the meat, bone and water to a boil in a soup pot. Do not skim. Simmer slowly for one hour until no more scum gathers at the top. Remove from heat and add 1 tablespoon of cold water. This will bring the fat to the top. The fat should be removed. Add rest of ingredients and continue to cook slowly until the meat is tender. Time of cooking will depend on the cut and quality of the meat. Strain soup and remove rest of fat. (Makes 3 pints of stock)

BLANCHE EHRENKREUTZ

Hot and Sour Soup

2 large dried black mushrooms*
6 tree ear mushrooms*
4 dried tiger lily stems*
1 tablespoon peanut, vegetable or corn oil
1/4 cup finely shredded pork
1 tablespoon light soy sauce
1/2 cup finely shredded bamboo shoots
5 cups good chicken broth
Salt to taste
2-3 tablespoons rice wine vinegar
1 teaspoon dark soy sauce
2 tablespoons cornstarch
3 tablespoons water
1/4 pound fresh tofu, cut in strips
2 eggs, lightly beaten
1 tablespoon sesame oil
1 teaspoon white pepper
2 tablespoons chopped scallions
Minced coriander for garnish

Place mushrooms, tree ears and tiger lily stems in a bowl. Cover with boiling water and let stand 15-30 minutes. Drain. Cut off stems and tough parts of tree ears. Cut mushrooms and tree ears in thin slices. Shred tiger lily stems with fingers. Heat wok or heavy skillet and when hot, add oil and shredded pork. Stir to separate and add light soy sauce. Add mushrooms, tree ears and tiger lily stems and bamboo shoots. Stir quickly, about 1 minute and add chicken broth and salt. Stir in vinegar and dark soy sauce. Combine cornstarch and water and stir into simmering broth. When slightly thickened, add bean curd, bring to boil and turn off heat. Let broth cool a bit so that eggs will not overcook when they are added. Add sesame oil and pepper. Stir to blend. After pouring soup in tureen, gradually add eggs in a thin stream, stirring. Sprinkle scallion and coriander on top. (6 servings)

*COOK'S TIP: Dried black mushrooms, tree ear mushrooms, tiger lily stems and tofu all available at Chinese grocery stores. (In Ann Arbor, Sing Tong Grocery Store in Maple Village.)

RHEKA BHISE

Susan's Vegetable Soup

3 quarts water
2-1/2 to 3 pounds chuck roast, cut into small chunks
2 cups carrots, sliced
1 large yellow onion, chopped
10 medium potatoes, peeled and diced
4 ribs celery, sliced
3/4 teaspoon thyme
1 teaspoon basil
10 (or more) black peppercorns
Salt to taste
4 whole cloves
1 quart ripe tomatoes, peeled (not juiced) and cut into quarters
2 cups corn (fresh or frozen)
1 (10-ounce) package frozen lima beans
1 cup green beans, cut up
Salt to taste
1/2 to 1 cup broken pasta (macaroni, rotini, etc.) (optional)

In a large stockpot, place water, meat, carrots, onions, potatoes, celery and spices. Simmer 1 hour. Add tomatoes, corn, lima beans, green beans and simmer another 1/2 hour. Add salt to taste. If you desire soup to be thicker, add broken pasta and cook only until pasta is done. Do not overcook.

SUSAN HURWITZ

Vegetable Barley Soup

3/4 cup barley
9 cups chicken stock
1-1/2 cups chopped onion
1 cup chopped carrot
1 cup sliced mushrooms
1/2 cup chopped celery
3 tablespoons butter
Salt and pepper to taste

Combine barley and 3 cups chicken stock. Cook on low heat for 1 hour, until liquid is absorbed. In a large covered saucepan or stockpot, cook onion, carrots, mushrooms and celery in butter until vegetables are softened. Add 6 cups (or more to taste) of chicken broth and simmer for 30 minutes. Add barley and simmer 5 minutes. Add salt and pepper to taste.

SUSAN HURWITZ

Corn Chowder

5 slices bacon, diced
1 onion, sliced in thin rings
2 cups creamed corn
1 cup diced cooked potatoes
1 (10-3/4 ounce) can cream of mushroom soup
2-1/2 cups milk
1 teaspoon salt and dash of pepper

Cook bacon in a large skillet. Remove all but 3 tablespoons of drippings. Saute onion. Add rest of ingredients. Heat and eat.

MARY WASKERWITZ

New England Corn Chowder

1/2 pound bacon, diced
1 medium onion, chopped (about 1/2 cup)
1/2 cup chopped celery, with tops
2 tablespoons all-purpose flour
4 cups milk (may use 2 cups skim milk plus 2 cans evaporated milk)
1 (16-ounce) can cream style corn
1 (16-ounce) can niblet corn
Salt and pepper to taste

In a large saucepan fry bacon until crisp; remove and drain. Pour all but 3 tablespoons drippings from pan. Add onion and celery to drippings; saute onion. Remove pan from heat; blend in flour. Cook over low heat briefly to heat through. Remove from heat and add milk. Boil and stir 1 minute. Stir in corn, salt and pepper; heat through. Stir in bacon. May sprinkle each serving with parsley. (6 servings)

PATTY PRUE

New England Clam Chowder

6 thin skinned potatoes, cut into 1-inch cubes (with skins)
7 (6-1/2 ounce) cans of chopped clams and their juices
1 (12-ounce) bottle of clam juice
1 (12-ounce) can of evaporated milk
1 cup milk
2 tablespoons all-purpose flour mixed with water to make a paste
2 tablespoons butter

Place potatoes in a large soup pot, cover with water. Boil until tender. Drain except for 2 cups, which will remain with the potatoes. Add the clams and clam juice to the potatoes and potato water. Bring to a boil. Then simmer for 20 minutes. Add evaporated milk and regular milk. Stir. Add flour paste and stir. Simmer for 30 minutes. Add butter. Stir. (8-10 servings) *"This is better when it is reheated 24 hours after you make it."*

DENISE CHARRON-PROCHOWNIK

33

SOUPS

Broccoli Soup I

2 (10-ounce) packages chopped broccoli (or 1 bunch fresh, sauteed)
2 (10-3/4 ounce) cans condensed cream of mushroom soup
2 soup cans of milk (2-2/3 cups)
1/2 cup dry white wine
4 tablespoons butter or margarine
1/2 teaspoon dried tarragon, crushed
Dash of white pepper

In a large saucepan, cook broccoli according to package directions. Drain. Add remaining ingredients and heat. (8 servings)   NANCY HOPWOOD

Broccoli Soup II

1 (10-ounce) package frozen broccoli
1/2 cup chopped onion
1 (14-1/2 ounce) can chicken broth
1/2 cup sliced almonds
2 tablespoons butter
2 tablespoons all-purpose flour
2 cups half-and-half cream (or 1 cup cream and 1 cup milk)
1 teaspoon salt
1/2 teaspoon basil
1/8 teaspoon white pepper

Combine broccoli, onions and broth in a saucepan. Heat to boiling; simmer 5 minutes. Cool slightly and blend in a blender with almonds until smooth. Melt butter; blend in flour with whisk and let bubble. Gradually stir in broccoli mixture, cream, salt, basil and pepper. Simmer 1 minute. (4-6 servings)
DIANE BAKER

Creamed Broccoli Soup

1 quart fresh broccoli heads, packed (2 bunches)
2/3 cup butter
1/3 cup all-purpose flour
2 cups hot chicken broth
Salt and white pepper to taste
3 tablespoons lemon juice
1 clove garlic, minced
1 tablespoon Worcestershire sauce
1/4 teaspoon Tabasco sauce

Saute washed broccoli in butter in a large skillet until soft. Blend in flour and simmer until smooth, stirring occasionally. Add remaining ingredients. Stir constantly until smooth and thick. Remove from burner. Process in blender. Return to pan to heat for serving or freeze for future use. (6 servings)
CAROLIN DICK

34

Noah's Favorite Cream of Broccoli Soup

4 cups fresh broccolli (stems peeled, flowerets separated from stems)
5 cups chicken stock
3 tablespoons butter or margarine
4 tablespoons all-purpose flour
1 cup half-and-half cream
2 cups milk, whole or skimmed
Salt and pepper to taste
Pinch of grated nutmeg

Slice stems and divide large flowerets into smaller ones. Place broccoli in saucepan with 3 cups chicken stock. Cover and cook until broccoli is tender. Set aside 1/2 cup flowerets to use as garnish. Strain most of liquid and set aside. Puree remaining broccoli. Melt butter or margarine. Whisk in flour and let bubble over medium heat for about 2-3 minutes. Stir in cream. Simmer, stirring for 3 minutes. Add milk and simmer 2 minutes. Stir in pureed broccoli and remaining chicken stock. Simmer 3 minutes more. Season to taste. Serve hot or cold garnished with reserved flowerets.

SUSAN HURWITZ

Cream of Garlic Soup

6 tablespoons butter, melted
2 cups chopped onion
1/2 cup minced garlic
1/2 cup all-purpose flour
6 cups beef broth
1 cup dry vermouth
1/2 cup sour cream
1/8 teaspoon grated nutmeg
Croutons
Chopped fresh chives

In a large saucepan saute onion and garlic in butter over low heat until onion is soft. Add flour and stir. Whisk in broth a little at a time. Increase heat to high and bring to boil. Reduce heat to medium-low, add vermouth and simmer 25 minutes. Puree soup in batches in blender or processor. Return to saucepan and place over very low heat. Whisk a little soup into sour cream in small bowl. Whisk sour cream slowly back into soup; do not boil. Remove from heat. Blend in nutmeg. Ladle into bowls. Garnish each with croutons and chives and serve. (4 servings)

JANET GILSDORF

Cream of Tomato Soup

1 small onion, chopped
1 tablespoon butter
3 tablespoons all-purpose flour
1 (28-ounce) can tomatoes
2 cups cold milk
Salt and pepper to taste
Fresh chopped parsley

Saute chopped onion in butter in a large skillet. Add flour and stir. Add canned tomatoes and bring to boil; stirring. Add cold milk to tomato mixture. Season with salt and pepper. Bring near boiling point. Sprinkle fresh parsley over soup and serve.

ELLA MAGAL

Zucchini Soup

5-6 small zucchini, chopped
1 small onion, chopped
1/2 teaspoon salt
1/2 teaspoon garlic powder (or 1 clove minced)
3 tablespoons butter
1 teaspoon curry powder
2 cups half-and-half cream
2 cups chicken broth

In a large skillet saute zucchini, onion, salt, and garlic in butter until tender. Puree well in blender until smooth. (Note: Only half can be mixed at one time in the blender.) Blend in curry, cream and broth. Serve hot. (Serves 4-6)

CATHERINE ANDREA

Senegalese Soup

3 large onions, chopped
1/4 pound butter
2 tablespoons curry powder
1 pound zucchini, sliced and cubed
3 cups chicken stock
1 cup sour cream
1 green apple, chopped (for garnish)

Saute onions in butter in a large skillet; do not brown. Add curry powder and cook slowly 5 minutes. Add zucchini and saute until tender (barely). Blend with chicken stock and sour cream. Continue cooking over low-medium heat for 15-30 minutes to blend flavors, stirring frequently. (4 servings)

JANET GILSDORF

36

SOUPS

Beer Cheese Soup

18 ounces water
9 ounces beer
2 ounces whipping cream
1 chicken bouillon cube
Pinch of thyme
Pinch of garlic powder
Pinch of white pepper
1/8 ounce Tabasco sauce
Salt to taste
7 ounces sharp cheddar cheese, grated
Roux (made of 2 tablespoon melted butter plus 2 tablespoon all-purpose flour)
Popped popcorn for garnish

Place water, beer, cream, bouillon cube and seasonings in top of double boiler and place directly on flame and boil for 15 minutes. Whip in cheese and add roux. Let stand for about 2 minutes, then whip until roux is fully dissolved. Cook in double boiler for 1/2 hour. Adjust roux and seasonings and salt to desired thickness and taste. (Makes 1 quart)

JANET GILSDORF

Canadian Cheddar Cheese Soup

2 tablespoons cornstarch
1 pound medium sharp cheddar cheese, grated
2 cups water
1 teaspoon salt
1/4 teaspoon pepper
1 teaspoon Worcestershire sauce
1 clove garlic, minced
8 tablespoons butter
3/4 cup diced cooked cauliflower
1 cup sliced mushrooms
1/2 cup chopped carrots
1 cup finely chopped onion
3/4 cup diced Canadian bacon (or fully cooked smoked ham)
2 cups half-and-half cream (or evaporated milk, undiluted)

Mix cornstarch with the grated cheese in a bowl. Heat water to boiling in a 4 to 6-quart Dutch oven. Add cheese mixture to boiling water a little at a time, stirring constantly. Continue to cook over medium heat, stirring constantly until cheese is melted and mixture is smooth. Add salt, pepper, Worcestershire and garlic. Saute each vegetable separately in 2 tablespoons butter until tender. Can be done in microwave. Add to soup along with bacon or ham. Heat, stirring constantly adding cream until desired thickness is reached. Serve. Do not overheat as it curdles. *"Wonderful hearty soup for cold winter days."*

CAROLIN DICK

37

SOUPS

Salads

SALADS

Grand Canyon Jello Salad

2 (3-ounce) packages orange gelatin
2 (3-ounce) packages lime gelatin
2 (3-ounce) packages lemon gelatin
2 (3-ounce) packages cherry gelatin
4 (5.3 ounce) cans evaporated milk (not skim evaporated milk)

Oil a 9 x 13-inch pan. (Do not use a glass pan as it is too shallow.) For each colored layer, add 1-1/2 cups boiling water to one package of gelatin. Mix well and pour into oiled pan. Let stand until firm (refrigerate or put in freezer, but do not allow to freeze). While this layer is setting, add 3/4 cup boiling water to second package of gelatin and cool in bowl. Add 3/4 cup evaporated milk. Pour over set plain layer. Repeat the above for each color, allowing enough time for setting in between layers. *"This is an easy recipe, but time-consuming. When done correctly, the layer effect is impressive."*

STEPHANIE MINERATH

Christmas Cranberry Crunch Salad

1 cup ground raw cranberries (use half bag of fresh)
1 orange (grind with peel and juice)
1 cup chopped celery
1 (3-ounce) package cherry gelatin (or lemon or strawberry)
1 cup hot water
1/2 cup pineapple juice (from 1 can of crushed pineapple)
1 tablespoon lemon juice
1 (13-ounce) can drained crushed pineapple
1/2 cup nuts, chopped
1 cup sugar

Use a food processor or blender to grind cranberries, orange and celery. Stir the gelatin, hot water, pineapple juice and lemon juice together in a large salad bowl and allow to partially set. Mix all other ingredients together. Combine with gelatin and set. (Makes a large mold or dish of salad)

ANN BETZ

41

Jello Fruit Salad

2 (3-ounce) packages gelatin (any flavor)
1 small can drained fruit (or 1-2 cups fresh fruit, any kind, cut in small pieces)
1 (8-ounce) container Cool Whip (or whipped cream)

Make gelatin as directed on package. Let set until firm. With a fork chop up gelatin. Add fruit and mix in gelatin. Add Cool Whip or whipped cream and mix all together. *"The fruit does not have to be all the same kind. If you are serving alot of people, double the gelatin and fruit."*

JUDY ROBERTS

Fresh Cranberry Salad

1 pound cranberries, ground
1 cup sugar
1 pint whipping cream or Dream Whip
3/4 pound marshmallows
1 (13-ounce) can drained, crushed pineapple

Combine ground cranberries and sugar in a mixing bowl. Let stand 2 hours. Whip cream and add the marshmallows which have been cut in small pieces (or use miniature marshmallows). Let stand 2 hours. Add the cranberry mixture and pineapple to whipped cream. Pour into a large mold. Let stand in refrigerator overnight. *"This makes a large salad and will keep several days."*

MARY CORNILS

Luscious Lemon Salad

1 (20-ounce) can crushed pineapple
1 (3-ounce) package lemon gelatin
1 (8-ounce) package cream cheese
1 (8-ounce) container Cool Whip
1/2 cup chopped nuts

Drain the pineapple, saving juice. Heat juice in a saucepan and dissolve gelatin in juice. Cool. Whip cream cheese and Cool Whip together. Fold into cooled gelatin juice mixture. Add nuts. Pour into jello mold and refrigerate at least 2 hours. (8 servings)

BARBARA DOERING

Shrimp Mousse

1 (3-ounce) package lemon gelatin
1/2 cup water
1 (11-ounce) can tomato soup
1/2 cup mayonnaise
1 (8-ounce) package cream cheese
1/2 cup chopped celery
1/2 cup chopped onions
1/2 cup chopped green pepper
2 (4-1/4 ounce) cans tiny shrimp
Lettuce

Dissolve gelatin in the water. Boil soup in a large saucepan. Add gelatin, mayonnaise and cream cheese. Stir and break up cream cheese so it melts. Remove from heat and stir until smooth. Let cool. Add rest of ingredients. Pour into well-oiled mold and refrigerate. Serve on lettuce for luncheon or with crackers for summer hors d'oeuvre.

SALLY WHITE

Seven-Layer Salad

1 head lettuce, torn
4 stalks celery, chopped
1 bunch scallions, chopped
1 (10-ounce) package frozen peas, thawed
1 pint jar mayonnaise
Parmesan or romano cheese
4 tomatoes, cut in wedges
Bacon bits

Using a large salad bowl or a 9 x 13-inch pan, arrange the first four ingredients in layers. Frost with one pint mayonnaise (not salad dressing). Sprinkle liberally with Parmesan or romano cheese. Refrigerate several hours or overnight. Garnish with tomato wedges and crumbled bacon. (8-10 servings)

STEPHANIE MINERATH

Caesar Salad

1 clove garlic, minced
2/3 cup olive or salad oil
2 medium eggs
1/3 cup lemon juice
1 teaspoon Worcestershire sauce
1 teaspoon salt
1/4 teaspoon pepper
5 ounces Parmesan cheese
1-1/2 heads of lettuce, torn into pieces
1/2 head endive, torn into pieces
1 head romaine, torn into pieces
3 cups croutons
5 anchovy fillets, cut in small pieces (optional)

In a small bowl marinate garlic at least 1/2 hour in oil. Whisk in eggs, lemon, Worcestershire, salt, pepper and mix until blended. Toss with cheese, greens and croutons. (10 servings)

ELIZABETH STONE

Orange-Spinach Salad

1 large bunch fresh spinach
1/2 pound bacon, diced and cooked
1 (11-ounce) can mandarin oranges
1/4 cup skinless peanuts

DRESSING:
1 cup oil
1/3 cup sugar
1/3 cup white vinegar
2 teaspoons grated onion
3/4 teaspoon salt
1/2 teaspoon celery salt
1/8 teaspoon pepper
1/2 teaspoon dry mustard
1 teaspoon paprika
1 tablespoon fresh lemon juice

Combine first four ingredients. Make dressing by whirling all dressing ingredients in blender a few seconds. Toss salad with dressing just before serving. *"This is always a hit."*

MARY DOYLE

Barb's Salad

SALAD:
1 head lettuce, shredded
1 cup chopped celery
1 (11-ounce) can mandarin oranges, drained
2 green onions (including tops), sliced
1 tablespoon minced parsley

DRESSING:
1/2 teaspoon salt
2 tablespoons vinegar
1/4 cup salad oil
3 tablespoons sugar

TOPPING:
1/4 cup almonds, blanched and cut
2 tablespoons sugar

Mix salad ingredients together. Blend all dressing ingredients well. In a heavy skillet, stir almonds and sugar constantly over low heat until sugar browns and carmelizes almonds. Remove, separate and cool on waxed paper. Add dressing and topping just before eating. (6-8 servings)

THOMAS SHOPE

Delicate Divine Salad

1 (10-ounce) package washed spinach (drained dry)
1 (8-ounce) can water chestnuts, sliced thin
1/2 pound bean sprouts
1/4 pound alfalfa sprouts
2 hard boiled eggs, sliced
6 fresh mushrooms, sliced
Almond slices or raw sunflower seeds

DRESSING:
1/4 cup honey
1 cup olive oil
1/3 cup ketchup
1/2 cup vinegar
1 medium onion, chopped fine
2 tablespoons Worcestershire sauce
Salt to taste

Mix all salad ingredients together in a large bowl. In a jar or bowl combine dressing ingredients and toss with salad. (8-10 servings)

DOROTHY BRAITHWAITE

SALADS

Wild Rice and Spinach Salad

2 cups fresh spinach, broken into medium pieces
Wild rice, cooked and cooled (1 cup rice plus 3 cups water)
1 pound mushrooms, thinly sliced
1/4 pound salted cashews
Salt and pepper to taste
MUSTARD VINAIGRETTE DRESSING:
6 tablespoons extra virgin olive oil
2 tablespoons red wine vinegar
1 tablespoon Pommery mustard

Combine salad ingredients. Blend dressing ingredients with a whisk and toss with salad.   JANET GILSDORF

Wilted Spinach Salad

1 bunch fresh spinach leaves
4 strips bacon, diced
2 teaspoons sugar
1/2 teaspoon salt
Dash of freshly ground black pepper
1/4 teaspoon dry mustard
5 tablespoons wine vinegar

Wash spinach and remove tough roots or stems. Break into bite-size pieces. Place the greens in a large bowl. Cook the bacon till crisp. (Do not drain off grease.) Add the rest of the ingredients. Simmer until sugar has dissolved. Pour the mixture over the greens and toss well. (4 servings)
                    ANN BETZ

Spinach Salad With Sweet and Sour Dressing

1 (10-ounce) package fresh spinach
1 (8-ounce) can water chestnuts, sliced
3 hard-boiled eggs, chopped
3/4 cup bacon bits (or crumbled bacon)

DRESSING:
2-1/2 teaspoons ketchup
3 teaspoons vinegar
1 small onion, finely chopped
1 tablespoon Worcestershire sauce
1/4 cup sugar
1/2 cup oil

Combine all dressing ingredients in a medium-sized jar; shake well. Combine salad ingredients. Pour dressing over salad when ready to serve.
                    KATHY JOY

46

Greens Tian

2-1/2 pounds greens (chicory, mustard greens, beet greens, spinach, escarole, chard or mixture)
1/3 cup plus 3 tablespoons olive oil
1 cup chopped onions
3 teaspoons minced garlic
1/2 cup rice, uncooked
3/4 cup grated Parmesan cheese (fresh is best)
Salt and freshly ground pepper to taste
1/2 cup fresh bread crumbs

Wash greens and chop. Heat 1/3 cup oil in a large saucepan and cook onions until wilted. Add garlic, stir; add greens 1/2 pound at a time, stirring to coat with oil. Cook until slightly wilted. Preheat oven to 400 degrees. Bring salted water to a boil, add rice and cook 5 minutes. Drain. Place wilted greens (do not drain) in a bowl, add rice and 1/2 cup cheese. Season with salt and pepper. Place in buttered 1-1/2 inch deep baking dish. Mix remaining 1/4 cup cheese with bread crumbs and sprinkle on top. Drizzle with remaining oil and bake for 30-40 minutes. (6-8 servings)

JANET GILSDORF

Tabbouleh Salad

1-1/2 cups bulgur wheat
3 cups hot water
1 cup finely chopped parsley
1/4 cup minced fresh mint
1/2 cup chopped green onions
2 large tomatoes, chopped
3 tablespoons chopped green pepper
1/2 cup lemon juice
1/2 cup olive oil
2 tablespoons salt
Pepper to taste

Soak bulgur in hot water until soft. Shake off excess water. Combine with remaining ingredients. Chill at least 2 hours before serving to blend flavors. May serve on lettuce as a salad or in Pita bread as a sandwich. (4-6 servings)

JANET GILSDORF

47

Artichoke Rice Salad

1 cup rice
2 cups water or chicken broth
1/4 cup green pepper, chopped
1/4 cup green onion, chopped
1/4 cup green olives, chopped
1/2 teaspoon dill weed
1/2 cup mayonnaise
2 (6-ounce) jars marinated artichokes, drained
Salt and pepper to taste
Lettuce

Cook rice in water or chicken broth until absorbed, about 25 minutes. Stir in pepper, onion, olives, dill, mayonnaise and artichokes, salt and pepper. Refrigerate and serve in lettuce-lined bowl with additional sliced olives on top. (6 servings)

JACK AND KATHY PASCOE

Artichoke Salad

1 (9-ounce) package frozen artichoke hearts, cooked and drained
1 (8-ounce) package cut green beans, cooked and drained
6 cups assorted salad greens, torn into bite-size pieces
1/4 cup thinly sliced onion
8-10 cherry tomatoes, halved
1/2 cup (2 ounces) crumbled bleu cheese

DRESSING:
3/4 cup oil
1/4 cup white wine vinegar
1 teaspoon sugar
1/2 teaspoon salt
1/2 teaspoon paprika
Dash of pepper

Combine all dressing ingredients. Add cooked artichoke hearts and beans; toss lightly. Refrigerate until chilled, about 3 hours. In a large bowl, toss dressing mixture with salad greens, onion, tomatoes and cheese; serve immediately. (8 one-cup servings)

KATHY SCHROEDER

Three-Layer Salad

1 head lettuce
1 (10-ounce) package frozen peas
1 (8-ounce) can water chestnuts
Celery
1 pound bacon
1 cup Hellman's mayonnaise
Parmesan cheese

Layer lettuce on bottom of oblong baking pan. Sprinkle peas over lettuce. Cut up water chestnuts and layer over peas. Cut celery and layer over chestnuts. Top with Hellman's mayonnaise. Fry bacon., crumble over Hellman's and sprinkle with Parmesan cheese. (Serves 12)   MICHELLE BARATONO

Mushroom-Broccoli Salad I

1 pound fresh mushrooms
2 heads fresh broccoli
1 purple onion
1 (8-ounce) bottle Italian dressing
Croutons

Slice mushrooms and break broccoli head into small pieces. Slice onion into rings. Mix together with Italian dressing. Marinate overnight or as long as possible. Before serving, top with plain croutons. (4-6 servings)
ROSWITHA BIRD

Mushroom-Broccoli Salad II

1 pound fresh mushrooms, sliced
1 head broccoli flowers
2 green onions, finely chopped

DRESSING:
1/3 cup sugar
1 teaspoon salt
1 teaspoon paprika
1 teaspoon celery seed
1 teaspoon onion powder
1 cup oil
1/4 cup cider or wine vinegar

Combine ingredients for dressing the night before or at least 2 hours before serving. Toss mushrooms, broccoli and green onions in large salad bowl. Pour dressing over salad one hour before serving. *"This salad is always a hit ."*
NELDA MERCER
JACKIE BREWER
BEVERLY SMITH

49

German Slaw

1 medium red cabbage
1 large onion
1-2 green peppers
3/4 cup vegetable oil
1/2 cup sugar
3/4 cup white vinegar
1 teaspoon celery seed

Chop cabbage, onion and green pepper. (It goes much faster if you have a food processor with a slicing blade.) In a medium saucepan, bring oil, sugar, vinegar and celery seed to a boil. Reduce heat and simmer uncovered 5 minutes. Cool oil-vinegar mixture slightly and pour over vegetables. Toss and chill. *"Great for summer barbecues and delicious with fish."*

ELIZABETH STONE

Permanent Slaw
(a saurkraut variation)

1 large head cabbage, shredded (about 4 pounds)
4 medium onions, chopped
1 (2-ounce) jar chopped pimento, drained

DRESSING:
1 pint vinegar
2 cups sugar
1-1/2 tablespoons celery seed
1/2 tablespoon turmeric
1 tablespoon salt
1 tablespoon whole mustard seed

Combine the slaw ingredients in a large bowl. In a saucepan combine dressing ingredients and boil 2 minutes. Pour hot mixture over vegetables. Let cool and refrigerate for at least 24 hours. Keeps for a month or two.

JO ZEISLER
SHELLY ROBBINS

Marinated Carrots

MARINADE:
3/4 cup ketchup
1/2 cup garlic-flavored olive oil
1/4 cup sugar
Salt and pepper to taste
1/2 cup white wine vinegar
1/2 cup water
2 tablespoon dill weed
VEGETABLES:
1/2 pound baby carrots
1 yellow onion, chopped
1 bell pepper, chopped

Mix all marinade ingredients well. Parboil carrots. Add onions, bell pepper and marinade; chill for at least 2 hours. (4-6 servings)

JANET GILSDORF

Peanut and Pea Salad

1 (10-ounce) package frozen peas (or equivalent fresh)
Salted water
1/2 pint sour cream
Dash of onion powder
Dash of celery salt
1 onion, chopped fine
1 package salted peanuts
Mayonnaise

Cook the peas slightly in salted water (leave them firm, green and shapely). Drain and cool. Mix with sour cream. Add a good shake of onion powder and celery salt. Add onion. Add peanuts. Combine with mayonnaise until desired consistency.

MARY CORNILS

Mim's Potato Salad

3 cups cooked potato, diced (6 potatoes)
2-3 tablespoons onion or green onion, chopped
1 tablespoon lemon juice
1/2 cup chopped sweet pickle
4 hard boiled eggs, chopped
1/3 cup French dressing
Mayonnaise to moisten

Mix all ingredients in a large bowl. Refrigerate before serving. (6 servings)

MARILYN ALLARD

Zucchini and Tomato Salad

6 small zucchini
1 green pepper, cut in strips
1/4 cup chopped green onion
1/4 cup chopped fresh parsley
1/4 cup vinegar
1/2 teaspoon salt
1/2 teaspoon garlic salt
1/2 teaspoon pepper
3/4 cup salad oil
4 tomatoes, cut in wedges
Lettuce

Cut unpeeled zucchini in very thin slices. Combine green pepper, onion and parsley in large bowl. Stir together remaining ingredients except tomatoes and lettuce. Pour over zucchini mixture. Chill several hours stirring occasionally. Serve with tomato wedges and lettuce.   JO ZEISLER

Golden Delicious Apple Salad

2 medium golden apples
1 (13-ounce) can pineapple tidbits (drained, reserve 1 teaspoon)
2 medium carrots, grated
1-1/2 teaspoons grated lemon peel
2 teaspoons lemon juice
2 teaspoons sugar
1/4 teaspoon nutmeg
1/4 teaspoon salt
2-3 teaspoons mayonnaise
Salted pecans for topping

Mix all ingredients together in a bowl except mayonnaise and pecans. Blend 1 teaspoon of reserved pineapple juice with the mayonnaise. Combine with salad and top with nuts. (Serves 6-8)   ANNA KELLY

Salad in a Pita

Carrots, bite-size pieces
Celery, bite-size pieces
Broccoli, bite-size pieces
Cauliflower, bite-size pieces
Cucumber, bite-size pieces
Green pepper, bite-size pieces
Hard cooked eggs, chopped
Pita bread

Marinate all vegetables in oil and vinegar dressing for several hours. Add eggs and spoon into halved Pita bread.   SALLY JOHNSTON

Veggie Taco Casserole

2 (15-ounce) cans refried beans
1 (1-pound) bag Dorito nacho corn chips
2 cups grated sharp cheddar cheese
1 medium onion, chopped
1/2 or 1 head lettuce, shredded
2 medium tomatoes, chopped

Preheat oven to 350 degrees. In a saucepan, heat beans until pouring consistency. Set aside. Gently crush 1/3 of taco chips and place into bottom of 10 x 13-inch pan. Pour and spread heated refried beans onto crushed chips. Spread one-half cup of cheese onto beans. Layer remaining ingredients in this order: onions, lettuce, tomatoes, remaining chips and then remaining cheese. Set in oven and bake about 15 minutes or until cheese is melted. Serve immediately. (8 servings) *"Kids love this. Party fare. Vegetarian."*

CONI HEIMANN

Taco Salad

1 pound ground beef
1 package taco seasoning mix
1/2 cup water
4 medium tomatoes
1 large onion
1 (8-ounce) can kidney beans
8 ounces cheddar cheese
1 head lettuce
1 (12-ounce) package Fritos corn chips
1/4 cup sugar
1 tablespoon taco sauce
1 (8-ounce) bottle Thousand Island dressing

Brown ground beef in a large skillet; drain grease. Add taco seasoning (saving 1 tablespoon for dressing) and 1/2 cup water. Cook 15 minutes over low heat and cool. Chop tomatoes and onion; rinse kidney beans, grate cheese, shred lettuce, crumble Fritos. Make dressing by combining taco seasoning mix with sugar, taco sauce and Thousand Island dressing. Just before serving, combine all ingredients and toss well. (10-12 servings)

GOLDER WILSON
STEPHANIE MINERATH

Chicken Salad

1 (6-ounce) package Uncle Ben's original long grain and wild rice
2 cups cooked chicken, cut up
1/4 to 1/2 pound fresh mushrooms, sliced
1 cup firmly packed fresh spinach leaves, cut into thin strips
2 green onions with tops, sliced
1/3 cup dry white wine
1/4 cup vegetable oil
2 teaspoons sugar
Salt and pepper to taste
10 cherry tomatoes, halved

Prepare rice according to package directions. Transfer to a large bowl. Cover and chill. Add chicken, mushrooms, spinach and green onions. Mix well. In a small bowl, blend wine, oil, sugar, salt and pepper. Add to rice mixture and mix well. Chill. Add tomatoes before serving. (6 servings)

DIANE BAKER

Cold Chinese Chicken Salad

BOTTOM NOODLE LAYER:
2 tablespoons peanut butter
4 tablespoons water
2 tablespoons soy sauce
1 tablespoon Chinese hot chili sauce
2 bunches cellophane noodles, cooked

Using a whisk, combine peanut butter, water, soy sauce and hot chili sauce. Mix this with the cooked cellophane noodles and place in bottom of 2-quart glass bowl.

SECOND LAYER:
1 tablespoon light soy sauce
1-1/2 teaspoons toasted sesame oil
1 tablespoon rice wine vinegar
Pinch of sugar
1 medium cucumber* cut in matchstick pieces

Combine a dressing of soy sauce, sesame oil, rice wine vinegar and sugar. Toss with cucumber pieces. Marinate for 1 hour. Sprinkle cucumbers (with dressing) on top of the noodles.

TOP LAYER:
2 cups cooked chicken, cut in pieces
1/2 cup chopped salted peanuts

Next, layer chicken and sprinkle peanuts on the top. (6-8 servings)
*COOK'S TIP: English cucumbers are burpless! *"Delicious light meal."*

ANN BETZ

Chicken Salad - Vietnamese Style

NUOC MAM SAUCE:
3 (1/4-inch) pieces fresh hot chili (jalapena)
1 clove garlic
1 teaspoon sugar
1/2 medium lime
1 tablespoon vinegar (rice vinegar preferred)
1 tablespoon water
4 tablespoons fish sauce

SALAD:
3 cups cooked noodles
2 Jerusalem artichokes, sliced
1 sweet red pepper, chopped
1 cup cooked chicken, chopped
1/8 cup chopped fresh coriander

Seed the chili and crush with garlic and sugar in mortar with pestle. Peel and seed the lime and mash the pulp in mortar with garlic and chili. Add vinegar and water and mix well. Add fish sauce. Let flavors blend for about 1/2 hour at room temperature before serving. Make Nuoc Mam sauce. Mix salad ingredients in a bowl with 2 tablespoons Nuoc Mam sauce. (Leftover sauce may be stored for 4 months in refrigerator.)

JANET GILSDORF

Chicken Salad Pie

1-1/2 cups diced cooked chicken
1-1/2 cups chopped fresh pineapple (or one 12-ounce can pineapple
    tidbits, drained)
1/2 cup chopped pecans
1/2 cup chopped celery
2/3 cup sour cream
2/3 cup mayonnaise
1 (8-inch) prebaked pie shell
3 tablespoons grated sharp cheddar cheese

In a large bowl combine chicken, pineapple, pecans and celery. In another bowl mix sour cream and mayonnaise. Add 2/3 cup of sour cream mixture to chicken mixture. Mix the salad until well-blended and place in the pie shell. Pat the mixture into the shell so that the top is as even as possible. Pour remaining sour cream mixture onto the chicken mixture and spread it evenly. Sprinkle grated cheese on top. Refrigerate the pie for at least 4 hours. (6-8 servings)

GRACE BRAND

Hot Chicken Salad

5 cups cooked, cubed chicken (4 breasts plus 4 thighs)
4 cups chopped celery
1 cup blanched almonds (or 1 can water chestnuts, chopped)
2/3 cup chopped green pepper (optional)
1/4 cup chopped pimento
1/4 cup chopped onion
2 teaspoons salt
1/4 cup lemon juice
1 cup mayonnaise
8 ounces American cheese
2 cups crushed potato chips

Preheat oven to 350 degrees. Combine chicken, celery, almonds, pepper, pimento, onion, salt, lemon and mayonnaise in a large bowl. Spread mixture in baking dish. Butter 9 x 13-inch baking dish and top with slices of cheese. Sprinkle potato chips on top and bake for 45 minutes.

JAN PITTELLI

Layered Chicken Salad

3 cups shredded lettuce
1 (10-ounce) package frozen peas
2 cups diced cooked chicken (or turkey)
1-1/2 cups diced tomatoes
1 cup cucumber slices, halved
1-1/2 to 2 cups mayonnaise
1 tablespoon sugar
1/2 teaspoon curry powder
1-1/2 cups croutons

Layer lettuce, peas, chicken, tomatoes and cucumber in a 2 to 3-quart casserole or salad bowl. Combine mayonnaise, sugar and curry; mix well. Spread over salad. Cover tightly with plastic wrap. Refrigerate overnight. Sprinkle with croutons before serving. (Makes 6 servings) May be doubled.

MARILYN CANHAM

Nancy's Turkey Salad

2-1/2 cups cooked turkey or chicken diced (cold)
1 cup green grapes, cut in halves
1 cup celery, diced
1 cup cubed pineapple
1/3 to 1/2 cup light Miracle Whip salad dressing (enough to coat)
Lettuce

Toss turkey salad ingredients in a large bowl. Chill. Serve on lettuce leaf.

NANCY NEWHARD

Curried Salmon Salad

Leaf lettuce
2 bananas, bias sliced
1 tablespoon lemon juice
2 cups cooked rice, chilled
1 (16-ounce) can salmon, chilled, drained, flaked, bone removed
1 (4-1/2 ounce) can tiny shrimp, chilled and drained
1 green pepper, cubed
2 carrots, shredded
2 apples, cubed

Line a bowl with lettuce. Toss bananas with lemon juice. Arrange bananas, rice, salmon, shrimp, green pepper, carrots and apples atop the lettuce. Serve with curry dressing. (8 servings)

CURRY DRESSING:
1 cup mayonnaise
1/4 cup milk
3-4 teaspoons curry powder

Mix mayonnaise, milk and curry in a bowl. Chill.

NANCY HOPWOOD

Curried Shrimp Salad

1/2 cup mayonnaise
2 tablespoons lemon juice
1 teaspoon curry powder
Salt and pepper to taste
1 (1-pound) package frozen shrimp, thawed
1 cup cooked rice
1 cup diced celery
1/4 cup chopped green pepper
1/4 cup chopped onion
Salad greens
4 tomatoes

Combine mayonnaise, lemon juice, curry, salt and pepper in a bowl. Gently toss the mayonnaise mixture with shrimp, rice, celery, green pepper and onion. Chill until ready to serve. Make bed of salad greens with circle of tomato wedges. Place shrimp mixture in center. (4 servings)

MARY ROLOFF

Mushroom and Shrimp Salad Dijon

2 cups fresh sliced mushrooms
1 pound cooked baby shrimp
1/3 cup salad oil
3 tablespoons red wine vinegar
2 tablespoons fresh lemon juice
2 tablespoons Dijon mustard
Pinch of salt
Crisp watercress or lettuce
1 medium cucumber, sliced

In a shallow glass pan, arrange mushrooms and shrimp. In a small jar, combine oil, vinegar, lemon juice, mustard and salt. Cover jar tightly and shake well. Pour over mushrooms and shrimp. Cover and refrigerate one hour. Line four salad plates with watercress. Divide cucumber slices evenly and arrange on plates. Top each plate with equal portions of shrimp-mushroom mixture. (4 servings)

FLO JOHNSTON

Eggs, Pasta and Grains

EGGS, PASTA AND GRAINS

Egg Casserole

2 cups soft bread cubes
1-3/4 cups milk
8 eggs, slightly beaten
2 tablespoons butter
1 teaspoon salt
1/4 teaspoon pepper
1/2 pound Swiss cheese, grated
2 tablespoons butter
1/2 cup fine dry bread crumbs
8 slices bacon

Preheat oven to 350 degrees. Soak bread cubes in milk for 5 minutes. Squeeze milk out of bread and set aside. Use 2 tablespoons butter, the reserved milk and scramble eggs until loose and wet. Season. Add bread and stir until combined. Put in buttered 9 x 13-inch pan. Put cheese on top. Melt remaining butter and brown the dry crumbs. Spoon over cheese. Top with bacon. Bake 30 minutes. (Freezes well; partially thaw before baking.) (6 servings) *"Delicious brunch recipe that can be made ahead of time."*   CAROL COLBY

Quiche Lorraine

4 strips bacon
3 large eggs
2 cups half-and-half cream
1/2 teaspoon salt
2 ounces Gruyere or Swiss cheese, grated
1 (9-inch) deep-dish pie shell

Preheat oven to 350 degrees. Fry bacon in a skillet until well done but not crisp. Chop into half-inch pieces. Combine eggs, cream and salt and beat until blended. Sprinkle bacon and cheese into deep dish pie shell. Pour egg mixture on top. Bake for 45 minutes.   KATHY JOY

Chile Rellenos

1 cup half-and-half cream
2 eggs, slightly beaten
1/3 cup all-purpose flour
3 (4-ounce) cans green chilies (split, rinsed and drained)
1/2 pound grated Monterey Jack cheese
1/2 pound grated sharp cheddar cheese
1 (8-ounce) can tomato sauce

Preheat oven to 350 degrees. Combine cream, eggs and flour. Pour into baking dish. Layer the chilies with the cheeses on top. Pour tomato sauce over all of this and bake until set, 1 hour.   JACKIE BREWER

Wine and Cheese Omelet

1/2 loaf day-old French bread
4 tablespoons melted butter
1/2 pound Gruyere cheese, grated
1/4 cup Swiss cheese, grated
4 slices Genoa salami, sliced and chopped
8 eggs
1 cup milk
1/4 cup dry white wine
3 tablespoons scallion tops, chopped
1/2 teaspoon salt
1/8 teaspoon pepper
2 teaspoons sharp German mustard
Dash of cayenne pepper
1 cup sour cream
1/2 cup Parmesan cheese

In well-greased 2-1/2 quart casserole, break bread and spread over bottom. Pour butter over bread. Sprinkle with Gruyere and Swiss cheeses and salami. In a mixing bowl beat eggs, milk, wine, scallion tops, salt and pepper, mustard and cayenne together. Pour over bread. Cover and refrigerate overnight. Remove 45 minutes before cooking. Bake at 325 degrees for 1 hour. Cover during baking. Uncover and spread top with sour cream. Sprinkle with Parmesan cheese and bake 10 minutes more. (6-8 servings)

DOROTHY BRAITHWAITE

Carbonara
(Pasta With Bacon and Eggs)

1 tablespoon cooking oil
1 medium onion, chopped
3/4 pound bacon, cooked and chopped
1 pound fettuccine
2 eggs, lightly beaten
2 tablespoons Parmesan cheese, grated
Pepper to taste

Heat oil in a skillet and cook onion until golden. Add bacon and heat several minutes. Meanwhile in a saucepan, heat water and cook fettuccine. Drain pasta. Add eggs, cheese and pepper to skillet and cook over low heat 2-4 minutes. Then add pasta, stir and serve. (4 servings)

CAROLINE BLANE

Cold Macaroni Salad

1 pound seashell macaroni (cooked)
1 pound medium sharp cheese, cubed
5-6 green onions with stems, chopped
2 stalks celery, chopped
2 tablespoons celery seed
Salt and pepper to taste
2 cups Miracle Whip

Cook, drain and rinse macaroni. Add other ingredients. Best if made the day ahead. It may be necessary to add more Miracle Whip the next day.

JO ZEISLER

Couscous Salad

3 tablespoons unsalted butter
1/8 teaspoon powdered saffron or turmeric
1-1/2 cups chicken stock (or canned chicken broth)
1-1/2 cups couscous
1-1/2 cups chopped celery
2/3 cup dried currants (plumped in hot water for 15 minutes and drained)
1/3 cup thinly sliced scallions
1/3 cup pine nuts, toasted lightly
1/4 cup minced fresh parsley leaves

DRESSING:
1/4 cup fresh lemon juice
1/4 teaspoon cinnamon
1/2 cup olive oil
Salt and pepper to taste

In a large skillet melt the butter with saffron over moderate heat. Stirring, add stock and bring liquid to a boil. Stir in couscous and cover the skillet and remove it from the heat. Let mixture stand 4 minutes and transfer it to a ceramic or glass bowl, breaking up any lumps with a fork. Add celery, currants, scallions, pine nuts and parsley. Toss to combine. In a small bowl, whisk together lemon juice and cinnamon. Add oil in a slow stream, whisking and whisk until dressing is emulsified. Drizzle dressing over salad, toss and season with salt and pepper. May be made a day ahead and chilled. (6 servings) *Best when made 24 hours ahead. Excellent when served with lamb, chicken or ham.*

RUTH SAUNDERS

Pasta E Fagiolini Con Pesto

1/2 pound butter, softened
1 (8-ounce) package cream cheese, softened
4 tablespoons chopped fresh basil (or 2 tablespoons dry basil)
2 tablespoons chopped fresh parsley (or 1 tablespoon dry parsley)
1 large or 2 small garlic cloves, minced
1/2 teaspoon salt
1/2 cup grated romano cheese
1 pound cooked spaghetti
1 pound cooked fresh string beans

Beat softened butter and cream cheese with a fork until well blended. Add basil, parsley, garlic, salt and romano cheese. Mix thoroughly. One or two tablespoons of hot water may be added to make ingredients blend better. Cook one pound spaghetti with one pound of fresh string beans. Drain and place in large bowl. Pour sauce over spaghetti and beans and toss together with two forks. Extra grated romano cheese may be sprinkled over spaghetti and beans. (6 servings)   CATHY MAZZOLINI

Stuffed Shells Marinara

1 (12-ounce) package large shells
1 (7-ounce) can tuna in oil
1 large onion, chopped
1 clove garlic, minced
1 (28-ounce) can tomato sauce
1 teaspoon salt
2 teaspoons leaf basil, crumbled
1/4 teaspoon pepper
1 (10-ounce) package frozen chopped spinach
2 eggs
1 cup soft bread crumbs (2 slices)
1 cup cream style cottage cheese
1 teaspoon salt
1/4 teaspoon pepper

Preheat oven to 350 degrees. Cook shells 9 minutes; drain and place in a large bowl of cold water. While pasta cooks, drain tuna oil into a large skillet; heat; saute onion and garlic in oil until soft. Stir in tomato sauce, tuna, salt, basil and pepper; simmer 15 minutes. Add water if it gets too thick. Cook spinach, following package directions; drain well. Beat eggs in a medium-sized bowl with a wire whip. Add cooked spinach, bread crumbs, cottage cheese, salt and pepper and stir until well blended. Drain shells. Fill each with spinach-cheese mixture. Arrange stuffed shells over half of the sauce in a 9 x 12-inch pan. Drizzle remaining sauce. Cover casserole with aluminum foil. Bake for 45 minutes or until shells are tender or until casserole is bubbly hot. (8 servings)
                                                                                    JOYCE TREPPA

Laurie's Pasta Salad From Chicago

1 pound cooked pasta, drained
1 small box cherry tomatoes, halved
1 (6-ounce) can black olives, drained
1/4 pound Genoa salami, diced
1 (6-1/2 ounce) jar marinated artichokes, with juices
1 (9-3/4 ounce) jar olive condite, with juices
Broccoli flowerets
Cauliflower flowerets
1/4 cup Parmesan cheese

Toss above ingredients in large bowl and marinate several hours.

JOANNE SONSTEIN

Asparagus Pasta Salad

1 pound asparagus, cut in 1-inch pieces
1 (8-ounce) package vermicelli*
1 tomato, chopped
4 green onions, chopped
1/2 green pepper, sliced thinly
1 (4-ounce) can black olives, sliced
4 ounces boiled ham, chopped
4 ounces mild white cheese, chopped
1/3 cup Parmesan cheese, grated
1 tablespoon parsley, chopped
1 teaspoon chives, chopped

Boil asparagus in a saucepan for 3-4 minutes; drain and cool. Cook vermicelli until al dente; drain and cool. Make the sauce.

SAUCE:
3/4 cup mayonnaise
Juice from 1 small lemon
1 teaspoon garlic powder
1/2 teaspoon celery salt
1/2 teaspoon basil
1/4 teaspoon Beau Monde seasoning
1/4 teaspoon pepper

Make sauce combining all ingredients. Toss sauce with all other ingredients. Chill. (4 servings)

*COOK'S TIP: Vermicelli is more easily handled if broken in half first. Can increase the amount of vermicelli if you prefer more pasta.

CHRISTINE BLACK

Macroni and Cheese

Of course you have to buy it. Then you put it in the stove. You take it back out to put cheese in it. Then you take it back in the stove and leave it for 45 minutes at <u>MED.</u> which is medium. You take it back out and it's ready.

CHRISTOPHER, AGE 7

Rice Pudding

3 cups milk
2 egg yolks, well beaten
Pinch of salt
1/2 cup sugar
2 cups cooked rice
1 teaspoon vanilla
1 teaspoon allspice
1 cup raisins
1 teaspoon white rum
2 tablespoons bread crumbs
2 tablespoons butter, melted
1/2 cup chopped pineapple (canned or fresh)

Preheat oven to 375 degrees. Mix milk with egg yolks, salt and sugar in a saucepan. Add rice, vanilla and allspice. Bring to a slow boil. Stir gently, simmer for 10 minutes. Add raisins and rum. Stir and remove from heat. Grease large deep baking dish. Sprinkle crumbs and butter in it. Pour pudding mix into pan and top with pineapple chunks. Bake for 30 minutes or until lightly browned. (6 servings)

DONOVAN BOWERBANK

Better-Than-Baked-Potato Rice

5 slices bacon
1 cup converted rice
1 clove garlic, minced
2-1/2 cups water
1 teaspoon salt
1/3 cup thinly sliced green onions, with tops (or chopped chives)
1/8 teaspoon white pepper
Dairy sour cream
Grated cheddar cheese

Cook bacon until crisp. Remove and set aside. Pour off all but 1 tablespoon drippings. Add rice and garlic. Cook over low heat until rice is lightly brown, about 5-7 minutes. Add water and salt. Bring to boil. Reduce heat and cover tightly; simmer 20 minutes. Remove from heat. Let stand, covered until all water is absorbed, about 5 minutes. Stir in onions, pepper and reserved crumbled bacon. Top with sour cream and cheese. (4-5 servings) *"This is nice served on a tray with shish kebobs."* SANDRA MERKEL

Rice With Lime and Ginger

1 tablespoon salt
1-1/2 cups raw long grain rice
2 tablespoons vegetable oil
4 carrots, peeled and trimmed
8 ounces snow peas

DRESSING:
1 clove garlic, peeled
1 piece fresh gingerroot (size of quarter and 1/2-inch thick), peeled
2 green onions (cut in 1-inch lengths)
3 tablespoons lemon juice
2 tablespoons lime juice
1 teaspoon salt
1/4 teaspoon freshly ground pepper
1 teaspoon Dijon mustard
2/3 cup olive oil

Bring large pot of water to a boil and add salt. Add rice and cook with water constantly boiling for 12-15 minutes. or until rice is tender. Drain and rinse with cold water. Shake dry and toss with oil. Set aside. Slice carrots and boil 2-4 minutes until barely tender. Drain and rinse with cold water. Pat dry and add to rice. Trim snow peas and cut in half. Blanch in boiling water for 30 seconds and drain. Rinse with cold water and pat dry. Add to rice. Prepare dressing by chopping garlic, ginger and green onion in a blender. Add lemon and lime juice, salt, pepper, mustard and oil. Combine dressing, vegetables and rice. Allow mixture to marinate in refrigerator till ready to serve.

ANN BETZ

Rice Pilaf

4 cups chicken stock
Handful of vermicelli (or pine nuts)
3 tablespoons butter
2 cups long grain rice
1 teaspoon salt

Bring chicken stock to boil. Crush vermicelli and brown in butter in a 2-quart saucepan. Add rice and coat grains with butter. Add salt and chicken stock. Cover and simmer 20 minutes or until stock is absorbed.

CAROL RAGSDALE

Coconut, Rice and Kidney Beans

1/2 pound kidney beans
1 cup coconut cream*
1/2 teaspoon salt
1/8 teaspoon thyme
2 cloves garlic, minced
1 small onion, chopped
1 pound rice, uncooked
Pepper (optional)

Cook beans in water until tender. Add coconut cream and all other ingredients except rice. Cook for 10 minutes. Add enough water to beans to cook rice. Reduce to medium heat, add rice and mix all together. Cook until rice is fluffy. Pepper can be added if desired. Peas can be substituted for kidney beans.

*Can be bought in health food stores.

DONOVAN BOWERBANK

Wheat Pilaf

2 cups chicken, beef or lamb stock
3 tablespoons butter
1 small onion, chopped
1 cup medium or coarse bulgur (cracked wheat)
1 teaspoon salt

Bring stock to boil. In a 1-quart saucepan saute onion in butter. Add bulgur and stir well. Add salt and stock. Cover and simmer 20 minutes or until stock is absorbed.

CAROL RAGSDALE

Uppuma

1 cup cream of wheat
1/2 teaspoon mustard seeds
20 cashew nuts
4 teaspoons vegetable oil
1/2 teaspoon ginger pieces, chopped fine
2 tablespoons onions, chopped
1 hot green pepper, chopped
2 cups water
3/4 teaspoon salt
1 tablespoon butter

Slightly cook the cream of wheat in a saucepan (until golden brown color) and set aside. In a nonstick pan, saute mustard seeds, cashew nuts in oil over heat until golden brown. Add ginger, onion, chopped green pepper and let simmer uncovered for 3 minutes. Add 2 cups of water and salt with the ingredients and bring it to a full boil. Add browned cream of wheat while constantly stirring to avoid clumps, keep stirring 5-7 minutes until cream of wheat is cooked. Add butter, mix well and serve hot. (4 servings)

Variation: Add cooked green peas or chopped and steamed potato.

VASANTHA PADMANABHAN

Breads

BREADS

Dill Irish Soda Bread

4 cups unsifted all-purpose flour
1 teaspoon salt
2 teaspoons baking powder
1 teaspoon soda
1/4 cup sugar
1/2 cup chopped fresh dill weed
1/4 cup butter
1 egg
1-1/2 cups buttermilk

Preheat oven to 350 degrees. Combine flour, salt, baking powder, soda and sugar in a large bowl. Add dill. Add butter, cut in until crumbly. Beat egg and buttermilk and add to dry ingredients. Stir until blended. Knead until smooth. Place loaf on a cookie sheet prepared with shortening and cornmeal. With a sharp knife, cut a cross on loaf about 1/2-inch deep. Bake for 50-60 minutes. (Makes 1 loaf)

JANET GILSDORF

Easy and Delicious Corn Bread

1-1/4 cups all-purpose flour
3/4 cup whole grain cornmeal
4 tablespoons sugar
5 teaspoons baking powder (yes, 5!)
3/4 teaspoon salt
1 egg
1 cup milk
2 tablespoons melted butter

Preheat oven to 375 degrees. Butter a 9-inch pie plate. Sift together all dry ingredients. Mix in egg and milk, then melted butter. Mix well. Spread batter into plate. Bake 30-35 minutes or until lightly browned around edges. *"This can be made with one wooden spoon and a bowl. It is so easy and great with soup on a cold winter night."*

SUSAN HURWITZ

73

BREADS

Lefse
(Norwegian Bread)

3 cups mashed potatoes
1 tablespoon sugar
1 teaspoon salt
1/2 cup shortening
1-1/2 cups sifted all-purpose flour

Mix all ingredients except flour in a large mixing bowl while the potatoes are hot. Chill thoroughly. Add flour to chilled mixture. Divide dough into 2-inch balls. Roll each out to a thin 8-inch round on a well-floured surface. Cook on a grill on the stove top for about 1 minute on each side. Wrap cooked lefse in a cloth to maintain soft moist texture. After lefse cools, it may be wrapped in a plastic wrap. (Makes two 8-inch rounds)

LILLIAN TUFTY PEARSON

Swope Bread

4 teaspoons baking soda
1 quart buttermilk
1 cup sugar
2 cups all-purpose flour
2 cups whole wheat flour
2 teaspoons salt

Preheat oven to 375 degrees. Dissolve baking soda in buttermilk in a large bowl. Add sugar; mix well. Add remaining ingredients and mix well. Pour into two well-greased loaf pans. Bake for 1 hour. (Makes 2 loaves)

PHYLLIS ASKEW

Toasted Cheese Loaf

1 loaf unsliced sandwich bread
1/4 cup softened butter
1 (5-ounce) jar sharp cheese spread
2 tablespoons chives
1 piece clean string!

Preheat oven to 400 degrees. Cut crusts from top and sides of unsliced sandwich loaf. Make 8 slices crosswise almost to bottom crust; make one vertical cut lengthwise down center almost to bottom. Place on baking sheet. Blend butter, cheese spread and chives. Spread between slices, over top and sides. Tie string around loaf. Bake for 10-12 minutes, until bread is crusty. Serve as pan rolls. (16 servings)

SISTER CAROLE FEDDERS

74

Cottage Cheese Pancakes

6 eggs
6 tablespoons melted butter
2 cups cottage cheese
6 tablespoons all-purpose flour (may use part whole wheat)
1 teaspoon lemon peel
Currant jelly

Whirl all ingredients in blender or food processor until smooth. Bake on hot griddle forming pancakes 2 inches in diameter. Flip once when golden. Serve with currant jelly. (Freezes beautifully after baking.) (Serves 4) *"Healthy quick breakfast for kids."*

KATHY CLARK

French Pan-cake

1/2 cup all-purpose flour
1/2 cup milk
1 egg
1/2 cup orange or lime juice
Confectioners' sugar

Preheat oven to 400 degrees. Beat the first three ingredients in a mixing bowl and pour into a buttered baking dish. Bake for about 15 minutes. Sprinkle with orange or lime juice and confectioners' sugar. (1 serving)

HAYDEE GHAZAL

Pumpkin Pancakes

2 cups all-purpose flour
2 tablespoons brown sugar
1 tablespoon baking powder
1 teaspoon salt
1 teaspoon ground cinnamon
1/4 teaspoon ground nutmeg
1/4 teaspoon ground ginger
1-1/2 cups milk
1/2 cup solid pack pumpkin
1 egg, slightly beaten
2 tablespoons oil

In a large bowl combine dry ingredients. In a separate bowl combine remaining ingredients and mix well. Add this to the flour mixture stirring just until blended. For each pancake pour one-fourth cup batter into hot pan and spread into a circle. Cook until surface bubbles and appears dry and flip.

SHEILA HAUSBECK

Bubble Buns

1/2 cup finely chopped walnuts (or your choice)
1/3 cup sugar
1/2 teaspoon cinnamon
1 package refrigerated biscuits
1/3 cup mayonnaise

Preheat oven to 400 degrees. Grease ten 2-1/2 inch muffin pan cups. In a small bowl combine first three ingredients. Separate biscuits. Cut into quarters; shape into balls. Coat each with mayonnaise. Then roll in nut mixture. Place 4 in each muffin pan cup. Bake for 15-17 minutes or until browned. Serve warm. (10 servings)   SISTER CAROLE FEDDERS

Gingerbread

1 cup sugar
1/4 teaspoon salt
1 teaspoon ginger
1/2 teaspoon cinnamon
1/2 teaspoon cloves
1 cup salad oil
1 cup molasses
2 teaspoons baking soda
1 cup boiling water
2-1/2 cups unsifted all-purpose flour
2 eggs, well beaten

Preheat oven to 350 degrees. In a bowl, combine the sugar, salt, ginger, cinnamon and cloves. Stir in the salad oil, then the molasses, mixing well. Mix the soda into the boiling water and immediately stir into the mixture. Gradually blend in the flour, to prevent lumping. Then mix in the eggs. Turn into a greased 9 x 13-inch pan and bake for 40-45 minutes. (12-18 servings)

LEMON SAUCE:
1/4 cup butter
1 cup sugar
2 tablespoons all-purpose flour
1-1/4 cups boiling water
1/2 teaspoon grated lemon peel
Dash of nutmeg (optional)
1-1/2 tablespoons lemon juice

In a saucepan, blend butter, sugar and flour. Gradually add boiling water. Add lemon peel and nutmeg. Boil 3 minutes. Remove from heat and stir in the lemon juice. (Makes 1-1/2 cups). Serve this rich lemon sauce with the Gingerbread for spooning on top.   ANN BETZ

Anise Toast

2 eggs
2/3 cup sugar
1 cup all-purpose flour
1 teaspoon anise seed

Preheat oven to 375 degrees. Grease and flour a 9 x 5 x 3-inch loaf pan. Beat eggs and sugar in a small mixing bowl until light and fluffy. Combine flour and anise seed and mix with sugar mixture. Spoon batter into prepared pan. Bake about 20 minutes until toothpick comes out clean. Remove from pan and cut into 1/4-inch slices. Place slices on buttered baking sheet. Bake 3-4 minutes until browned on underside. Flip over. Bake 3-4 minutes on other side. (32 servings)

TONIE LEEDS

Butterscotch Bread

24 frozen dinner rolls (dough balls)
1 (3-ounce) package butterscotch pudding (not instant)
1/2 cup margarine
1/2 teaspoon cinnamon
3/4 cup brown sugar
1/2 cup chopped nuts

Grease a Bundt pan or tube pan. Place all frozen rolls in pan. Sprinkle dry pudding on rolls. Melt margarine, cinnamon, sugar and nuts until sugar is dissolved. Pour over rolls. Cover with foil. Set out overnight or eight hours. Bake at 350 degrees for 30 minutes or until done. Remove from oven. Wait 5-10 minutes and invert.

DANA KREMM

Shortbread

1 pound butter (at room temperature)
5 cups all-purpose flour
1 cup sugar

Preheat oven to 400 degrees. Add flour and sugar together. Slowly add butter and knead until you have a ball of dough and sides of bowl are clean. (The making of this recipe is in the kneading.) Flatten into a 12 x 18-1/2-inch lip cookie sheet, ungreased. Bake for 10 minutes, reduce temperature to 350 degrees and bake for 20 minutes until lightly brown.

ELLEN MACDONALD

BREADS

Wasem's Apple-Oat Bread

1-1/2 cups all-purpose flour
1 teaspoon baking powder
1 teaspoon baking soda
1 teaspoon salt
1 teaspoon cinnamon
1/2 teaspoon nutmeg (freshly grated, if possible)
1 egg
1/3 cup vegetable oil
1/2 cup brown sugar
1 cup applesauce
1 cup rolled oats
1/2 cup raisins

Preheat oven to 350 degrees. Sift together first 6 ingredients. Combine remaining ingredients and beat in dry ingredients. Pour into greased 9 x 5-inch loaf pan and bake for about 60 minutes. *"When cool, I drizzle loaf with my Maple Glaze."*

SUSAN'S MAPLE GLAZE:
1-1/2 to 2 cups sifted confectioners' sugar
Maple syrup (amount varies according to thickness of syrup)

Place sugar in a mixing bowl. Mix in enough maple syrup so that mixture can be drizzled over Apple-Oat Bread.   SUSAN HURWITZ

Banana Nut Bread

1/3 cup margarine
1-1/4 cups sugar
2 beaten eggs
1-1/2 cups all-purpose flour
1/2 teaspoon baking powder
3/4 teaspoon baking soda
1/2 teaspoon salt
1 cup mashed bananas
1 teaspoon vanilla
1/2 cup sour milk*
1 cup chopped walnuts (optional)

Preheat oven to 350 degrees. Cream margarine and sugar together in a bowl. Add eggs. Sift together flour, baking powder, soda and salt. Add to creamed mixture alternating with bananas, vanilla and milk. Add nuts last. Pour into greased and floured loaf pans or 9 x 13-inch cake pan. Bake for 30 minutes. (Makes 2 loaves or 1 sheet pan)

*COOK'S TIP: Sour milk can be made with 1/2 cup of milk plus 2-3 drops of vinegar.   PAULA FINK

Coconut Banana Bread

1/3 cup soft butter
2/3 cup sugar
2 eggs
3 tablespoons milk
1 teaspoon lemon juice
1/2 teaspoon almond extract
1-1/2 cups all-purpose flour plus 1/2 cup whole wheat flour
1 teaspoon baking powder
1/2 teaspoon baking soda
1/2 teaspoon salt
1 cup mashed ripe bananas
1 cup toasted coconut

Preheat oven to 350 degrees. Cream the butter and sugar together in a bowl and add eggs, milk, lemon juice and almond extract. Combine the flour, baking powder, baking soda and salt in another bowl. Mix the wet ingredients with the dry ingredients. Stir bananas and coconut into batter. Pour into a well-greased 9 x 5-inch loaf pan. Bake for 55 minutes. Cool in pan a few minutes, then finish cooling on rack. (Makes 1 loaf)   KATHY CLARK

Maize 'N Blueberry Bread

2 cups all-purpose flour (may use 1/4 cup whole wheat flour)
1 cup sugar
1 teaspoon baking powder
1/4 teaspoon baking soda
1/2 teaspoon salt
2 tablespoons melted butter
1/4 cup hot water
1/2 cup orange juice
1 tablespoon grated orange rind
1 beaten egg
1 cup blueberries

Preheat oven to 350 degrees. Mix all dry ingredients in a large bowl. In another bowl mix all wet ingredients except blueberries. Fold dry and wet ingredients together only until just mixed. Fold in 1 cup blueberries (or more). Bake in greased and floured large loaf pan for 60-70 minutes. (Makes 1 loaf)

ORANGE GLAZE:
2 tablespoons orange juice
1 teaspoon orange rind
2 tablespoons honey

Boil glaze ingredients for 1 minute. Immediately remove bread from pan and spread with glaze.   KATHY CLARK
PHYLLIS ASKEW

Demie's Orange Bread

1/2 cup shortening
1 cup sugar
2 eggs, slightly beaten
1-1/4 cups sifted all-purpose flour
1 teaspoon baking powder
1/2 teaspoon salt
1/2 cup milk
1/2 cup chopped nuts
1 orange peel, grated

Preheat oven to 350 degrees. Cream shortening and sugar in a mixing bowl until fluffy; blend in eggs. Sift flour again with baking powder and salt. Add flour mixture alternately with milk to creamed mixture, stirring constantly. Mix in chopped nuts and orange peel. Bake in 5 x 9-inch loaf pan for 1 hour.

TOPPING:
1/2 cup sugar
Juice of 1 orange

Remove bread from oven and poke a few holes in the top and pour topping on.

DEMETRA RATLIFF

Orange Pecan Bread

1 egg
1 cup orange juice
1 cup raisins, finely cut
1 tablespoon orange rind, grated
2 tablespoons shortening, melted
1 teaspoon vanilla
2 cup all-purpose flour, sifted
1 teaspoon baking powder
1/2 teaspoon baking soda
1/4 teaspoon salt
1 cup sugar
1 cup pecans, chopped

Preheat oven to 350 degrees. Beat egg in a mixing bowl; stir in orange juice, raisins, orange rind, shortening and vanilla. Sift flour, baking powder, baking soda, salt and sugar into the liquid mixture and mix well. Stir in pecans. Pour into a well-greased 5 x 9 x 2-1/2-inch loaf pan. Bake for about 1 hour. (Makes 1 loaf)

ETHEL JOHNSTON

Buttermilk Caraway-Raisin Bread

5 cups sifted all-purpose flour
1 cup sugar
1 tablespoon baking powder
1-1/2 teaspoons salt
1 teaspoon soda
1/2 cup butter
2-1/2 cups white seedless raisins (washed and dried)
3 tablespoons caraway seeds
2-1/2 cups buttermilk
1 egg, slightly beaten

Preheat oven to 350 degrees. Sift flour, sugar, baking powder, salt and soda in a large bowl. Cut butter with pastry blender until mixture resembles coarse cornmeal. Stir in raisins and caraway seeds. Add buttermilk and egg to dry mixture, blending only until flour is moistened. (Mixture will appear lumpy.) Butter generously an 11 x 9-inch heavy cast iron skillet. Turn batter into skillet. Bake until firm and brown, about 1 hour. Serve warm or cold. Butter spread on while bread is still warm is delicious. *"This is an old-fashioned recipe. Delicious with casseroles or serve for breakfast for an extra-special treat."*

PEG GRIFFIN

Rhubarb Nut Bread

1-1/2 cups brown sugar
2/3 cup oil
1 egg
1 cup sour milk (or buttermilk)
1 teaspoon salt
1 teaspoon baking soda
1 teaspoon vanilla
2-1/2 cups all-purpose flour
1-1/2 cups rhubarb, diced
1/2 cup chopped nuts

TOPPING:
1/3 cup sugar
1 tablespoon butter
Cinnamon

Preheat oven to 325 degrees. In a large mixing bowl stir together first 8 ingredients. Add rhubarb and nuts. Pour into 2 greased loaf pans. Cut together with pastry cutter the ingredients for the topping and sprinkle over the batter. Bake for 60 minutes. Do not overbake. (Makes 2 loaves)

JOYCE TREPPA

Strawberry Bread

3 cups all-purpose flour (may use 2-1/2 cups whole wheat flour plus
   3/4 cup wheat germ)
1 teaspoon salt
2 cups light brown sugar
1 teaspoon soda
3 teaspoons cinnamon
4 eggs
2 (10-ounce) packages frozen strawberries
3/4 cup salad oil
1/2 cup butter, softened

Preheat oven to 350 degrees. Mix dry ingredients in a large bowl. Make a well in the center and add the eggs, thawed strawberries, salad oil and butter. Mix until well blended. Grease and flour two loaf pans. Bake 1 hour. (Makes 2 loaves)

JO ZEISLER

Carrot Bread

1-1/2 cups Mazola oil
2 cups sugar
3 eggs
2 cups finely grated raw carrots
3 cups all-purpose flour
1 teaspoon baking soda
1 teaspoon salt
2 teaspoons baking powder
2 teaspoons cinnamon
1 teaspoon vanilla

Preheat oven to 350 degrees. Mix oil and sugar together in a small bowl. Let set a few minutes. In a mixing bowl with an electric beater, beat the oil and sugar, add eggs and carrots and the dry ingredients. Blend well. Then pour into greased 9-inch loaf pans and bake for about 55 minutes. *"This recipe freezes well."*

KAY SHAW

Chocolate Zucchini Bread

4 eggs
3 cups sugar
3 (1-ounce) squares unsweetened chocolate, melted
1-1/2 cups oil (I prefer sunflower)
2 teaspoons vanilla
3 cups all-purpose flour
1-1/2 teaspoons baking soda
1 teaspoon salt
3 cups zucchini, chopped
1 cup nuts, chopped

Preheat oven to 350 degrees. Beat the eggs in a mixing bowl until thick and light. Add sugar a quarter cup at a time. Add chocolate, oil and vanilla. Combine flour, soda and salt together. Alternate additions of the flour mixture with the chocolate and zucchini mixture and nuts. Pour into a greased and floured loaf pan and fill no more than two-thirds full. Bake for one and a quarter hours or until a toothpick comes out clean. (Makes 1 loaf)

NIKKI WOODROW-RUSH

Zucchini Bread

3 eggs
2 cups sugar
2 cups zucchini, grated
1/4 teaspoon salt
2 teaspoons vanilla
1 teaspoon baking powder
1 teaspoon baking soda
1 teaspoon cinnamon
1/2 teaspoon nutmeg
3 cups all-purpose flour
1 cup oil
1 cup walnuts (optional)

Preheat oven to 325 degrees. Mix eggs, sugar, zucchini, salt and vanilla together in a large bowl. Add remainder of ingredients. Fold into greased and floured loaf pans or 9 x 13-inch cake pan. Bake 50-60 minutes. (Makes 2 loaves or 1 sheet pan) *"Makes a moist bread or cake."*

PAULA FINK

Lucy's Bran Muffins

2 cups Kellogg's all-bran cereal
2 cups Nabisco 100 all-bran cereal
1 cup boiling water
2 cups buttermilk
1-1/4 cups sugar
1/2 cup Crisco
2 eggs
2-1/2 cups all-purpose flour
2-1/2 teaspoons baking soda
1/4 teaspoon salt
1/2 cup raisins
1/2 cup dates, chopped

Combine all-bran cereal and Nabisco 100 all-bran, boiling water and buttermilk in a large mixing bowl. Let this mixture soak for 1 hour. Preheat oven to 350 degrees. While this is soaking, combine sugar, Crisco and eggs. Beat till smooth. In a separate bowl, combine flour, baking soda and salt. Combine everything together adding raisins and dates. Place batter in greased muffin tins. Bake for 30 minutes. (Makes 24 muffins)

LUCY CHARTIER

Plain Muffins

3 cups bread flour
2 teaspoons salt
2-1/2 teaspoons baking powder
1 teaspoon baking soda
1-1/2 cups sugar
3/4 cup all-purpose shortening
2 cups water
2 small eggs

Preheat oven to 400 degrees. Place first 5 ingredients in bowl. Mix together. Add shortening, water and eggs and mix by hand until the dry ingredients are moistened. Do not overmix. Portion into greased muffin cups and bake for 20-25 minutes. (Makes 20-24 muffins)

UNIVERSITY OF MICHIGAN HOSPITALS
DEPARTMENT OF DIETETICS

Apple Muffins

1/4 cup shortening
1/2 cup sugar
1 egg
2 cups sifted all-purpose flour
4 teaspoons baking powder
1/2 teaspoon salt
2/3 teaspoon cinnamon or apple pie spice
1 cup milk
1 cup chopped apples mixed with 1/4 cup sugar

Preheat oven to 375 degrees. Cream shortening in a large bowl, add sugar gradually, add egg. Sift flour, baking powder, salt and cinnamon together. Add alternately with milk. Add apples. Bake in muffin tins about 24 minutes. (Makes 12 muffins)

ETHEL JOHNSTON

Banana Muffins

3 cups bread flour
2 teaspoons salt
2-1/2 teaspoons baking powder
1 teaspoon baking soda
1-1/2 cups sugar
3/4 cup all-purpose shortening
2 cups mashed bananas
1-2/3 cups water
2 small eggs

Preheat oven to 400 degrees. Combine first 5 ingredients and mix well. Add shortening, mashed bananas, water and eggs and mix well. Portion into greased muffin cups and bake for 20-25 minutes. (Makes 20-24 muffins)

UNIVERSITY OF MICHIGAN HOSPITALS
DEPARTMENT OF DIETETICS

Blueberry Muffins

3 cups bread flour
2 teaspoons salt
2-1/2 teaspoons baking powder
1 teaspoon baking soda
1-3/4 cups sugar
3/4 cup all-purpose shortening
1-2/3 cups water
2 small eggs
1/2 pound frozen or fresh blueberries

Preheat oven to 400 degrees. Combine first 5 ingredients in a bowl and mix well. Add shortening, water and eggs and mix. Add blueberries last. Portion into greased muffin cups and bake for 20-25 minutes. (Makes 20-24 muffins)

UNIVERSITY OF MICHIGAN HOSPITALS
DEPARTMENT OF DIETETICS

Cherry Muffins

3 cups bread flour
2 teaspoons salt
2-1/2 teaspoons baking powder
1 teaspoon baking soda
1-1/2 cups sugar
3/4 cup all-purpose shortening
1 cup chopped maraschino cherries
1-2/3 cups water
2 small eggs

Preheat oven to 400 degrees. Mix first 5 ingredients well in a bowl. Add shortening and cherries to dry ingredients. Add water and eggs and blend. Portion into greased muffin cups and bake for 20-25 minutes. (Makes 20-24 muffins)

UNIVERSITY OF MICHIGAN HOSPITALS
DEPARTMENT OF DIETETICS

Date Nut Muffins

3 cups bread flour
2 teaspoons salt
2-1/2 teaspoons baking powder
1 teaspoon baking soda
1-1/2 cups sugar
3/4 cup all-purpose shortening
1-2/3 cups water
2 small eggs
1/2 cup dates, chopped
1/2 cup nuts, chopped

Preheat oven to 400 degrees. Combine first 5 ingredients in a bowl and mix
well. Add shortening, water and eggs and blend. Add dates and nuts to
mixture. Pour into greased muffin cups and bake for 20-25 minutes.
(Makes 20-24 muffins)

UNIVERSITY OF MICHIGAN HOSPITALS
DEPARTMENT OF DIETETICS

Orange Muffins

3 cups bread flour
2 teaspoons salt
2-1/2 teaspoons baking powder
1 teaspoon baking soda
1-1/2 cups sugar
3/4 cup all-purpose shortening
1/2 pound oranges, ground
1-2/3 cups water
2 small eggs

Preheat oven to 400 degrees. Mix first 5 ingredients together in a bowl. Add
shortening, oranges, water and eggs and mix. Portion into greased muffin cups
and bake for 20-25 minutes. (Makes 20-24 muffins)

UNIVERSITY OF MICHIGAN HOSPITALS
DEPARTMENT OF DIETETICS

Six-Week Muffins

2 cups boiling water
2 large shredded wheat biscuits
1/2 pound raisins or chopped dates
3/4 cup shortening
2-1/2 cups sugar
4 eggs
5 cups all-purpose flour
1 quart buttermilk
4 teaspoons salt
5 teaspoons soda
4 cups bran buds (or all bran)

Pour boiling water over shredded wheat biscuits. Add raisins or dates. Cool. Cream shortening and sugar. Combine with eggs, flour, buttermilk, salt, soda and bran. Mix and store in refrigerator covered with waxed paper. Spoon as needed into muffin cups, but do not stir. Batter improves with age. Bake at 425 degrees for about 15 minutes. (Makes a total of 4 dozen muffins)

DEE CORNISH
JUDY MOYER

Bagels

1 package dry yeast
1 cup warm water (105-115 degrees F)
2 tablespoons sugar
1-1/2 teaspoons salt
2-3/4 cups all-purpose flour

Dissolve yeast in warm water in large bowl. Stir in sugar, salt and 1-1/4 cup of the flour. Stir until smooth, add remaining flour. Knead dough on lightly-floured surface until smooth and elastic, about 15 minutes. Punch down dough and divide into 8 equal parts. Make each part into a bagel shape, place on greased pan and let rise in warm place for 20 minutes. Preheat oven to 375 degrees and heat 2 quarts of water in a large kettle. Heat to boiling. Reduce heat and drop in 4 bagels. Simmer 7 minutes, turning once. Repeat with remaining bagels. Bake on a greased baking sheet until golden brown, 30-35 minutes, turning once.

Variations: When mixing in sugar and salt, add 1 egg and/or raisins.

SHEILA HAUSBECK

Raised Pretzels

1 quart milk
1 cup sugar
2 tablespoons coarse salt
1/2 cup solid shortening
1/2 cup margarine
2 packages dry yeast
1/4 cup warm water
12 cups all-purpose flour
4 eggs
1-1/2 teaspoons baking powder

Heat milk to boiling in a large saucepan; add sugar, salt, shortening and margarine. Cool to lukewarm. Dissolve yeast in warm water and add to milk mixture. Combine flour, eggs and baking powder. Add to milk mixture. Let rise. Punch down and knead; then let rest 10 minutes. Roll into pretzels. Let rise. Preheat oven to 450 degrees. (Makes 6 dozen)

DIPPING SOLUTION:
1-1/2 teaspoons lye
1 quart warm water
Pinch of soda
Pinch of salt
1 tablespoon instant coffee (optional if you want them browner)

Dip pretzels in solution and bake for 5-7 minutes. Grease pans with beeswax. Use coarse salt which you can either put on just before baking or when they are reheated from the freezer.

SHELLY ROBBINS

Overnight Yeast Rolls

4 cups all-purpose flour
1/2 cup sugar
1 package dry yeast
2 cups warm water
3/4 cup margarine, melted
1 egg

Place flour and sugar in a bowl and create a shallow hole. Place yeast in shallow hole and pour warm water and melted magarine in. Stir gradually including flour. Add egg when all combined. Place dough in covered container and refrigerate for a minimum of 1-1/2 hours, maximum 24 hours. Preheat oven to 350 degrees. Pour mixture into greased muffin tins and bake for 20 minutes or until brown. (Makes 2 dozen rolls)

PAULA FINK

German Bread

2 cups milk
1 tablespoon sugar
3 packages dry yeast
7 cups all-purpose sifted flour
1 cup sugar
1 teaspoon salt
3 eggs
4 tablespoons butter (at room temperature)
1 egg (to brush on top of bread)

Heat milk lukewarm in a medium saucepan; add sugar. Add yeast and let stand for 10 minutes. Mix flour, sugar and salt. Add eggs and mix well. Add milk to the flour mixture and beat with electric mixer on slow speed till all blended. Add butter Dough is now complete. Sprinkle flour on board and knead dough for about 10 minutes. After this is done, place dough in a bowl and let rise for 1 hour in a warm place and cover after punching down dough. Let rise again for 1 more hour. Cover dough. Preheat oven to 350 degrees. Place dough on board and separate into 3 parts. Elongate to criss-cross dough. Beat egg and glaze top of bread after it is in the pan. Use a greased Bundt pan to bake. Let dough rise for 30 minutes more before baking. Bake for 40 minutes in center of oven. (18 servings)

JEANNINE CHARRON

Buttermilk Cheese Bread

1 cup buttermilk
2 tablespoons sugar
2-1/2 teaspoons salt
1 tablespoon shortening
1-1/2 cups grated cheddar cheese (6 ounces)
1 package dry yeast
1 cup lukewarm water
1/2 teaspoon baking soda
6 cups sifted all-purpose flour

Scald buttermilk with sugar, salt and shortening in a saucepan; let cool a bit, then add grated cheese if it is real cold (if at room temperature beat in after you add the first amount of flour). Dissolve the yeast in warm water and add, then stir in 2 cups of flour to which the baking soda has been mixed and beat to a smooth soft dough. Gradually add the remaining flour, then knead until smooth and elastic. Grease bowl,.add dough and grease top, let rise about an hour, until about double in bulk. Punch down, divide dough in half and knead each a few times. Put in greased pans and grease top. Let rise until about double (1 hour). Bake at 350 degrees about 1 hour or until bread gives a hollow sound when tapped. Grease top and remove from pans to cool on wire rack.

ESTHER SCHULZ

Herb-Parmesan Bread

2 packages dry yeast
2 cups warm water
2 tablespoons sugar
2 teaspoons salt
2 tablespoons soft butter
1/4 cup plus 1 tablespoon grated Parmesan
1-1/2 tablespoons oregano
1 teaspoon basil
4-1/4 cups sifted all-purpose flour

Sprinkle yeast over water in large bowl of electric mixer. Let stand a few minutes, then stir to dissolve yeast. Add sugar, salt, butter, 1/4 cup cheese, oregano, basil and 3 cups flour. Beat at low speed until blended or process in food processor. At medium speed, beat until smooth, about 2 minutes. Scrape bowls and beaters. With a wooden spoon, gradually beat in the rest of the flour to make a smooth, but sticky, dough. Cover the bowl with wax paper and towel. Let rise in a warm place 45 minutes or until double in bulk. Preheat oven to 375 degrees. Grease a 1-1/2 to 2 quart casserole or bowl. With wooden spoon, stir down batter. Beat about 1/2 minute. Turn batter into casserole. Sprinkle with 1 tablespoon Parmesan. Bake about 45-55 minutes or until browned. (Makes 1 round loaf)

NANCY BUNIN

Dixie Biscuits

1 cup mashed potatoes
1 cup potato water (water in which potatoes were boiled)
1 cup water
2/3 cup sugar
1 package dry yeast
2 eggs
2 teaspoons salt
1 cup minus 1 tablespoon shortening
7-1/2 cups all-purpose flour, sifted
Melted butter

Mix potato, potato water and water, sugar and yeast in a large bowl. Let stand 2 hours. Then add beaten eggs and salt. Cut shortening into flour (like biscuits) and add to yeast mixture. Store in refrigerator and use as desired by rolling out and cutting like biscuits. Leave about 3-inch space between them in pan. Brush tops with melted butter and let rise about 2 hours. Bake in a 325 degree oven 20-25 minutes. (Makes 5 dozen biscuits) *"Dough is also good for cinnamon buns."*

ETHEL JOHNSTON

Portuguese Sweet Bread

1 cup diced pared potato
2 cups boiling water
7-1/4 to 7-1/2 cups all-purpose flour
2 packages dry yeast
2/3 cup sugar
6 tablespoons margarine
2 teaspoons salt
3 eggs
1-1/2 cups raisins
1 beaten egg (for brushing on loaves)
Slivered almonds for top

Cook potato in a saucepan until tender; drain and reserve 1-2/3 cups liquid. Mash potato. Stir together 2-1/2 cups flour and yeast. Heat liquid, sugar, margarine and salt until warm. Add to yeast mixture, then add eggs and potatoes. Beat with electric mixer 1/2 minute; beat at high speed for another 3 minutes. Stir by hand; add raisins and enough flour to make a moderately stiff dough. Knead until smooth, about 8-10 minutes. Let rise until double, about 1 to 1-1/4 hours. Divide into thirds. Let rest 10 minutes. Shape into round loaves; cover and let rise until double. Preheat oven to 375 degrees. Brush tops of loaves with beaten egg. Sprinkle with almonds. Bake for 35-40 minutes. Cover with foil after 20 minutes to prevent excessive browning. (Makes 3 loaves) *"This bread freezes well."*

SANDRA MERKEL

Brewer's Rye Bread

5-6 cups unsifted all-purpose flour
4 cups unsifted rye flour
2 cups milk
1 tablespoon salt
1/3 cup dark molasses
1/4 cup margarine
1-1/4 cups warm ale (105-115 degrees)
2 packages dry yeast
1/2 teaspoon fennel seed

Combine flours in a large bowl, set aside. Scald milk; stir in salt, molasses and margarine. Cool to lukewarm. Measure ale into large warm bowl. Sprinkle in yeast; stir until dissolved. Stir in warm milk mixture, fennel seed and 4 cups flour mixture. Beat until smooth. Let batter rise in warm place, until doubled in bulk, about 30 minutes. Stir batter down, stir in additional flour mixture to make a stiff dough. Turn out onto lightly floured board; knead until smooth and elastic about 12 minutes. Place in greased bowl, turning to grease top. Cover; let rise until doubled in bulk, about 45 minutes. Punch dough down; divide in half. Form each half into a smooth ball. Flatten into a mound, about 7 inches in diameter. Place on 2 greased baking sheets. Cover; let rise in warm place, until doubled, about 50 minutes. Bake at 375 degreees about 35 minutes. Cool on racks. (Makes 2 loaves) *"Best part is finishing off remaining ale while dough rises."*

THOMAS SHOPE

Swedish Rye Bread

4 cups milk
1/2 cup sugar
1/2 cup butter
1 tablespoon salt
1/4 cup molasses
2 packages dry yeast plus 1/4 cup warm water
1 cup rye flour plus enough all-purpose flour for a medium-stiff dough

Scald milk in a saucepan and pour over sugar, butter, salt and molasses. Cool to lukewarm. Dissolve yeast in water and add to above mixture. Add flour. Let rise until double in bulk in a greased bowl. Make into loaves and let rise again. Bake 50 minutes in 350 degree oven.

JANET GILSDORF

BREADS

New Orleans French Quarter Beignets

3 cups all-purpose flour
1 package dry yeast
1/2 teaspoon ground nutmeg
1 cup milk
1/4 cup sugar
1/4 cup cooking oil
3/4 teaspoon salt
1 egg
Confectioners' sugar

In a large bowl, combine 1-3/4 cups flour, yeast and nutmeg. In a saucepan, heat milk, sugar, oil and salt just until warm, stirring occasionally. Add to yeast mixture and add egg. Beat well (may use food processor). Stir in enough additional flour to make a soft dough. Turn into greased bowl and chill. Turn dough out onto well-floured surface; form into ball. Cover and rest about 10 minutes. Roll dough to 18 x 12-inch rectangle. Cut in 3 x 2-inch rectangles. Cover and let rise 30 minutes (will not be double). Fry a few at a time in deep fat (375 degrees), turning once until golden, about one minute. Drain on paper toweling; sprinkle with confectioners' sugar. (36 servings) *"Best served freshly made."*

JANET GILSDORF

English Tea Ring

1 package dry yeast
1/4 cup warm water
1/2 cup milk, scalded
1/4 cup sugar
1/4 cup shortening
1 teaspoon salt
2-1/2 plus 3/4 cups all-purpose flour
1 beaten egg
1/2 teaspoon vanilla
1/4 cup sugar
1 teaspoon cinnamon
1/2 cup walnuts, chopped
1/2 cup candied fruit or raisins

Soften yeast in water. Combine milk, sugar, shortening and salt. Cool. Beat in 1 cup flour, yeast, egg and vanilla. Mix in enough flour to make soft dough. Knead lightly. Place in greased bowl. Let rise until double (1-1/2 to 2 hours). Roll out to 13 x 9-inch rectangle. Brush on a little melted butter. Combine sugar, cinnamon, walnuts and fruit. Sprinkle with sugar mixture. Roll into loaf. Shape in circle and seal edges. Put in greased cookie sheet. Snip evenly around on top. Let rise until double. Preheat oven to 375 degrees. Brush top with milk. Bake for 20-25 minutes.

SALLY JOHNSTON

94

Christmas Stollen

1-1/2 cups scalded milk
1 cup sugar
1-1/3 cups margarine or butter
2 teaspoons salt
2 packages dry yeast (or 2 cakes)
1/2 cup lukewarm water
9 cups all-purpose flour
4 eggs, well beaten
1-1/2 cups blanched almonds, chopped
1-1/2 cups white raisins
Grated rind of 1 lemon (or 2 teaspoons dried peel)
4 ounces finely diced citron peel
4 ounces diced candied berries
1/4 cup diced candied pineapple
2 teaspoons vanilla
1/2 cup sugar
2 teaspoons cinnamon
Melted margarine (to brush on top)
Confectioners' sugar glaze

In a large bowl mix together the scalded milk, sugar, margarine and salt. Cool to lukewarm, then add the yeast dissolved in lukewarm water and 2 cups flour and mix well. Raise until light and bubbly, about 1-1/2 hours. Add in order given: 6 cups flour, eggs well beaten, blanched almonds, chopped, white raisins, grated rind or peel, citron peel, candied cherries, candied pineapple and vanilla. Mix well and use about 1 cup of flour in kneading the dough well, then divided in 4 equal parts. Taking one part at a time, roll out 1/2-inch thick in oval shape and sprinkle with a sugar-cinnamon mixture (1/2 cup sugar with 2 teaspoons cinnamon until well-blended) or buy mix at store. Fold over as you would for a Parker House roll and press edges firmly together. Brush with melted margarine. Raise until doubled in bulk and bake at 350 degrees about 45 minutes. Ice with a thick confectioners' sugar glaze. I use regular bread pans and roll them up like a jelly roll, with the seam side down. If folded over, bake them on a cookie sheet.

ESTHER SCHULZ

Sweet Roll Dough

1/2 cup warm water
2 packages dry yeast
1-1/2 cups lukewarm milk
1/2 cup sugar
2 teaspoons salt
2 eggs
1/2 cup soft shortening
7 to 7-1/2 cups sifted all-purpose flour

Measure the warm water and yeast into a mixing bowl. Stir in the milk, sugar, salt, eggs, shortening and half of the sifted flour. Mix with spoon until smooth. Add enough remaining flour to handle easily; mix with hand. Turn onto lightly floured board; knead until smooth and elastic (about 5 minutes). Round up in greased bowl, greased side up. Cover with damp cloth. Let rise in warm place (85 degrees) until double (about 1-1/2 hours). Punch down; let rise again until almost double (about 30 minutes). Divide dough for desired rolls and coffee cakes. Shape, let rise, bake at 400 degrees, 12-15 minutes. (Makes 2 dozen rolls) *"Can be used for dinner rolls or coffee cake."*

KATHERINE KERSEY

Sweet Rolls

3/4 cup scalded milk
4-1/2 teaspoons shortening
4-1/2 teaspoons sugar
1-1/2 teaspoons salt
3/4 cup water or milk
1-1/2 packages dry yeast
2 eggs, well beaten
4-1/2 cups sifted all-purpose flour
1 tablespoon butter, cut in small pieces
3-4 tablespoons brown sugar
1 tablespoon cinnamon
3/4 cup brown sugar
3 tablespoons light corn syrup
1-1/2 tablespoons butter
1/2 cup chopped nuts

Combine scalded milk, shortening, sugar and salt. Cool to lukewarm by adding water or milk. Add yeast. Blend in eggs. Gradually add flour. Mix until well-blended and soft. Let rise in warm place until light. Roll out on board in rectangle and sprinkle with butter, brown sugar and cinnamon. Beginning with long edge, roll up. Cut in 3/4-inch slices. Combine and heat in saucepan, brown sugar, light corn syrup and butter. Spread evenly in bottom of 9 x 13-inch pan. Add nuts. Place rolls on top of filling; let rise and bake at 375 degrees for 24-30 minutes.

FLO JOHNSTON

96

Poultry

97

POULTRY

Apricot Chicken

1 (6-ounce) jar apricot preserves
1 package Lipton onion soup mix
1 (8-ounce) bottle Kraft French dressing
2 fryer chickens, cut up
Cooked noodles or rice

Preheat oven to 350 degrees. In a bowl mix apricot preserves, onion soup mix and French dressing together. Place chicken in a roasting pan. Bake for 1 to 1-1/2 hours. Baste every 10-15 minutes with apricot preserve mixture. Serve with noodles or rice. (Serves 8) *This recipe was given to our office staff by Dr. William Weintraub who practiced in Pediatric Surgery from 1974-79. It is wonderful and sticky."*

JODI MATTIS

Debbie's Chicken a L'Orange

3 pounds chicken, cut up
1/4 cup all-purpose flour
1/4 cup cooking oil
Salt and pepper to taste
3 oranges, peeled and cut into cartwheels (for garnish)

Preheat oven to 350 degrees. Dust chicken lightly with flour. In a large skillet, brown chicken in oil. Season to taste. Remove chicken from skillet and put into a 3-quart baking dish.

ORANGE SAUCE:
1 cup orange juice
1/2 cup chili sauce
1/4 cup chopped green pepper
1 teaspoon dry mustard
2 tablespoons soy sauce
1/2 tablespoon honey

Place all ingredients of sauce into a saucepan and simmer 2-3 minutes. Pour sauce over chicken. Cover and bake for 60 minutes. Before serving, decorate with cartwheels. (4 servings)

CAROLINE BLANE

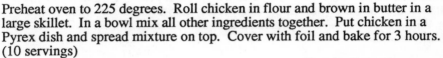

Charleston Chicken

5-6 chicken breasts, split
Flour for dredging
3 tablespoons butter
1 (10-3/4 ounce) can cream of chicken soup
1 cup white wine or sherry
1 (16-ounce) jar onions, drained
1 (4-ounce) can mushrooms, drained
Dash of paprika

Preheat oven to 225 degrees. Roll chicken in flour and brown in butter in a large skillet. In a bowl mix all other ingredients together. Put chicken in a Pyrex dish and spread mixture on top. Cover with foil and bake for 3 hours. (10 servings)

SHARON SHANNON

Chicken and Pasta

4 boneless chicken breasts
2 tablespoons olive oil
2 cloves garlic, minced
1 (14-ounce) can artichoke hearts
1/2 pound fresh mushrooms
1/2 cup white wine
1 cup butter
2 pints heavy cream
2 cups freshly grated Parmesan cheese
Salt and pepper to taste
1 (1-pound) package herbal pasta (tomato/spinach/herb)
Parsley for garnish

Cut chicken in bite-size pieces and saute in a large skillet in olive oil and garlic for approximately 10 minutes. Add artichoke hearts (quartered), mushrooms, white wine and simmer, uncovered until most of the liquid is reduced (15 minutes). While chicken, artichokes and mushrooms are simmering, melt butter in large saucepan. When melted, add cream and cheese. Simmer until almost creamy. Salt and pepper. Boil pasta to al dente and combine chicken, sauce and pasta together in large bowl. Garnish with parsley. (Serves 6)*"This recipe was made up after eating a similar dish at Maude's. Very easy to prepare."*

COOK'S TIP: I use the fresh tomato/spinach/herbal type of pasta sold at Kroger's.

SARA HICKEY

Chicken Veronique

2 pounds boned breast of chicken
1/2 cup all-purpose flour
4-5 tablespoons olive oil
1 clove garlic, minced
2 (14-ounce) cans artichoke bottoms (well-washed in water),
    quartered
1 pound fresh mushrooms, sliced
1/2 cup white wine
Salt and pepper to taste
Cooked pasta

Cut chicken into bite-sized pieces. Cover with flour. Heat olive oil in Teflon pan. Add chicken to hot oil. Add minced garlic. Stir-fry until chicken is well-browned. Set aside. Stir-fry artichoke bottoms and mushrooms briefly. Reduce heat. Add chicken and white wine. Simmer, covered, for 10-15 minutes. Season to taste. Serve with pasta. (4 servings)

ED PROCHOWNIK

Chicken Breasts Tarragon

4 chicken breasts, skinned, boned and halved
4 tablespoons all-purpose flour (seasoned with paprika and salt)
4 tablespoons cooking oil
1 (4-ounce) can mushrooms
1 medium onion, chopped
1 teaspoon dried tarragon
1/4 cup white wine
1 cup chicken broth
1/2 pint heavy cream
Cooked rice

Dredge chicken breasts in seasoned flour. Heat oil in a large skillet. Lightly brown chicken turning once. Add mushrooms and onions; saute until onion becomes clear. Sprinkle tarragon on chicken breasts, add wine and simmer until wine evaporates. Add chicken broth and simmer mixture one hour or until breasts can be cut with fork. Add cream and simmer until sauce thickens. Serve over rice cooked in chicken broth (broth may be made with bones and skin removed from chicken breasts). A green salad and apricot-glazed carrots are excellent accompaniments. *"Elegant fare served with a Pinot Chardonnay or Champagne."*

RONALD HALL

Chicken Cordon Bleu I

3 whole chicken breasts, split, boned, skinned
3 slices Swiss cheese, cut in half
3 slices boiled ham, cut in half
2 tablespoons butter or margarine
1 (10-3/4 ounce) can cream of chicken soup
1/2 cup milk
Chopped parsley

Flatten chicken breasts with flat side of knife. Top each with half slice of cheese and ham. Roll and secure with toothpicks. In a large skillet, brown chicken in butter. Stir in soup and milk. Cover. Cook over low heat for 20 minutes. Stir occasionally. Top with parsley. (Serves 6)

PHYLLIS MULHOLLAND

Chicken Cordon Bleu II

4 thin slices boiled ham (about 3 x 3 inches)
2 slices Swiss cheese, cut in half (each half sliced and stacked to form a small rectangle or triangle)
2 whole boneless chicken breasts, cut in half
1/4 cup margarine
3/4 cup dry bread crumbs
1/2 teaspoon salt
1/8 teaspoon paprika

Preheat oven to 400 degrees. Fold ham around cheese. Wrap half of chicken breast around ham and cheese. Melt margarine in pie plate. Mix bread crumbs, salt and paprika in second pie plate. Roll stuffed chicken breasts first in margarine, then in crumb mixture to coat well. Place in single layer in buttered baking dish. Bake for 40 minutes. (4 servings)

COOK'S TIP: For a quick and easy gravy, heat one can or jar of prepared chicken gravy with a 4-ounce jar sliced mushrooms and serve over chicken.

CAROL DROGOWSKI

Chicken Divan I

4 whole chicken breasts, stewed and boned
3 (10-ounce) packages broccoli, cooked
2 (10-3/4 ounce) cans cream of mushroom soup
3/4 cup mayonnaise
1/4 teaspoon curry
1 cup grated cheddar cheese

Arrange chicken and broccoli in layers in a 9 x 12-inch baking dish. Preheat oven to 350 degrees. Combine soup, mayonnaise and curry. Pour sauce mixture on top of broccoli and chicken. Sprinkle with cheese and bake for 1 hour. (4 servings)

GEORGIA KASKO

Classic Chicken Divan II

2 bunches fresh broccoli (or two 10-ounce packages frozen)
1/4 cup butter
1/4 cup all-purpose flour
2 cups chicken broth
1/2 cup heavy cream
3 tablespoons sherry
1/2 teaspoon salt
Pepper to taste
3 chicken breasts, cooked and thinly sliced
1/2 cup grated Parmesan cheese

Cook broccoli in a large saucepan until barely tender. Drain and place broccoli spears crosswise into a rectangular casserole dish. Melt the butter. Add flour and blend in with a wire whisk. Add all the chicken broth and continue to stir. Cook until the mixture thickens. Stir in cream, sherry, salt and pepper. Preheat oven to 350 degrees. Pour half of the sauce over the broccoli. Top with chicken slices. Add 1/4 cup Parmesan cheese to the rest of the sauce. Pour the remainder of the sauce over the chicken slices. Sprinkle the top with more Parmesan cheese. Bake 20 minutes or until it is bubbly hot.

JOAN ROTH
(SUBMITTED AT REQUEST OF
DONITA SULLIVAN)

Easy Poulet de Broccoli
(Easy Chicken and Broccoli Casserole)

6 cooked chicken breasts, boned and skinned, cubed
2 packages fresh or frozen broccoli (if fresh, cook 5 minutes)
2 (10-3/4 ounce) cans cream of chicken (or mushroom soup)
1 cup mayonnaise (not Miracle Whip) or sour cream
1 teaspoon lemon juice
1/2 teaspoon tarragon

TOPPING:
1-1/4 cups cheddar cheese
1-1/4 cups bread crumbs
2 tablespoons melted butter

Preheat oven to 350 degrees. Layer chicken and broccoli in buttered casserole. Combine sauce ingredients in a bowl and pour over chicken and broccoli. Top with cheddar cheese. Combine bread crumbs and melted butter. Cover cheese with bread crumbs mixture. Bake for 30 minutes.

NANCY COLLINS

Chicken Florentine

1 pound chicken breasts, skinned and boned
1/8 teaspoon pepper
3/4 cup chicken broth
2 tablespoons dry white wine
1 pound fresh spinach (or 10-ounce package frozen)
1 tablespoon water
2 teaspoons cornstarch
3 ounces Neufchatel cheese, cut up (or cream cheese)
Lemon juice
Paprika
Lemon slices (optional)

Place chicken in a skillet. Sprinkle with pepper. Add broth and wine, bring to boiling. Reduce heat; cover and simmer 25-30 minutes. Remove chicken with slotted spoon. Cover and keep warm. Reserve broth in skillet. Meanwhile, wash spinach. Cook in large saucepan, covered, with just the water that clings to the leaves. Reduce heat when steam forms. Cook and toss 3 minutes. Drain, set aside and keep warm. Combine water and cornstarch. Stir into broth in skillet. Cook and stir until thickened and bubbly. Cook 2 minutes more. Add Neufchatel cheese; stir until cheese is melted. Arrange spinach on serving plate; sprinkle with lemon juice. Top with chicken and sauce. Sprinkle with paprika. Garnish chicken with lemon slices if desired. (4 servings)

FRANK MOLER

Terry's Easy Chicken

1 medium onion, chopped
1/2 cup celery, diced
2 tablespoons oil
1 cup mushrooms, sliced
6 chicken breasts, boneless
1 cup bread crumbs
1 cup cooking oil
1 can French green beans
1 (10-3/4 ounce) can cream of mushroom soup
1 soup can water
Salt and pepper to taste

Preheat oven to 300 degrees. Saute onion and celery together in a large skillet in oil. Stir in mushrooms; set aside. Dip chicken breasts in water; roll in bread crumbs and fry in oil quickly. Brown both sides. Lay breasts in baking dish or pan; spoon onion, celery and mushrooms on top. Add drained green beans from can. Dilute mushroom soup with one can of water and pour on top. Bake approximately 45 minutes to 1 hour or until breasts are tender.

TERRY PERDUE

Chicken-Rice Casserole

2 whole cut-up chickens (or only legs or breasts)
1 cup rice, uncooked
1 package onion soup mix
1 (10-3/4 ounce) can cream of mushroom soup
2 soup cans water

Preheat oven to 375 degrees. Remove skin from chicken, if desired. Place chicken pieces in 9 x 13-inch baking dish. Sprinkle rice and soup mix over top of chicken. Dilute cream of mushroom soup with 2 cans of water. Heat to boiling. Pour over chicken. Cover pan with foil. Bake for 1-1/2 hours. (4 servings)

MARILYN DEAN KENNEDY

Crab-Stuffed Chicken

4 (12 ounces each) large chicken breasts, halved, skinned and boned
3 tablespoons butter or margarine
1/4 cup all-purpose flour
3/4 cup milk
3/4 cup chicken broth
1/3 cup dry white wine
1/4 cup chopped onion
1 tablespoon butter or margarine
1 (7-1/2 ounce) can crabmeat, drained, flaked and cartilage removed
1 (3-ounce) can chopped mushrooms, drained
1/2 cup coarsely crumbled saltine crackers (10 crackers)
2 tablespoons snipped parsley
1/2 teaspoon salt
Dash of pepper
1 cup (4 ounces) grated Swiss cheese
1/2 teaspoon paprika

Place one chicken piece, boned side up, between 2 pieces of waxed paper. Working from center out, pound chicken lightly with meat mallet to make cutlet about 1/8-inch thick (8 x 5 inches). Repeat with remaining chicken. Set aside. In a saucepan melt the butter or magarine; blend in flour. Add milk, chicken broth and wine all at once; cook and stir until mixture thickens and bubbles. Set aside. Preheat oven to 350 degrees. In a skillet, cook onion in the remaining butter until tender but not brown. Stir in crab, mushrooms, cracker crumbs, parsley, salt and pepper. Stir in 2 tablespoons of the sauce. Top each chicken piece with about 1/4 cup crab mixture. Fold sides in; roll up. Place seam side down in a 12 x 7-1/2 x 2-inch baking dish. Pour remaining sauce over all. Bake, covered, for 1 hour or until chicken is tender. Uncover; sprinkle with cheese and paprika. Bake 2 minutes longer or until cheese melts. (8 servings)

FRANK MOLER

Oven-Fried Chicken With Honey

1/4 cup margarine
1/3 cup honey
1 tablespoon soy sauce
2/3 cup sesame seeds
2-1/2 to 3 pounds chicken, cut up

Heat oven to 400 degrees. Melt margarine in a saucepan and combine with honey and soy sauce. Dip chicken in mixture and roll lightly in sesame seeds. Place skin side up in 9 x 13-inch pan. Bake uncovered for about one hour or until tender. Baste occasionally. (4-6 servings)

MARIE BAZIL

106

Sour Cream Chicken

2-1/2 to 3 pounds of chicken (preferably 4-6 chicken breasts)
2 tablespoons melted butter
2 large onions, chopped
1/2 cup chicken broth (or chicken bouillon)
1/2 pint sour cream
Salt and pepper to taste
1 tablespoon paprika

Brown chicken in butter in a large skillet. Remove chicken and brown the onions. Add chicken broth and chicken. Cover and cook over medium low heat about 30 minutes. Remove chicken to warm platter or warm bowl. Blend sour cream into chicken broth and onions and stir until heated through. Pour over chicken. Salt and pepper to taste. Sprinkle paprika over top. (4 servings)

KAREN EPSTEIN

Chicken in Paprika-Sour Cream Gravy

3 pounds chicken pieces
1/3 cup all-purpose flour
4 tablespoons salad oil
2 onions, sliced very thin
2 cups water
2 teaspoons chicken broth concentrate
1 teaspoon salt
1/8 teaspoon pepper
2 tablespoons paprika
1/2 cup sour cream
Cooked noodles or spaetzle

Coat chicken with flour and brown in oil in a large skillet. Remove from pan. Stir onions and remaining flour into oil and cook 2 minutes. Stir in water, broth, salt, pepper and paprika. Add chicken. Reduce heat to low, cover and simmer 1/2 hour, turning once. Stir in sour cream. Serve over noodles or spaetzle.

MARY WASKERWITZ

U-Quo-Chow-Gai Ding
(Chicken With Walnuts)

1/4 cup cooking oil
1 cup coarsely broken walnuts
2 boned chicken breasts, cut up
2 tablespoons cooking oil
1 cup sliced onion
1-1/2 cups celery, cut on the bias
1-1/4 cups chicken broth
1 tablespoon cornstarch
1 teaspoon sugar
1/4 cup soy sauce
2 tablespoons sherry
1 (8-ounce) can bamboo shoots
1 (8-ounce) can water chestnuts

Heat 1/4 cup cooking oil in wok. Stir-fry walnuts. Drain on paper towel.
Wash out wok. Stir-fry chicken in 2 tablespoons cooking oil for 8-10 minutes.
Remove the chicken. Add onion, celery, half of chicken broth. Cook 5
minutes uncovered until tender. Separately, mix cornstarch, sugar, soy sauce,
sherry and remainder of chicken broth. Pour this mixture over the vegetables.
Cook and stir until thickened. Add chicken, bamboo shoots, water chestnuts
and walnuts. Mix and serve. (6 servings)

JOAN ROTH

Chinese Chicken

1 pound cubed chicken breasts
2 tablespoons butter or margarine
1 tablespoon cornstarch
1 (28-ounce) can mixed Chinese vegetables, drained
1 (10-3/4 ounce) can cream of mushroom soup
1/4 teaspoon ground ginger
1 teaspoon brown sugar
1/2 teaspoon salt
1 tablespoon soy sauce
Cooked rice
Chinese noodles (optional)

Cook chicken in butter or magarine in a large skillet. Add cornstarch. Add
vegetables. Add mushroom soup. Heat through and stir until thickened. Add
ginger, sugar, salt and soy sauce. Serve over rice. Can add additional soy
sauce. Can top with Chinese noodles. (2-3 servings) *"May omit salt if desired.
Low cholesterol meal."*

CAROL SANDERS

Oriental Chicken and Rice

1-1/2 cups sliced green pepper
3/4 cup sliced onions
3 tablespoons oil
1/4 cup cornstarch
2 cups chicken stock
3 tablespoons soy sauce
2 cups slivered cooked chicken
3 ripe tomatoes, cut in wedges
Cooked rice

Saute green pepper and onion in oil in a large skillet until tender crisp. Blend cornstarch with a small amount of chicken stock. Add remaining stock and soy sauce. Gently stir chicken and sauce into vegetables. Cook and stir until sauce is clear and thickened. Add tomatoes and cook until heated through. Serve over rice. *"Bob's favorite recipe."*

JERI KELCH

Chicken With Wine and Cheese

2 pounds chicken parts
2 (10-3/4 ounce) cans cream of chicken soup
1/2 cup sherry
1 cup grated sharp cheddar cheese

Preheat oven to 300 degrees. Wash and dry chicken and put in a baking dish skin side up. In a bowl mix together soup and sherry and pour over all. Sprinkle with cheese. Bake for 1-1/2 hours uncovered. *"That is all there is to it and it is delicious. Quick company recipe."*

NANCY MORIN

Oven Fried Chicken

1-1/2 cups potato flakes
1 teaspoon seasoned salt
1/2 teaspoon paprika
1/2 teaspoon pepper
1/2 teaspoon garlic powder
1/4 cup butter, melted
1 tablespoon water
1 egg
3 pounds chicken, cut up

Preheat oven to 400 degrees. In a large bowl, combine potato flakes and seasonings. Stir in melted butter. In another bowl, beat together water and egg. Add all ingredients together. Coat chicken pieces. Bake for 1 hour.

SHELLY ROBBINS

Chicken, Gravy and Vegetables

3 pounds chicken pieces
2 tablespoons margarine
1 (10-3/4 ounce) can cream of chicken soup
1/4 cup red wine
1-1/2 cups chicken broth
1 teaspoon thyme
Salt and pepper to taste
2 cups sliced celery
5 carrots, 1/2-inch slices
3 onions, quartered
Cooked noodles, rice or potatoes

In a large skillet or Dutch oven brown chicken in margarine. Add soup, wine, broth, seasoning. Cover and simmer 30 minutes. Add vegetables, cover and cook 45 minutes. Serve over noodles, rice or potatoes.

MARY WASKERWITZ

Chicken Enchilada Crepes

2 tomatoes, peeled and chopped
2 tablespoons green onions, chopped
1/2 cup butter
1 cup chicken broth or bouillon
3 cups cooked chicken, diced
1 dozen flour tortillas
1/2 pound Jack cheese, grated
1/2 pound Swiss or cheddar cheese, grated
1 pint half-and-half cream

Preheat oven to 350 degrees. Saute tomatoes and onion in butter for 5 minutes in a large skillet. Add bouillon and chicken and simmer 10 minutes. Fill tortillas, roll and place seam side down in a 9 x 13-inch baking dish. Cover enchiladas with cheese. Pour half-and-half over enchiladas. Cover with foil. Bake for 1/2 hour. (If these are assembled ahead of time and are cold in the refrigerator, they may need to cook longer.) Remove foil and brown 10 minutes. (Makes 12 enchiladas)

NUGGET BURKHART

Zhender's Chicken Livers

1 pound chicken livers
1 cup all-purpose flour
1/2 cup shortening
1/3 medium onion, chopped
Seasoned salt to taste

Roll chicken livers in flour. Heat shortening in a skillet. Place chicken livers, not crowded, in hot fat and saute until half-done. Then add the onion and seasoning salt and continue cooking until livers are browned.

NANCY MORIN

Stupid Chicken

6 chicken breasts or 2 fryers
1 (10-1/2 ounce) can mushroom soup
1 cup sour cream
1/3 cup vermouth (or 1/2 cup sherry)
1 package slivered almonds

Preheat oven to 350 degrees. Place chicken in 9 x 13-inch glass or metal baking dish. Mix all liquid ingredients. Pour over chicken in one layer. Cover with almonds. Cook one hour. (Serves 6)

JAMES SKINNER

Chicken Mushroom

5-1/2 ounces chipped beef
6 slices bacon
6 boned and skinned chicken breasts
1 (10-3/4 ounce) can undiluted cream of mushroom soup

Preheat oven to 300 degrees. Scald and drain chipped beef. Shred by hand and line a 9 x 13-inch baking pan. Wrap one slice of bacon around each chicken breast and place in pan. Pour mushroom soup over chicken. Cover pan with foil. Bake for 2 hours. Remove foil and finish until crisp, about 1/2 hour.

MRS. THOMAS KELLEHER
THERESA KELSCH

Glazed Cornish Hens

8 (1 pound) Cornish hens
Salt and pepper to taste
1/3 cup butter, melted

ORANGE SAUCE:
1/4 cup lemon juice
1-1/2 cups orange juice
3 tablespoons lemon peel
3 tablespoons orange peel
2 cups currant jelly
1 cup Madeira wine
2 teaspoons dry mustard
1 teaspoon ginger
1/2 teaspoon salt
1/8 teaspoon Tabasco sauce

Preheat oven to 500 degrees. Sprinkle the body cavity of each hen with salt and pepper and tie the legs together. Arrange the hens, breast side up, in a roasting pan and brush them with butter. Bake, uncovered, for 15 minutes. Remove the hens from the oven and reduce oven temperature to 400 degrees. Turn them breast side down and pour 1/2 cup water over the hens. Bake, covered, for 30 minutes. Turn the hens breast side up and baste them with the pan juices. Bake the hens, uncovered, for 25 minutes. In a medium saucepan over medium heat, combine the lemon juice, orange juice, lemon peel and orange peel and bring the mixture to a boil. Reduce the heat and simmer for 20 minutes. Add the remaining sauce ingredients and cook over low heat for 2 hours, stirring occasionally, or until the sauce is thickened. Brush the hens with the sauce and continue baking for 5 minutes. Transfer them to a heated platter and serve accompanied by the remaining sauce in a heated bowl. (8 servings)

ANN BETZ

Herbed Duckling With Strawberry Sauce

2 (4-1/2 to 5 pound) fresh or frozen (thawed) ducklings
1/2 teaspoon ground sage
1/2 teaspoon pepper
12 juniper berries, crushed
2 teaspoons salt

2 hours before serving, remove giblets and necks from ducklings. Rinse ducklings with running cold water; pat dry with paper towels. Cut each duckling into quarters. Place skin side down on rack in large open roasting pan. Preheat oven to 350 degrees. In a cup, combine sage, pepper, crushed juniper berries and salt. Evenly sprinkle half of sage mixture on duckling. Roast for 1 hour, turn duckling, sprinkle remaining sage mixture on duckling and roast about 45 minutes longer or until duckling is fork-tender. 15 minutes before duckling is done, prepare sauce. (8 servings, 490 calories per serving)

STRAWBERRY SAUCE:
2 pints strawberries
1/3 cup water
1/4 cup orange-flavored liqueur
3 tablespoons sugar
2 teaspoons cornstarch
1/2 teaspoon salt
Watercress sprigs for garnish

Reserve 6 strawberries for garnish. Hull remaining strawberries; thinly slice 6 hulled strawberries and set aside. In blender at high speed or in food processor with knife blade attached, blend hulled whole strawberries, water, orange-flavored liqueur, sugar, cornstarch and salt until smooth. Pour strawberry mixture into 2-quart saucepan. Cook over medium heat, stirring constantly, until sauce is boiling, stir in sliced strawberries. To serve, spoon some sauce onto warm platter; arrange duckling pieces on sauce; garnish with watercress and reserved whole strawberries. Pass remaining sauce in small bowl to spoon over servings.

JOYCE LONDON

113

Baked Pheasant and Rice

1 (10-3/4 ounce) can condensed cream of mushroom soup
3/4 cup milk
3/4 cup long grain rice, uncooked
14 ounces fresh mushrooms
1 (1-1/2 ounce) envelope dehydrated onion soup mix
2 pheasants in serving pieces
Melted butter
Paprika

Preheat oven to 325 degrees. Blend mushroom soup and milk in a bowl.
Combine this with rice, mushrooms and onion soup. Mix and pour into 13 x 9-inch baking dish. Arrange pheasant on top. Brush with melted butter, sprinkle with paprika and bake uncovered for 1-1/2 hours. (6-8 servings)

JANICE CHAPMAN

Marinated Turkey Breast

2 cups soy sauce
4 cups sautern wine
2 cups peanut oil
Dash of lemon pepper
Dash of celery salt
1 teaspoon chicken bouillon
Turkey breast

Mix all marinade ingredients well in a bowl and marinate turkey breast for 24 hours, turning often. Cook turkey breast on a grill. Baste the meat at the end of the cooking time as it will get too black if basted at the beginning. (Serve remaining sauce with the cooked turkey.)

ANNA KELLY

Turkey Mole

12-16 pound turkey (or 1-pound turkey breast)
4 tablespoons lard
10-12 dried Ancho chilies (or other chilies - 50 species exist)
4-6 dried Serrano chilies
1 large tomato
1/2 cup raisins
1/2 cup blanched almonds
1 medium onion, coarsely chopped
1 sprig fresh coriander (cilantro) or 1 tablespoon dried coriander
1/2 teaspoon salt
1/8 teaspoon anise
1/8 teaspoon powdered coriander seed
1/8 teaspoon dried cloves
1/4 teaspoon cinnamon
1 shredded tortilla
1-1/2 ounces unsweetened chocolate
Tortillas

Remove turkey meat from carcass or slice breast into 1/2-inch strips. Saute in 2 tablespoons melted lard; drain and simmer 30 minutes with 6 tablespoons salted water in casserole over low heat. Keep warm. Soak dried chiles in tepid water for 1 hour. Remove stems, seeds and veins. Combine chilies, tomato, raisins, almonds, onion, spices, and tortilla in food processor (easier) or blender, mix until a thick, even paste is formed. Melt 2 tablespoons lard in skillet; stir in paste gradually and cook 5 minutes over medium heat. Add crushed chocolate and stir until melted. Season to taste with salt or hot sauce. Add to turkey, eat with hot tortillas. (8-10 servings)

COOK'S TIP: May be used as filling for enchiladas, tacos, etc. Chicken can be substituted. The flavor (and kick!) is always different, depending on the chilies available. The mole and other sauces form the basis for Mexican haute cuisine, quite different from the country fare we have imported as Tex-Mex.

GOLDER WILSON

Meats

MEATS

Beef	119
Lamb	137
Pork	139

Bigos

1 quart sauerkraut
1/4 pound bacon
1 large onion, chopped
1/2 pound each pork, veal, beef and lamb
1/2 pound venison (optional)
Water or vegetable stock
1/2 pound Polish sausage, cut in small pieces
Salt and pepper to taste
1/2 pound mushrooms, sauteed

Wash sauerkraut and cook until tender. Cut bacon and fry. Add onion and meat and fry until meat is slightly brown. Add water or vegetable stock and cook until meat is tender. Add Polish sausage and sauerkraut and boil until the flavors blend. Season to taste. Add sauteed mushrooms.

BLANCHE EHRENKREUTZ

Cornish Pasty

CRUST:
3 cups all-purpose flour
1 cup suet, ground fine
1/4 cup shortening
1 teaspoon salt
6-8 tablespoons cold water

Combine crust ingredients as for pie pastry in a bowl. (Should be slightly softer than pie dough.) Roll out into 1/8-inch circle. Preheat oven to 400 degrees.

FILLING:
1 pound thinly sliced round or sirloin steak
1 small rutabaga, diced
5-6 potatoes, diced
4 onions, chopped
Chopped parsley
Salt and pepper to taste
1 teaspoon butter

Slice beef steak. Round steak works well if cut thinly on the diagonal (or splurge and use sirloin!). Peel and dice vegetables. Place diced vegetables and meat on half of the circle of rolled crust dough. Add parsley, salt and pepper and butter. Fold over and seal edges, turnover style. Pierce top several times with fork tines. Bake on cookie sheet for 1 hour or bake 30 minutes, cool and wrap for the freezer; then finish baking before serving. (4 servings)

ELLEN MCDONALD

119

Sherried Beef

3 pounds stewing beef (or pot roast)
3 (10-3/4 ounce) cans cream of mushroom soup
1 envelope onion soup mix
3/4 cup sherry wine
1/4 cup water
Cooked rice or egg noodles

Preheat oven to 325 degrees. Place all ingredients (except rice or noodles) in a covered roasting pan. Bake 3 hours. Pour over rice or noodles. (4-6 servings)

GERRIE PROCHASKA

Standing Rib Roast

Standing rib roast, 5-6 pounds
Salt and pepper

Take roast out of refrigerator and allow to reach room temperature. Preheat oven to 375 degrees. Salt and pepper roast rolling it in seasoning. Place in oven in large pan uncovered. Cook for 1 hour and turn off oven. Do not open oven door for 2 hours (opening door allows heat to escape). This is minimum amount of time. 45 minutes prior to serving, turn on oven to 350 degrees and warm meat. Meat will be medium-rare to rare. (8-10 servings) *From the kitchen of my mom, Lyn Fink."*

PAULA FINK

Beef Pepper Steak

1/4 cup vegetable oil
1 pound round steak (pounded to about 1/8-inch thick)
1 medium onion, sliced
2 green peppers, sliced
1 tablespoon cornstarch
1/2 cup cold water
2 tablespoons soy sauce
1 teaspoon sugar
1 teaspoon garlic salt
1/4 teaspoon black pepper
Cooked rice

Preheat oil in electric skillet, uncovered at 325 degrees. Add meat and brown. Remove to serving dish. Add onion and pepper slices and cook until just tender. Dissolve cornstarch in water and soy sauce. Add sugar, garlic salt and pepper. Pour into skillet with vegetables, stirring until sauce is thickened and clear. Add meat and cook several minutes longer or until heated through. Serve over hot rice. (4 servings)

GEORGIA KASKO

Montego Pepper Steak

2 teaspoons freshly ground black pepper
3 pounds boneless beef steak
3/4 cup red wine
1/4 cup rum
2 tablespoons beef consomme
2 tablespoons melted butter

Press ground pepper firmly into steak so that it is heavily coated on both sides. Let stand at room temperature for 30 minutes. Combine wine, rum and consomme and set aside. Melt butter in a large skillet. When very hot, cook steak over high heat for 5 minutes on each side. Reduce heat and let steak cook until done to your taste. Place on warm platter. Stir wine and consomme into drippings left in skillet. Heat and pour over steak and serve. (6 servings)

DONOVAN BOWERBANK

Sweet and Sour Steak

1-1/2 pounds round steak, cubed
1 medium onion, chopped
1 envelope brown gravy mix
1 tablespoon brown sugar
1/2 teaspoon ginger
1 bay leaf
1 tablespoon vinegar
Salt and pepper to taste
1 teaspoon Worcestershire sauce

Brown steak with onion in a large skillet. Put into crockpot. Combine gravy mix with water according to package directions. Add remaining ingredients to steak. Cook on low setting all day.

CAROL COLBY

Hungarian Steak

1 tablespoon margarine
1 to 2 pounds sirloin tip steak
Dash of Lawry's seasoned salt
1 cup warm water
1 large yellow onion (sliced thin horizontally)
Dash of salt and pepper
1 tablespoon paprika

Using an electric skillet (325 degrees) or large frying pan, melt margarine over medium heat. Add steak which has been seasoned with Lawry's. Brown on both sides. Add warm water. Add sliced onion over top. Sprinkle salt, pepper, paprika and cover. Simmer for 1/2 hour on low heat. (4 servings)
"Quick one-pot meal . Add potatoes or green pepper; or make a sour cream gravy for stroganoff."

PHYLLIS NEWBERRY

121

Chinese Beef

2 pounds flank or round steak (cut in thin strips)
1 tablespoon oil
1 clove garlic, minced
1/4 teaspoon ginger
1 teaspoon sugar
1/4 cup soy sauce
2 green peppers, cut in strips
2 tomatoes, quartered
1 (14-ounce) can bean sprouts
Chow Mein noodles

Brown steak in oil in a large skillet. Add garlic and ginger. Then add sugar and soy sauce and simmer covered for 5 minutes. Add green peppers and simmer additional 5 minutes. Add tomatoes and bean sprouts. Cook an additional 5-10 minutes until heated through. Serve on noodles. (4 servings) *"Very nice company meal served with cole slaw, hot rolls and a nice white wine."* DOROTHY LAMERSON

Real Texas Chili

2 tablespoons vegetable oil
3 pounds boneless chuck, cut into 1-inch cubes (never use hamburger)
2-3 cloves garlic, minced
4-6 tablespoons chili powder
2 teaspoons ground cumin
3 tablespoons all-purpose flour
1 tablespoon leaf oregano
2 (13-3/4 ounce) cans beef broth
1 teaspoon salt
1/4 teaspoon pepper
Optional:
1 (15-ounce) can pinto beans
1 cup dairy sour cream
1 lime, cut into wedges

Heat oil in a 4-quart kettle over medium heat. Add beef, stirring frequently with a wooden spoon until meat changes color but does not brown. Lower heat; stir in garlic. Combine chili powder, cumin seed and flour. Sprinkle meat with chili mixture, stirring until meat is evenly coated. Crumble oregano over meat. Add 1-1/2 cans of the broth and stir until liquid is well-blended. Add salt and pepper. Bring to a boil, stirring occasionally. Reduce heat, simmer partially covered over low heat, 1-1/2 hours. Add remaining broth, cook 30 minutes longer or until meat is almost falling apart. Cool thoroughly, cover, refrigerate overnight to ripen flavor. Reheat chili when ready to use. Heat beans, drain; stir into chili. Garnish chili with sour cream and add wedges of lime to squeeze over each portion. (8 servings) KATHERINE KERSEY

Great Chili

3 pounds ground beef
1 pound round steak, cut into small cubes
2 pounds Italian sausage (hot or sweet, bulk not links)
1 large Spanish onion, chopped
3 celery stalks, chopped
2 red pimento peppers, chopped
2 cloves garlic, minced
4 (16-ounce) cans stewed tomatoes
1 (46-ounce) can V-8 juice
2 packages dried onion soup mix
1/2 cup white vinegar
1 bay leaf
3 ounces chili powder
2 teaspoons cumin
1 teaspoon oregano
1/2 teaspoon paprika
2 teaspoons beef bouillon granules
1/4 cup barbecue sauce
1/4 cup Red Hot sauce (optional)
Salt to taste
Dash of crushed red pepper
Dash of basil
Dash of thyme
3-4 (16-ounce) cans kidney beans
6 ounces beer

Brown meat in a large skillet; drain and set aside. Saute vegetables in some of the meat drippings and set aside. (Vegetables may be blended if desired.) In a large stockpot, combine all ingredients except beans and beer. Heat to boiling, reduce heat and simmer 3-4 hours stirring occasionally to avoid scorching. Add beans and beer and simmer another hour. The longer it cooks, the better the flavors blend. (Makes 7 quarts)   NANCY COLLINS

Stayabed Stew

2 pounds beef stew meat
1 cup sliced carrots
2 chopped medium onions
3 potatoes sliced or cubed
1 teaspoon salt and dash of pepper
1 bay leaf (optional)
1 (10-3/4 ounce) can mushroom, tomato or celery soup (thinned with
    1/2 can water)
1 (8-1/2 ounce) can tiny peas (optional)

Mix all ingredients in a casserole with a tight lid. Bake at 275 degrees for 5 hrs. Add the peas the last half-hour. (4 servings) *"I prefer using mushroom soup."*
                    KAY NEFF

Beef Bourguignon

1/4 cup diced bacon
1/4 cup all-purpose flour
1 teaspoon paprika
2 teaspoons salt
3 pounds lean beef chuck (cut in 1-1/2 inch cubes)
6 tablespoons margarine
1/3 cup chopped carrot
1 medium onion, chopped
1 clove garlic, minced
1/2 teaspoon thyme
1/2 teaspoon celery flakes
1/4 cup chopped parsley
1 bay leaf, broken in half
1/2 teaspoon Tabasco sauce
2 cups beef bouillon
1 cup dry red wine
1/2 pound mushrooms, sliced

In a Dutch oven cook the bacon until crisp, remove and reserve it. In a bowl combine the flour, paprika and 1-1/2 teaspoons of the salt. Roll the beef cubes in the flour mixture. To the bacon grease in the Dutch oven, add 4 tablespoons of the margarine and melt it over medium-high heat. Add the beef cubes and brown on all sides. Add the chopped carrot, chopped onion and garlic and saute until the onion is limp. Add the thyme, celery flakes, half of the parsley, bay leaf, Tabasco sauce, bacon, bouillon, and wine. Simmer the mixture, covered for 2 hours or until the meat is nearly tender. Add more bouillon and wine if the liquid does not cover the meat. In a small pan saute the mushrooms in the remaining margarine. Add the mushrooms and 1/2 teaspoon salt to the beef mixture. If a thicker consistency is desired, stir in 1 tablespoon flour dissolved in 2 tablespoons water and cook until the mixture is thickened. Serve the dish sprinkled with the remaining parsley. (8 servings)

ANN BETZ

Easy Beef Stew

3 pounds stew meat
3 (10-1/2 ounce) cans mushroom soup
1 cup dry vermouth
1 package onion soup mix
Cooked rice

Mix all ingredients together in a large bowl. Cook in large, covered casserole three hours at 325 degrees. Serve over rice. (Serves 6)

JAMES SKINNER

Beef Stew

2 pounds beef chuck or stew meat (1-inch cubes)
1/4 cup all-purpose flour
1-1/2 teaspoons salt
1/2 teaspoon pepper
1-1/2 cups beef broth
1 teaspoon Worcestershire sauce
1 clove garlic, minced
1 bay leaf
1 teaspoon paprika
4 carrots, sliced
3 potatoes, diced
2 onions, chopped
1 stalk celery, sliced
2 teaspoons Kitchen Bouquet (optional)

Place meat in crockpot. In a bowl mix flour, salt and pepper and pour over meat; stir to coat meat with flour. Add remaining ingredients and stir to mix well. Cover and cook on low 10-12 hours or high 4 to 6 hours. Stir stew occasionally. (6-8 servings)

JOYCE LONDON

My Own Beef Stroganoff

2 to 2-1/2 pounds sirloin (or other high quality beef)
Salt to taste
Pepper to taste
1/2 to 3/4 cup all-purpose flour
1/2 cup butter or margarine
1/2 pound mushrooms, quartered
4-6 green onions, chopped
2 cloves garlic, finely minced
1 teaspoon lemon juice
2 tablespoons all-purpose flour
1 cup beef stock or consomme
1/4 cup Madeira wine
2 teaspoons Dijon mustard
1 teaspoon dried dill (or more to taste)
1/2 cup sour cream
Cooked rice or noodles

Cut steak into bite-sized pieces and toss with salt, pepper and 1/2 to 3/4 cup flour. In large skillet, melt 3 tablespoons butter. Brown meat quickly and remove from skillet. Leave meat rare. Add rest of butter to skillet and saute mushrooms, onions, garlic and lemon juice. Sprinkle with 2 tablespoons flour and cook, stirring for 1 minute. Add beef stock and Madeira wine. Bring to a boil, stirring until thickened, about 5 minutes. Stir in mustard, dill, sour cream and browned sirloin. Heat over low heat until hot. Serve over rice or noodles. (6-8 servings)

SUSAN HURWITZ

Burgundy-Glazed Hamburgers

2 English muffins
Soft butter
1 pound lean ground beef
1 teaspoon salad oil or olive oil
2 tablespoons chopped shallots (or green onions)
1 clove garlic, minced
1 teaspoon beef stock base
1/2 teaspoon Dijon mustard
3/4 cup dry red wine
3 tablespoons butter

Split muffins and spread with soft butter. Broil until lightly browned and keep warm on a serving platter. Shape meat into 4 patties slightly wider than the muffins. Using a large skillet cook patties in oil over medium heat, until browned on both sides and done to your liking. Transfer patties to toasted muffins and keep warm. Add shallots and garlic to pan; cook a few minutes, stirring. Combine beef stock base, mustard and wine and pour into pan; boil rapidly, uncovered, until reduced by half. Add the 3 tablespoons of butter and heat, stirring, until melted. Spoon sauce over hamburgers and serve open-faced. (Makes 4 servings) *"A very good, quick and easy meal."*

ANN BETZ

Meat Loaf (That Even Kids Like!)

1 pound ground chuck
1 pound ground veal
1 to 1-1/2 teaspoons salt
1 teaspoon basil
1 teaspoon chives
1 tablespoon parsley
1 cup rolled oats
1/2 to 3/4 cup Hunt's tomato sauce
1 onion, finely chopped
1 cup mushrooms, finely chopped
1 (6-ounce) can tomato paste

Preheat oven to 350 degrees. Combine all ingredients except tomato paste in large bowl. Shape into 2 oval-shaped loaves. Freeze one and bake the other in a 5 x 8-inch baking pan lined with foil for 50-60 minutes. Spread tomato paste all over meat loaf and put back in oven for 15 minutes. (Makes two 5 x 8-inch size loaves)

SUSAN HURWITZ

Cran-Meat Loaf

2 pounds lean ground beef
4 slices bread, crumbled
2 teaspoons salt
1/4 teaspoon pepper
1 small onion, chopped
2 eggs, beaten
1 (16-ounce) can whole cranberry sauce

Preheat oven to 350 degrees. Mix ground beef, bread, seasonings, onion and eggs in a large bowl. Add half can of cranberry sauce and mix well. Line shallow pan with foil and shape mixture into loaf on foil. Bake for 1 hour. Mash remaining cranberry sauce and spoon over loaf. Bake 15 minutes longer. (6 servings)

JILL FLYNN

Meatball Carbonade

2 slices bacon
1 beef bouillon cube
1 cup water
1 pound ground beef
1 egg, slightly beaten
1/4 cup fine dry bread crumbs
1/2 teaspoon salt
Dash of pepper
2 medium onions, thinly sliced
2 tablespoons all-purpose flour
3/4 cup beer
1 teaspoon brown sugar
1 teaspoon vinegar
1/2 teaspoon salt
1/4 teaspoon crushed dried thyme
Dash of pepper
2 tablespoons snipped parsley

Preheat oven to 350 degrees. Cook the bacon until crisp; crumble and set aside, reserving drippings. Dissolve the beef bouillon cube in boiling water. Combine 1/4 cup of the beef broth with ground beef, the beaten egg, bread crumbs, salt and pepper; mix well. Shape meat mixture into small meatballs; brown on all sides in bacon drippings. Transfer meatballs to 1-1/2 quart casserole. In same skillet, saute sliced onions till golden; spoon atop meatballs. Stir flour into bacon drippings; add the remaining beef broth and beer. Stir in brown sugar, vinegar, salt, thyme and pepper. Cook and stir until mixture thickens and bubbles. Pour over onions and meatballs. Cover and bake for 45 minutes. Top with snipped parsley and the crumbled bacon just before serving. (4 servings)

ANN BETZ

Baked Chop Suey

3 pounds ground chuck
2 cups chopped celery
3 medium onions, chopped
2 (10-3/4 ounce) cans cream of chicken soup
2 (10-3/4 ounce) cans golden mushroom soup
2 cups water
2 cups Minute Rice, uncooked
6 tablespoons soy sauce
1-2 tablespoons Worcestershire sauce
Chow mein noodles

Preheat oven to 350 degrees. Brown ground chuck. Add rest of ingredients.
Place in 11 x 15-inch baking dish or 4-quart casserole. Generously sprinkle
chow mein noodles on top and bake for 30-45 minutes. *"Ideal for a large
group."* DOROTHY LAMERSON

Enchilada Casserole

2-1/2 pounds lean ground beef
1 medium onion, chopped
1 clove garlic, minced
2 (10-3/4 ounce) cans cream of mushroom soup
2 (10-3/4 ounce) cans cream of chicken soup
2 cans enchilada sauce (hot or mild, depending on your taste)
2 (4-ounce) cans chopped green chilies
2 packages soft corn tortilla shells
1 pound grated cheddar cheese

Brown ground beef, onions and garlic in a large saucepan. Add soups and
sauces and simmer for 30 minutes. Preheat oven to 350 degrees. Cut tortilla
shells in quarters. In a large cake pan, layer sauce, chilies and shells with
cheese. Continue layering until all ingredients are used. Bake for 30 minutes.
"Dish may be made ahead. Great for buffets. Freezes well also."
SARA HICKEY

Intern's Casserole

2 pounds ground beef
Salt and pepper ad lib
1 box frozen Tater Tots
1 (10-3/4 ounce) can mushroom soup

Preheat oven to 350 degrees. Brown ground beef in a skillet; drain fat and
season to taste. Spread in bottom of 8 x 10-inch flat baking pan. Top with
undiluted mushroom soup. Top with Tater Tots. Bake for 30 minutes.
(Servings p.r.n.) *"This dinner saved many H.O. 1's from starvation but did not
help their cholesterol."* JESS THOENE

128

Ground Beef 'N Tater Casserole

1 pound ground beef
1 (9-ounce) package frozen cut green beans, cooked and drained
1 (10-3/4 ounce) can condensed tomato soup
1/4 cup water
1/2 teaspoon salt
1/8 teaspoon ground black pepper
2 cups prepared mashed potatoes
1 cup French fried onions
1/2 cup grated cheddar cheese

Preheat oven to 350 degrees. Brown beef in skillet; drain. Combine beef, green beans, soup, water, salt and pepper. Pour into 1-1/2 quart casserole. Combine mashed potatoes and 1/2 can French fried onions. Can be spread all over the top of the beef, green bean and soup mixture or spooned in a mounded ring around top outer edge of casserole. Bake, uncovered, for 25 minutes. Top potatoes with cheese and remaining onions and bake 5 minutes longer.

AUDREY MITZELFELD

Ground Beef Casserole

1 (16-ounce) package noodles
1 (3-ounce) package cream cheese, cut in chunks
1 pound ground beef
2 tablespoons butter
1/2 teaspoon garlic salt
1 tablespoon salt
1 large onion, chopped
1 cup sour cream
3 (8-ounce) cans tomato sauce
Parmesan or romano cheese

Preheat oven to 375 degrees. Cook noodles in a saucepan and drain well. Put cream cheese in the noodles to melt. Fry the hamburger in butter until no longer pink. Combine all ingredients except cheese. Place in a casserole dish. Grate enough cheese to cover the top. Bake for 45 minutes. (8 servings) *"Excellent for a football buffet. Can be made ahead of time and reheated."*

MARY ELLEN BOTSFORD

Spaghetti

First you put squiggly noodles in a bowl and put some tomato sauce on and hamburger and get some Chinese noodles and then heat it all together.

JENNY OSTROWSKI
AGE 7

Quad Rettini

2 pounds ground beef
1 large onion, chopped
1 clove garlic, minced
2 tablespoons olive oil
1 (1-pound) can cream style corn
1 (8-ounce) can tomato sauce
1 (8-ounce) package egg noodles, cooked and drained
1 (4-1/4 ounce) can ripe chopped olives
1/2 pound fresh mushrooms (or 4-ounce can)
1 (10-ounce) package frozen spinach, defrosted and drained
1 teaspoon oregano
2 teaspoons salt
Dash of liquid red pepper seasoning
1 pound grated sharp cheddar cheese

Saute meat, onion and garlic in olive oil in a skillet until brown. Drain fat. Add corn and tomato sauce. Simmer 5-10 minutes. Preheat oven to 300 degrees. Add egg noodles, olives, mushrooms, spinach, oregano, salt and red pepper seasoning. Add half of the cheese and mix well. Place in greased casserole and put rest of cheese on top. Bake for 1 hour. *"Excellent for potlucks."*

CAROLIN DICK

Stuffed Pasta Shells

1 (12-ounce) box jumbo pasta shells
1 pound ground beef
1/2 teaspoon onion salt
1/2 teaspoon garlic salt
1/4 teaspoon pepper
3 teaspoons sweet basil
3/4 cup minced onion
3 slices day-old bread, cubed
1 (16-ounce) jar prepared spaghetti sauce (or your own)
1/4 cup Parmesan cheese, grated
1/4 cup romano cheese, grated
1/2 pound cubed mozzarella cheese
1 egg, slightly beaten

Preheat oven to 350 degrees. Cook jumbo pasta shells al dente. Brown ground beef with next 4 ingredients. Add minced onion, cooking until just tender. Remove from heat. Add bread cubes. Mix thoroughly. Add 1/4 cup spaghetti sauce. Mix. Allow mixture to cool slightly; then add Parmesan and romano cheese, mixing thoroughly. When mixture is cooled, add mozzarella cheese and egg. Mix. Fill cooked shells with the beef-cheese mixture. Put a thin layer of spaghetti sauce on the bottom of 9 x 13-inch pan. Place shells in pan using sauce between layers. Bake for 30 minutes. (6-8 servings)

FRAN RUPP

Pyrizhky
(Meat-Filled Pastry)

DOUGH:
2 packages dry yeast
1/2 cup water
1/2 pound unsalted butter
3 cups all-purpose flour
1 cup sour cream
Salt

Dissolve yeast in lukewarm water. Cut butter into flour. Add sour cream, salt and yeast and mix together. Roll out immediately and cut out with doughnut cutter. Preheat oven to 375 degrees.

FILLING:
1 pound ground chuck (sauteed)
1 medium onion (sauteed)
Salt and pepper to taste

Mix all filling ingredients well. Place 1 teaspoon of meat mixture in the middle of the round. Fold the round in half and seal the edges, forming a half-moon. Place on greased cookie sheet and bake for one-half hour.

STEPHANIE ROHACZ

Quick and Easy Lasagne

1-1/2 pounds ground chuck
1 cup chopped onion
1 green pepper, cut into strips
1 teaspoon seasoned salt
1/2 teaspoon pepper
1 tablespoon sugar
1/2 teaspoon garlic powder
1/2 teaspoon oregano
1 quart tomatoes
1 (15-ounce) can tomato sauce
1 (8-ounce) box uncooked lasagne noodles
12-16 ounces sliced mozzarella cheese

Saute ground chuck, onions and pepper in a large skillet. Drain off fat. Add seasonings, tomatoes and tomato sauce. Simmer 15 minutes. Preheat oven to 350 degrees. Spoon small amount of sauce on bottom of 9 x 13-inch baking dish. Layer noodles, sauce, cheese ending with cheese. Noodles must be covered by sauce. Cover with foil. Bake 45 minutes." *A family favorite. Fast and easy since noodles do not have to be precooked.*"

JERI KELCH

Lasagne

1 pound Italian sausage or ground beef
1 medium onion, chopped
2 cloves garlic, minced
1 tablespoon parsley flakes
1 tablespoon sweet basil
1/2 teaspoon salt
1 (28-ounce) can tomatoes
2 (6-ounce) cans tomato paste
1 (10-ounce) box lasagne noodles
3 cups ricotta cheese
2 beaten eggs
1 teaspoon salt
1/2 teaspoon pepper
2 tablespoons parsley flakes
1/2 cup grated Parmesan cheese
1 pound grated mozzarella cheese
1-2 packages pepperoni, sliced thin

In a Dutch oven brown meat and onion slowly. Spoon off excess fat. Add next six ingredients. Simmer uncovered about 30 minutes stirring occasionally. Cook noodles until tender; drain; rinse in cold water. Meanwhile combine ricotta cheese with eggs, seasonings and Parmesan cheese. Preheat oven to 375 degrees. Spread a very small amount of meat sauce in a 9 x 13-inch pan, place 1/3 of the noodles over it in a single layer; spread 1/3 of the ricotta cheese mixture over this, layer pepperoni, add 1/3 of the mozzarella, then 1/3 meat sauce. Repeat layer twice more. Garnish with mozzarella. Bake for 30 minutes. (Serves 8)

COOK'S TIP: Do not use pepperoni on the third layer. The pan will be very full; place a cookie sheet under it to bake. Glass pans are the best for baking lasagne.

RIE HARDING
PHYLLIS MOONEY
JULIE SCHIEBOLD
ROBERTA YOUNG

Lasagne

Lasagne is my favoritest food. You take a long strip of noodles and you put sauce on the bottom and put noodles all around it and then you bake it in the oven and it's lasagne.

DAVID OSTROWSKI
AGE 6

Deep-Dish Pizza

CRUST:
1 package dry yeast
1 cup warm water
1 teaspoon sugar
1 teaspoon salt
2 tablespoons oil
2-1/2 cups all-purpose flour

FILLING:
1 pound hamburger, browned and drained
1 (28-ounce) can whole tomatoes (strained)
1 (8-ounce) can tomato sauce (optional)
1 tablespoon minced onions
1 teaspoon dry oregano
1/4 teaspoon each salt and pepper
1/8 teaspoon garlic powder
1 small green pepper, chopped
1 (8-ounce) can mushrooms or fresh mushrooms
1 cup grated mozzarella cheese

Preheat oven to 350 degrees. Dissolve yeast in water. Stir in remaining ingredients. Let dough rest for 5 minutes. Pat dough in a greased and floured 9 x 13-inch pan. Put hamburger on top of dough. Combine tomatoes, tomato sauce, onions, oregano, salt, pepper and garlic powder in a large bowl and spread over hamburger. Layer green peppers and mushrooms. Top with grated cheese. Bake 30-45 minutes.   KATHY DUNN

Crazy Crust Pizza

CRUST:
1 cup all-purpose flour
1 teaspoon salt
1 teaspoon Italian seasoning or leaf oregano
2 eggs
2/3 cup milk

TOPPING:
1/4 cup chopped onion, if desired
1 (4-ounce) can mushroom pieces
1 cup pizza sauce
Meat of your choice (hamburger, ham, pepperoni, sausage)
1 cup (4 ounces) shredded mozzarella cheese

Mix dry crust ingredients together; add eggs and milk. Pat onto greased pan. Preheat oven to 425 degrees. Sprinkle first three topping ingredients on top. Brown meat and drain fat. Bake for 25-30 minutes. Sprinkle with cheese and set in oven for 10-15 minutes.   DIANE SEBERT

133

Pizza

CRUST:
1 package dry yeast
2 cups warm water
1 beaten egg
2 teaspoons salt
1 tablespoon sugar
1 tablespoon oil
5 cups all-purpose flour

Dissolve yeast in warm water in a large bowl. Beat egg in a small bowl and add to yeast-water mixture. Add salt, sugar, oil and mix well. Add flour a cup at a time and stir vigorously with a table knife. When dough becomes too hard to stir, put remaining flour on board, add dough and knead rest of flour until the dough is smooth. Let dough rise until light before rolling out on greased pizza pan. Roll out on a lightly-floured board. Be careful not to use too much flour as this prevents dough from stretching. Shape dough as desired. Pat excess flour off dough before placing on greased pan. Note: If you grease your hands and flour them before kneading, it helps to keep the dough from sticking to your hands. (Makes 3 large pizzas)

SAUCE:
1 (12-ounce) can tomato paste
1-1/2 cans of water
2 teaspoons oregano
1/2 teaspoon dried hot pepper (optional)
1/2 teaspoon garlic salt
Mozzarella cheese (as much as you desire)

Place all sauce ingredients except cheese in a saucepan. Simmer on stove, stirring occasionally. Taste. Add more seasoning if desired. Smear sauce on top of crust. Sprinkle grated cheese on top. Bake 15-20 minutes at 450 degrees. Pizzas are done when top is browned nicely and bubbly. Check under crust by lifting up with pancake turner; under-crust should be slightly brown with "freckles".

TRICIA LAIBLE

Barbeques for a Crowd

5 pounds boned pork (roasted till done)
5 pounds bone beef (roasted till done)
3 cups onions, chopped
6 cups canned tomatoes
1-1/2 cups tomato paste
3/4 cup vinegar
6 ounces brown sugar, packed
1 teaspoon oregano
1 tablespoon Worcestershire sauce
1 tablespoon A-1 sauce
Dash of Tabasco
1 tablespoon salt

Shred meat. Add rest of ingredients to a large kettle. Cook slowly for 2-3 hours. (Makes 60 sandwiches)

DOROTHY LAMERSON

Mom's Barbecue

4 pounds chuck roast
4 pounds pork shoulder
1 (14-ounce) bottle ketchup
1 (12-ounce) bottle chili sauce
1-1/2 cups celery, sauteed
1-1/2 cups onion, sauteed
Shot of lemon juice
1 tablespoon vinegar
1/4 cup brown sugar
2 tablespoons sugar
Shot of Worcestershire sauce

In a roasting pan cook the chuck roast and pork shoulder until tender enough to fall off the bone. Cut into small pieces. Combine rest of ingredients and add to juices left in the pan along with the meat. Cook 1 hour.

JACKIE BREWER

Sloppy Joes

You take hamburger and then you let it cook until it gets brown and then you add Open Pit, then ketchup and mustard and mix it and let it cook for a few minutes and its done and then you put it in a bun.

MONICA MCGRATH
AGE 7

Stuffed Grape Leaves

1/2 cup uncooked long grain rice
6 tablespoons olive oil
1/2 cup finely chopped onion
1/2 pound lean ground beef
1/2 cup finely chopped green onion
1/2 cup finely chopped parsley
2 tablespoons dried dill
2 teaspoons finely snipped fresh mint (optional)
3 tablespoons lemon juice
1/2 teaspoon turmeric
1/2 teaspoon oregano
1 teaspoon salt
Pepper to taste
40 preserved grape leaves
2 tablespoons olive oil
Lemon wedges (for garnish)

Boil the rice in 1-1/2 cups briskly boiling water for 10 minutes, drain and
reserve it. In a heavy skillet, heat the olive oil over moderate heat until a haze
forms. Add the onion and cook, stirring, until golden brown. Stir in the
ground beef, breaking up lumps and cook until browned. Drain off the excess
grease. Reduce the heat and add the rice, green onion, parsley, dill, mint,
lemon juice, turmeric, oregano, salt and pepper. Cook the stuffing for 3-4
minutes and reserve it. In a large pot bring 2 quarts of water to a boil. Drop in
the grape leaves and remove from the heat. Soak the leaves for 1 minute and
transfer them to cold water. Separate the leaves and drain them on paper
towels. To stuff the leaves spread 30 leaves dull side up, flat on a plate. Place
1 tablespoon of the stuffing on the center of each leaf. Turn up the stem end
and fold the leaf over the stuffing. Layer the bottom of a 2-3 quart casserole,
with a tight fitting cover, with the 10 unstuffed leaves. Arrange the stuffed
leaves, with the seam side down, in the casserole. Sprinkle the dish with the
remaining 2 tablespoons of oil and 2 tablespoons water. Simmer, tightly
covered, for 50 minutes. Serve the stuffed grape leaves hot or at room
temperature garnished with lemon wedges. (6-8 servings)

ANN BETZ

Leg of Lamb Deluxe

1 (5-1/2 pound) partially boned leg of lamb
1/2 pound ground veal
1/2 pound ground cooked ham
1/2 cup fine dry bread crumbs
1/2 pound fresh mushrooms, finely chopped
1 egg
1 teaspoon salt
1/2 teaspoon oregano
1/4 teaspoon pepper
1 small clove garlic, minced
1 tablespoon Worcestershire sauce
1 tablespoon orange marmalade

Bone the leg of lamb, leaving about 3 inches of shank bone in place so roast will retain its characteristic shape. Preheat oven to 325 degrees. Mix ground meats, bread crumbs and remaining ingredients. Pack tightly into lamb leg. Secure opening with skewers and string or cover lamb leg with aluminum foil and tie with string. Place fat side up on rack in shallow pan. Bake 30 to 35 minutes per pound. Let lamb stand about 10 minutes before carving. (12-14 servings)

SHARON SLAGEL

Shish Kebabs

Leg of lamb (cut into 1 to 1-1/2 inch cubes)
Tomatoes, quartered
Green peppers, quartered
Onions, quartered

MARINADE:
1/2 pound onions, chopped
1 tablespoon salt
1/2 teaspoon pepper
1/3 cup pale dry sherry
2 tablespoons oil
1 teaspoon oregano

In a bowl combine ingredients of marinade and pour over lamb. Mix well and marinate 2-16 hours. Place meat on skewers and cook over hot coals. Skewer vegetables separately and cook similarly. (4-8 servings)

CAROL RAGSDALE

Lamb Curry

1 cup plain yogurt
1 teaspoon paprika
1 teaspoon ground coriander
1/2 teaspoon ground cumin
1/2 teaspoon garam masala*
1/2 teaspoon crushed red pepper flakes
1/2 teaspoon ground turmeric
1/4 teaspoon ground black pepper
2-1/2 pounds boneless lamb (cut into 1-inch pieces)
1 small lime
1 small onion
1/4 cup packed fresh coriander leaves (or parsley sprigs)
2 cloves garlic
1 slice fresh gingerroot (1-inch thick, pared, cut into chunks)
2 medium onions, quartered
1/2 cup ghee* or butter
1/2 cup chicken stock
1/2 cup water
Condiments (peanuts, eggs, coconut, bacon, bananas, onion,
   avocado, kumquats)

Mix yogurt, paprika, ground coriander, cumin, garam masala, red pepper flakes, turmeric and pepper in a bowl. Pour over lamb. Stir until lamb is coated with yogurt mixture. Refrigerate covered, stirring occasionally, 3-4 hours. Slice lime and small onion; reserve for garnish. Mince coriander; reserve for garnish. Mince garlic, gingerroot and onions. Saute onion mixture in ghee in large saucepan until tender, about 5 minutes. Stir in lamb, stock and water. Heat to boiling, reduce heat and simmer covered until lamb is tender, about 1 hour. Arrange lamb in deep platter. Garnish with reserved lime, onion and coriander. Serve with condiments (peanuts, eggs, coconut, bacon, bananas, onion, avocado, kumquats). (Serves 8-10)

*Available at A and M Foods in Ann Arbor.

CAROLE MOONEY

Sze-Chuan Pork With Garlic and Ginger Sauce

10 ounces pork tenderloin
1 tablespoon soy sauce
2 teaspoons cornstarch
2 tablespoons dried woodear (black fungus)*
6 water chestnuts
1 cup peanut oil plus 3 tablespoons peanut oil
1 teaspoon minced garlic
1 teaspoon freshly minced ginger

Cut pork into thin slices and marinate with soy sauce and cornstarch for about 15 minutes. Soak dried woodear in warm water for about 15 minutes. Then discarding stems, slice them when expanded. Also slice the water chestnuts. Heat peanut oil in a skillet or wok. Stir-fry pork for about 1 minute or until pork changes color. Then remove and put aside. Drain off oil from pan. Heat 3 tablespoons oil to fry garlic and ginger. Then add water chestnuts, woodear and pork. Stir.

GARLIC AND GINGER SAUCE:
1 tablespoon chopped green onion
1 tablespoon soy sauce
1 tablespoon vinegar
1 tablespoon hot bean paste*
1/2 tablespoon red wine
1 teaspoon sugar
1/2 teaspoon salt
2 teaspoons cornstarch
1 teaspoon sesame oil
1/4 teaspoon black pepper

In a bowl mix together all ingredients for the sauce. Add to meat mixture in a skillet or wok, stirring thoroughly for about 1 minute. Serve. *"Hot and spicy."*

*Available at Chinese grocery stores.   CHIACHEN WU

Orange Pork Chops

6 pork chops
1/2 cup orange juice
1 teaspoon salt
1/4 teaspoon pepper
1/2 teaspoon dry mustard
1/4 cup brown sugar

Preheat oven to 350 degrees. Place chops in a roasting pan. Mix other ingredients and pour on top. Bake for 1 hour. Cover them with foil for the first 40 minutes. Baste occasionally.   MARY ELLEN BOTSFORD

Pork Chops on the Ritz

1 or 1-1/2 rolls of Ritz crackers (small box)
2 eggs
1/4 cup milk
6-8 pork chops
Salt and pepper to taste
1/2 cup butter

Preheat oven to 350 degrees. Crumble crackers in a plastic bag with a rolling pin or large glass. Mix eggs and milk in a medium-size bowl. Season pork chops. Dip pork chop in milk and eggs and put in bag with the crackers. Shake until covered. Place pork chops in baking pan and place two slices of butter on top of each. Bake until done (approximately 45 minutes). (Serves 6) *"Once you've tasted 'Pork Chops on the Ritz' you will not eat them any other way. They are truly delicious!"*

NICHOLE LEE

Pork Tenderloin With Mustard Sauce

2-1/2 to 3 pounds pork tenderloin
MARINADE:
2 tablespoons brown sugar
1/4 cup soy sauce
1/4 cup bourbon

Combine brown sugar, soy sauce and bourbon together in a mixing bowl. Marinate meat several hours, turning occasionally. Preheat oven to 325 degrees. Bake one hour basting with marinade.

MUSTARD SAUCE:
1/3 cup sour cream
1/3 cup mayonnaise
1 tablespoon dry mustard
2-3 chopped green onions

Mix sauce ingredients thoroughly and let sit for 30 minutes in the refrigerator. Serve meat with chilled sauce. (4 servings)

V. MARC TSOU

Veal Patties

You take veal pork and then brown 'em. Put cheese on 'em and then put some tomato sauce on 'em and cook 'em. Then bring them out.

JANET OSTROWSKI
AGE 9

140

Ham and Cheese Casserole

16 slices Pepperidge Farm bread (regular, sliced)
2 cups ground ham
1/2 pound grated cheddar cheese
1/2 pound grated Swiss cheese
4 eggs
Salt to taste
1/2 teaspoon dry mustard
1-3/4 cups milk
1 heaping tablespoon brown sugar
1/4 teaspoon paprika
1 finely chopped green onion (including tops)
1/2 teaspoon Beau Monde seasoning
1/2 teaspoon salt
1/4 cup butter
1-1/2 cups crushed cornflakes

Grease sides of 9 x 13-inch pan with softened butter. Trim crust from bread slices; use enough bread to completely cover bottom of pan. Butter one side of each slice. Place slices, buttered side down, in the pan. Firmly pack the ground ham on the bread layer. Sprinkle cheddar cheese over ham. Place second layer of bread, crust trimmed off, buttered side down over cheese and ham. Sprinkle with Swiss cheese. Beat the eggs, salt, dry mustard and milk together with wire whisk. Mix brown sugar, paprika, green onion, Beau Monde and salt. Pour mixture over everything. Refrigerate overnight. The next day before baking, melt 1/2 stick butter. Mix with crushed cornflakes. Sprinkle on top. Bake at 350 degrees for 45 minutes. *"Great way to use leftover ham. Delicious brunch."*

COOK'S TIP: May be reheated, but will not puff up again.

CAROL MESZAROS

Ham and Cheese Quickies

1/4 pound softened butter
1 medium onion, chopped
2 tablespoons prepared mustard
1-1/2 tablespoons poppy seeds (optional)
1 teaspoon Worcestershire sauce
Hamburger buns
1 pound shaved ham
Grated Swiss cheese

Preheat oven to 300 degrees. Mix the first five ingredients together in a small bowl and spread on split hamburger buns. Top with shaved ham, then grated Swiss cheese. Wrap in foil. May freeze at this point. Bake for 20 minutes or perhaps longer if frozen. (10 servings)

PHYLLIS ASKEW

141

Ham and Cheese Yum-Yums

16 slices bread with crusts off
Prepared mustard
8 slices boiled ham
8 slices sharp cheddar cheese
6 eggs, well-beaten
3 cups milk
2 teaspoons salt
1 cup crushed cornflakes
1/2 cup melted butter

Butter 8 slices of bread. Put buttered side down in baking dish. Spread a little mustard on top of each of these slices. Then place slice of ham on mustard, then slice of cheese, then another slice of bread buttered side up. Blend eggs, milk and salt together. Pour all of egg mixture over top. Let set in refrigerator for 24 hours. Preheat oven to 350 degrees. Just before serving, sprinkle mixture of cornflakes and melted butter over top of bread. Bake for 45 minutes. (8 servings) *"Very tasty for breakfast or light lunch. Can be prepared a day ahead. Our family uses this for holiday breakfast."*

MARION GRAHAM

Ham-Scalloped Potato Casserole

4 tablespoons margarine
1/4 cup all-purpose flour
1 teaspoon salt (optional)
Dash of Tabasco sauce (or pepper)
2 cups milk
1 (8 to 10-ounce) package sharp cheddar cheese, grated
4-5 medium potatoes, peeled and sliced thin
2-3 cups diced cooked ham (1/2-inch cubes)
1 medium onion, chopped
1 (10-ounce) package frozen green beans

Preheat oven to 350 degrees. Spray a 3-quart casserole dish with Pam. Melt margarine in saucepan; add flour, salt and pepper. Stir one minute. Add milk and simmer, stirring constantly, one minute. Add grated cheddar and stir till melted. Put potatoes, ham, onion and green beans in casserole dish; pour cheese sauce over all and mix together well. Bake for 2 to 2-1/2 hours until potatoes are tender. (4-6 servings) *"A good way to use leftover ham."*

CAROL DROGOWSKI

PORK

Ham and Cheese Strata

8 slices bread (crusts trimmed)
4 slices ham
8 slices sharp cheddar cheese
1 quart half-and-half cream
8 eggs
1 teaspoon dry mustard
1 teaspoon Worcestershire sauce
1 teaspoon salt

Trim crusts from bread. Butter 4 slices and lay buttered side down in casserole dish. Place slice of ham, then slice of cheese on bread. Cover with remaining bread and put buttered side up. Grate last 4 slices of cheese and sprinkle over top. Mix cream, eggs, mustard, Worcestershire sauce and salt and pour mixture over bread. Let soak overnight. Take out of refrigerator 2 hours prior to baking. Bake at 350 degrees for 1 hour. Let set 5-10 minutes before serving. (4-6 servings)

GERALDINE CROWLEY

Ham Souffle

6 tablespoons butter
1/2 cup all-purpose flour
2/3 cup milk
3 eggs, separated
1/4 pound cooked chopped ham
1 teaspoon dry mustard
Salt and pepper to taste

Preheat oven to 350 degrees. Melt butter in small saucepan. Add flour and cook 1 minute, stirring constantly. Stir in milk with wire whisk. Bring to a boil and simmer until thickened. Remove from heat and set aside to cool. Beat egg whites until stiff. Pour milk mixture into a heat-proof bowl and blend in ham. Stir in egg yolks and blend in mustard, salt and pepper to taste. Carefully fold in stiffly beaten whites. Turn into a buttered 1-quart souffle dish. Run a teaspoon around the outside edge of the mixture, pushing it inwards. Bake for 40 minutes until golden and well-risen. Serve at once. (4-6 servings)

KATHY DUNN

Sausage and Cheese Brunch Dish

1/2 to 1 pound bulk sausage
6 eggs
2 cups milk
1 teaspoon salt
1 teaspoon dry mustard
6 slices white bread
1 cup grated cheddar cheese

Brown the sausage in a skillet and drain. Beat the eggs. Add milk, salt and mustard. Break bread into pieces and add to egg mixture. Add cheese and sausage. Pour into a 9 x 13-inch pan. Refrigerate overnight. Bake at 350 degrees for 45 minutes. (Serves 6-8)

LYNDA CATTELL
PATTY PRUE

Sausage Casserole

1 pound bulk pork sausage meat
1 onion, chopped
1 green pepper, diced
1-2 cans stewed tomatoes (about 20 ounces)
1 cup uncooked elbow macaroni
1 tablespoon sugar
1-1/2 cups sour cream
Salt and pepper to taste
Parsley (optional)

In a large skillet cook sausage until lightly browned. Pour off most of the fat. Add onion and green pepper and cook 5 minutes longer. Add tomatoes, macaroni, sugar and bring to a boil. Cover and simmer for 30 minutes, stirring occasionally. (May be made ahead of time up to this point.) Add sour cream, heat, and season to taste. Serve with parsley if desired. Good reheated. (4 servings)

NANCY LIVERMORE

Hot Dogs (Well-Done)

Pour water in a pail. Put hot dogs in a pan. Cook seven days and then eat them.

JIM DENNIS
AGE 7

Hot Cajun Sausage Calzone

PASTRY DOUGH:
1 tablespoon active dry yeast
Pinch of sugar
3/4 cup warm water (105-110 degrees)
1 tablespoon olive oil
2-1/2 cups all-purpose flour
1/2 teaspoon salt

In a small bowl, mix the yeast and sugar with the water. Let stand for about 10 minutes, until foamy. Add the oil to yeast mixture. Place the flour and salt in a food processor. Process briefly to combine. With the machine on, add the yeast mixture through the feed tube and mix until a ball of dough forms on the blade. Remove the dough and knead lightly for about 3 minutes. Place the dough in an oiled bowl; turn to coat. Cover and let rise in a warm, draft-free place until doubled in bulk.

FILLING:
3 tablespoons olive oil
1 pound hot Louisiana or Italian sausage, sliced
2 medium onions, thinly sliced
1 large red bell pepper, sliced
3/4 teaspoon thyme
3/4 teaspoon oregano
1 teaspoon paprika
2/3 cup hot spiced pinto beans, drained
Salt and freshly ground black pepper
Cornmeal

In a large skillet, heat the oil. Add the sausage and saute until cooked through, about 8 minutes. Remove the sausage with a slotted spoon and set aside. Add the onions, bell pepper, thyme, oregano and paprika to the oil in the skillet. Cook over low heat until the onion is very soft, about 15 minutes. Add the reserved sausage and the beans and mix. Season with salt and pepper to taste. The filling can be made a day ahead and refrigerated covered. Let return to room temperature before proceeding. Preheat oven to 500 degrees. Divide the dough into 4 equal portions. On a lightly floured surface roll out each piece to a circle about 1/4-inch thick. Mound 1/4 of the sausage filling on half of each circle, leaving a 1/2-inch margin. Fold the dough over the filling to make a semicircle. Pinch and crimp the edges well to seal. Sprinkle cornmeal over a large baking sheet and arrange the calzone on top. Bake for 13 minutes, or until golden brown. (Makes 4 calzone)

CAROLE MOONEY

Sauerkraut and Spareribs

2 pounds spareribs
6 large potatoes
1 (16-ounce) can sauerkraut
1 pound smoked sausage
2 cups hot water
Lawrey's seasoned salt or garlic salt (optional)

Preheat oven to 350 degrees. Place spareribs on cookie sheet. Season and bake for 60 minutes to brown. Drain fat. Peel and slice potatoes. Cover sauerkraut with water and drain. Lightly grease casserole dish and layer sliced potatoes, sauerkraut, spareribs and sliced sausage. Repeat layers ending with a mixture of sauerkraut and potato slices to keep meat moist. Pour hot water over and cover tightly. Bake until tender. If casserole seems too dry, add additional hot water.

ELLA MAGAL

Seafood

SEAFOOD

Cioppino

1/4 cup chopped green pepper
2 tablespoons chopped onion
1 clove garlic, minced
1 tablespoon oil
2 (16-ounce) cans tomato sauce
1/2 cup red wine
2 tablespoons parsley
1/2 teaspoon salt
1/4 teaspoon oregano
1/4 teaspoon basil
Dash of pepper
1 pound chopped skinned perch
1 (4-1/2 ounce) can drained shrimp
1 (6-1/2 ounce) can clams with juice

Brown green pepper, onion, garlic in oil in a large skillet. Add the tomato sauce, red wine, parsley, salt, oregano, basil and pepper. Simmer for 20 minutes. Add the perch and simmer for 5 minutes. Add the shrimp and clams and simmer for 3 minutes. (4-6 servings) *"Serve with garlic bread and a green salad. Tastes even better the next day re-warmed. No "fishy" taste. Easy! Even Jenista can make it right every time. Much more filling than it looks."*

JERRI JENISTA

Caribbean Snapper

1-1/2 pounds snapper
1 teaspoon salt
1 teaspoon black pepper
1/2 cup butter
1 large onion, chopped
2 medium tomatoes, chopped
1 medium green pepper, chopped
1/4 cup tomato sauce

Season fillets with salt and pepper. If broiling, dot with 1/4 cup butter; if frying, saute in 1/4 cup butter until done. Heat the remaining 1/4 cup butter in a large saucepan or frying pan. Saute onions, tomatoes and peppers until soft but not brown. Add tomato sauce. Simmer an additional 10 minutes. Pour sauce over fish. Return to preheated oven, 350 degrees, for 15 minutes. (Serves 4)

DONOVAN BOWERBANK

Grouper en Papillote
(Fish in a Bag)

4 lunch-size brown paper bags
Vegetable oil
1 egg, beaten
1/2 cup half-and-half cream
1-1/2 cups toasted buttered bread crumbs
1/2 cup grated Parmesan cheese
Lemon pepper to taste
4 (6-8 ounce) grouper fillets (may substitute red snapper, haddock, halibut or flounder)

Preheat oven to 450 degrees. Open bags and lay on sides. Brush oil on one interior side of each bag. Combine egg, cream, bread crumbs, cheese and lemon pepper. Roll fish in bread crumb mixture to thoroughly coat. Place 1 fillet on the oiled side of each bag. Tie bags and place directly on rack in oven. Bake 25 minutes. Remove from oven. Carefully cut open with scissors and serve immediately in bags. (4 servings)

ELLEN DANIEL

Sole Veronique

1 large onion, finely chopped
2 cloves garlic, minced
2 pounds sole fillets
Chopped parsley to taste
Salt and pepper to taste
1/2 pint dry white wine (1 cup)
2 tablespoons all-purpose flour
1/4 cup butter
Juice of 1 lemon
1/2 pound large white grapes, peeled*

Preheat oven to 425 degrees. Butter an oval baking dish. Make a layer on bottom of onion and garlic. Lay fish fillets (1-layer thick) on top. Season. Pour over wine. Bake for 20 minutes. In a small bowl mash flour into the butter. Remove fillets from oven and transfer fish to a heated serving plate. Pour juices into a saucepan and simmer adding lemon juice and flour-butter mixture. Stir until thickened. Add grapes. Heat 2-3 minutes and pour over fish and serve. (4 servings)

*COOK'S TIP: To peel grapes plunge in boiling water for 20 seconds and then peel.

CAROLINE BLANE

Salmon Mold With Cucumber Dressing

1 envelope unflavored gelatin
1/4 cup cold water
1 teaspoon salt
1 teaspoon dry mustard
Dash of cayenne
2 tablespoons all-purpose flour
2 tablespoons sugar
2 egg yolks
1 cup milk
3 tablespoons vinegar
1-1/2 tablespoons butter
2 cups flaked canned red salmon
Lettuce

Soften the gelatin in the cold water. Mix the dry ingredients in a saucepan; add the egg yolks and mix well. Add the milk, stir, and add the vinegar. Cook over a low heat, stirring until thickened. Add the gelatin and stir until dissolved. Add the butter and stir until melted. Fold in the salmon and turn into six individual molds or one large mold. Chill until firm or at least 4 hours. Unmold on a bed of lettuce. Serve dressing with salmon mold.

CUCUMBER DRESSING:
1 large cucumber, peeled and chopped fine
1 cup mayonnaise (or 1 cup sour cream)

Blend cucumber and mayonnaise or sour cream together.

CAROLE MOONEY

Linguine and Clam Sauce

4 tablespoons olive oil
3 large cloves garlic, mined
1 tablespoon anchovy paste
1/4 cup fresh chopped parsley
1 (28-ounce) can tomatoes
1 (10-ounce) can tomatoes
1 (6-ounce) can tomato paste
Fresh pepper (6-8 twists of mill)
1 teaspoon basil
2 cans Doxsee minced clams (save liquid) or 1/2 pound fresh but you
   will need a bottle of clam juice
8-9 frozen cooked shrimp (chopped coarsely, size of end of little
   finger)
Cooked linguine*

In a large saucepan combine oil and garlic. Cook till transparent over medium heat. Add anchovy paste and parsley and sizzle about 30 seconds. Add tomatoes, paste, pepper, basil and 1 cup of juice from clams. (If you use fresh clams you will have to use bottled clam juice that is available at all supermarkets.) Let this simmer for about 20 minutes to half an hour uncovered. At this point you can shut down and put together anything else you plan to serve. *(We generally have an oil and vinegar salad and garlic bread. This is very filling.)*

*COOK'S TIP: When you start the water for your linguine, start the heat under the sauce and when it starts to bubble, add the clams and cut-up shrimp. When shrimp is done (about 10 minutes), your linguine should also be ready and you can eat, eat, eat. Serve individually or you can put it all in a big bowl, Italian-style. Either way, this is a terrific dish and I know you will enjoy it. (4 servings)

FAT BOB TAYLOR

Linguine With Oysters

1/4 cup butter
6 green onions, chopped
1 clove garlic, minced
1 pint select oysters with liquid (not Pacific)
2 tablespoons parsley
Salt and pepper to taste
1/2 pound linguine, cooked

Saute onion and garlic in butter in a large skillet. Add oysters and parsley and seasonings. Simmer 4 minutes. Add pasta and toss.

MARY WASKERWITZ

152

Oyster Crisp

16 ounces oysters (shucked with liquor)
1/4 teaspoon salt
1/8 teaspoon pepper
1/8 teaspoon nutmeg
6 strips bacon (cooked, drained and crumbled)
1 cup Swiss cheese, grated
1/2 pint whipping cream
14 saltine crackers, coarsely crushed
2 tablespoons butter or margarine

Preheat oven to 400 degrees. Pour oysters and liquor into greased shallow 1-1/2 quart baking dish. (If oysters are large, break into bite-size pieces.) Sprinkle salt, pepper and nutmeg over oysters, then scatter bacon over them and top with cheese. Pour cream over all, cover with cracker crumbs and dot with butter. Bake uncovered for 15 minutes or until the edges of oyster begin to curl. *"Simple and quick casserole."*

GERALDINE CROWLEY

Scalloped Oysters

2 pints fresh oysters and their liquor
9 tablespoons coffee cream
1 cup dry white bread crumbs
1-3/4 cups saltine cracker crumbs
1/2 to 3/4 cup melted butter
Salt, pepper and paprika to taste

Put oysters in a sieve over a bowl to collect the liquid. Mix the liquid with the coffee cream. Combine home-made bread crumbs (simply use good white bread and buzz in blender) and cracker crumbs (crumble your own saltines) and pour melted butter over them. Blend well. (They should not be soggy.) Lightly grease Pyrex baking dish. Cover the bottom with a layer of combined crumb mix. Over the top of this, arrange half of the oysters and then pour over them half of the oyster-cream mixture. Season lightly with salt, pepper and slight drifting of paprika. Next another layer of crumbs, then oysters, the remaining liquor-cream, and a repeat of seasonings. Top this last layer with crumbs and dot with butter and paprika. Easy with the butter and paprika to suit your taste. At this point oysters may be stored in refrigerator or placed in a preheated 400 degree oven for exactly 20 minutes. *"Sliced baked ham (hot or cold) should accompany each serving of scalloped oysters. Raspberry sherbet is very good with it!"*

MARILYN CANHAM

Scallops Sauteed

1/4 cup butter
2 cloves garlic, minced
1 pound bay scallops
1/2 teaspoon salt
1/4 teaspoon pepper
1/4 cup chopped parsley
Cooked rice

Melt butter in a large skillet. Add garlic and salt. Cook until garlic is brown.
Add scallops and cook 6 minutes. Sprinkle with salt and pepper. Add parsley
and cook 1 minute. Serve hot over rice.

MARY WASKERWITZ

Scallops in Wine

2 pounds scallops
2 cups dry white wine
4 minced shallots
24 finely sliced mushroom caps
2 tablespoons minced parsley
1/4 cup butter
2 tablespoons all-purpose flour
2-4 tablespoons whipping cream
Cooked pasta

Simmer scallops in wine. Drain and reserve the liquid. Saute shallots,
mushrooms and parsley in butter in a large skillet. Stir in flour till blended.
Add the reserved liquid and cream. Add scallops. Serve with pasta (linguine or
fettucine, homemade is best). (6 servings)

JANET GILSDORF

Scallops With Tomatoes, Olives and Capers

1 small onion, chopped
2 tablespoons olive oil
1 bell pepper, chopped
1 sweet red pepper, chopped
2 cloves garlic, minced
2 large tomatoes, chopped
1/2 cup pimento-stuffed olives, chopped
2 tablespoons small capers
Salt and pepper to taste
1 pound fresh bay scallops
Cooked pasta*

In a large skillet saute onion in olive oil until soft. Add peppers, garlic and tomatoes and cook for 5 minutes. Add olives and capers, salt and pepper. Simmer 30 minutes. Add scallops the last 5-10 minutes and cook till scallops are just done. Serve over fresh pasta. (4 servings)

*COOK'S TIP: Homemade pasta made with semolina flour is the best.

JANET GILSDORF

Shrimp and Scallop Pilaf

2 tablespoons butter or margarine
1 medium onion, chopped
1 (13-3/4 ounce) can chicken broth plus 1 cup water
1 cup uncooked long grain rice
1/4 teaspoon turmeric
1/2 teaspoon salt
Dash of pepper
1/4 teaspoon garlic powder
8 ounces shrimp, peeled and deveined
8 ounces sea scallops
Cooked rice

In a large skillet, melt butter and cook onions until clear. Add broth mixture, rice, turmeric, salt, pepper and garlic powder, stirring to mix. Bring to a boil, reduce heat, cover and simmer for 15 minutes. Stir. Add shrimp and scallops. Heat 5 minutes or longer until scallops are opaque and shrimp are pink. Toss with rice and serve. (4 servings) *"May microwave scallops and shrimp. Serve with peas and baby onions, bread and tossed salad."*

PAMELA OLTON

Baked Stuffed Shrimps Miller

16 large raw shrimp
1 teaspoon salt
1 garlic clove
2 cups croutons
1 (6-ounce) can crabmeat (or 1 cup fresh crabmeat, flaked)
1 teaspoon parsley
1/2 cup butter, melted
6 tablespoons dry white wine
6 tablespoons water
Chopped parsley
Paprika

Preheat oven to 400 degrees. Peel the raw shrimp, leaving the tails intact.
Wash and devein the shrimp, split them slightly and spread them out. Butter 4
individual casseroles and arrange 4 shrimp in each one, standing them upright,
split side down, in a circle, with the tails around the top of the rim. Rub salt
with garlic clove, split and let the garlic stand in the salt for a few minutes until
the salt is well-flavored and discard the garlic. Combine croutons, crabmeat,
the garlic-flavored salt and parsley and blend in melted butter. Combine the
wine and water and add enough of the liquid to the crabmeat mixture to make a
moist but not wet stuffing. Divide the mixture among the casseroles, spreading
it over the split ends of the shrimp and sprinkle the shrimp and stuffing with
chopped parsley and paprika. Bake the casseroles for 20 minutes or until the
shrimp are done and the stuffing is hot and lightly browned. Serve the shrimp
with melted butter. (4 servings)

JACKIE BREWER

Shrimp and Cheese Casserole

6 slices white bread
1/2 pound Old English cheese (usually comes sliced)
1 pound prepared shrimp (cooked)
1/4 cup butter or margarine, melted
3 eggs, beaten
Salt to taste
1/2 teaspoon dry mustard
2 cups milk

Break bread into quarter-sized pieces. Break cheese into bite-sized pieces.
Arrange shrimp, bread and cheese in several layers in greased casserole. Pour
margarine or butter over this mixture. In a large bowl beat the eggs. Add salt
and mustard to eggs. Then add milk. Pour this mixture over ingredients in
casserole. Let stand minimum of 3 hours, preferably overnight, covered, in
refrigerator. Bake 1 hour, covered, at 350 degrees. *"If you increase the amount
of shrimp, this dish is better than ever, but if you decrease the amount of
shrimp, it is still good."*

ELIZABETH STONE

156

Linguine With Shrimp and Clam Sauce

3 tablespoons olive oil
3 cloves garlic, minced
1 (6-1/2 ounce) can chopped clams with juice
1 pound cooked shrimp (salad size)
1/4 cup chopped fresh parsley
1/4 teaspoon oregano
Juice from 1/3 lemon
3 tablespoons half-and-half cream
1 teaspoon cornstarch
Salt and pepper to taste
3 tablespoons freshly grated Parmesan cheese
Linguine

In a large skillet heat oil over medium low heat. Add garlic. Cook gently for
about 5 minutes. Add clams and liquid, shrimp, parsley, oregano and lemon
juice and heat until low boil. Decrease heat. Add half-and-half cream to the
cornstarch. Mix well. Add slowly to the clam-shrimp mixture. Simmer for a
few minutes. Add salt and pepper to taste and the Parmesan cheese. Cook
linguine according to package directions. Toss pasta with sauce and serve.
(4 servings)

NANCY JOHNSON

Shrimp Scampi

6 tablespoons butter
1 tablespoon oil
4-5 cloves garlic, minced
2 teaspoons lemon juice
1/4 teaspoon salt
1/4 teaspoon grated lemon peel
1 pound shrimp (peeled, washed and deveined)
2 tablespoons parsley
Tabasco sauce to taste
Cooked rice

Melt butter in a large skillet. Add oil, garlic, lemon juice, salt and grated lemon
peel. Cook until bubbly and add the cleaned shrimp. Cook 4-5 minutes. Stir
in parsley and Tabasco sauce. Serve over hot white rice. *"Quick and easy."*

NANCY MORIN

157

Magic Crust Shrimp Pie

6 ounces cooked baby shrimp
1 cup cheddar cheese, grated
1/2 cup mozzarella, grated
1/4 cup sliced green onion
1/4 cup chopped pimento
2 tablespoons parsley
2 cups buttermilk
2 tablespoons butter
4 eggs
1/2 tablespoon baking powder
1 cup all-purpose flour
1/2 teaspoon soda

Preheat oven to 350 degrees. Combine shrimp, cheese, onion, pimento and parsley and place in lightly greased 10-inch pie plate. Put remaining ingredients in blender or food processor. Blend on high 15 seconds. Pour over ingredients in pie plate. Bake for 35-40 minutes. Cool 5 minutes before cutting. (6-8 servings)   TAMI BETZ

Shrimp and Scallops Over Linguine

1-1/2 tablespoons butter
1-1/2 tablespoons olive oil
1/2 pound shrimp
1/2 pound scallops
8 shallots, finely chopped
8 green onions, finely chopped
2 large cloves garlic, finely minced
2 teaspoons dried basil
1 teaspoon dried tarragon
1/4 teaspoon thyme
1/2 cup white wine
10 peeled, seeded and juiced very ripe tomatoes, chopped (or 4 cups
  drained, crushed canned high quality tomatoes)
1/2 cup half-and-half cream
1-2 tablespoons sugar
Salt and pepper to taste
1 to 1-1/2 pounds fresh linguine

Heat water in a large stockpot for linguine. In skillet, heat butter and oil and saute shrimp and scallops until barely firm. Transfer to a bowl. Add shallots and onion to skillet and saute until soft. Over medium heat, add garlic and herbs and cook 1 minute. Add wine and cook 2 minutes. Stir in tomatoes. Increase heat to high and boil briefly until sauce thickens. Stir in cream and sugar and heat through, about 20 seconds. Then take off the heat and add salt and pepper to taste. Put pasta in boiling salted water. Cook until done but still firm. Drain, heat seafood mixture briefly and serve over linguine.
                    SUSAN HURWITZ

Shrimp Creole

2 tablespoons all-purpose flour
2 tablespoons butter
1 can stewed tomatoes with onions and green peppers
2 teaspoons garlic powder
1/8 teaspoon thyme
1/2 teaspoon oregano
2 tablespoons minced onion
2 bay leaves
Salt and pepper to taste
1 pound small shrimp (peeled, washed and deveined)
Cooked rice

Combine all ingredients in a large saucepan and simmer for 25 minutes. Serve over rice. (4 servings)

MARY ELLEN BOTSFORD

Camarao a Bahiana
(Shrimp Dish From Brazil)

3 tablespoons oil
1 onion, finely chopped
6 small tomatoes, peeled, seeded and chopped
1/4 cup finely chopped parsley
2 pounds shrimp, shelled and deveined
1/2 teaspoon salt
Freshly ground black pepper
1 tablespoon butter
1 tablespoon all-purpose flour
1 cup coconut milk*
2 small, very hot red peppers, minced (or use dried red peppers, to
   taste)
Cooked rice

Heat oil in a large saucepan and saute the onion until softened. Add the tomatoes and parsley and saute 5 minutes. Add the shrimp and cook, stirring constantly, 3 minutes. Season with salt and pepper. In a small saucepan, melt the butter. Add the flour and cook, stirring 1 minute. Add the coconut milk gradually, stirring constantly until slightly thickened. Add the sauce and peppers to the shrimp mixture. Simmer 2 minutes. Transfer to a heated serving dish and surround with rice. (Serves 4)

*COOK'S TIP: To make coconut milk, simmer equal amounts of grated unsweetened coconut and milk together for 30 minutes. Strain the milk and use as directed.

FLORENCE JOHNSTON

159

Vegetables

VEGETABLES

Baked Beans

1 (16-ounce) can pork and beans
4 tablespoons brown sugar
1 tablespoon Worcestershire sauce
2 teaspoons prepared mustard
1/4 cup ketchup
1 medium onion, chopped
Bacon slices

Preheat oven to 325 degrees. Mix all ingredients except the bacon. Lay bacon on top of beans and bake in a bean pot or casserole dish for about 1 to 1-1/2 hours. (4 servings)   MARY ELLEN BOTSFORD

Stir-Fried Broccoli

2-3 stalks of broccoli, cut into pieces
1 tablespoon oil
1 tablespoon white wine
1 teaspoon lime or lemon juice
1 teaspoon salt
1/4 teaspoon pepper
1 teaspoon cornstarch in 1 tablespoon water
1/4 cup broth or water
Onion, carrots, sweet peppers (optional)

Heat oil to about 300 degrees. Add washed bite-sized broccoli. Stir vigorously and heat for about 1 minute. Add wine and lemon juice; cover, cook on low heat for 5 minutes. Test for doneness. Add salt, pepper, water and cornstarch. Stir until thickened and serve hot, plain or over rice. May add onion and/or sliced carrots and/or sweet pepper for color.
                              INTA ERTEL

Broccoli Casserali I

1 pound fresh broccoli
1 (4-ounce) can mushrooms
1 (10-3/4 ounce) can cream of mushroom soup
1/2 cup milk
8 ounces grated cheese
1/2 cup margarine or butter
1 cup Bisquick or Jiffy mix

Cook broccoli till crisp tender. Preheat oven to 400 degrees. In a bowl combine mushrooms, soup and milk. Drain broccoli and place in baking dish. Pour mushroom mixture over broccoli. Top with grated cheese. Cut margarine into Jiffy mix and sprinkle over cheese. Bake for 20 minutes. (4 servings)
                              NORMA ABRAM

163

Broccoli Casserole II

1-1/2 pounds broccoli, cut up
1 (10-3/4 ounces) can cream of mushroom soup
1/4 cup mayonnaise
1/4 cup sharp cheddar cheese, grated
1 tablespoon chopped pimento
1-1/2 teaspoons lemon juice
1/3 cup Ritz cracker crumbs

Preheat oven to 350 degrees. In a saucepan cook broccoli 10-15 minutes in salt water. Drain. Put in 1-1/2 quart casserole. Combine soup, mayonnaise, cheese, pimento and lemon juice. Pour over broccoli. Crumble cracker crumbs over top. Bake for 35 minutes.

GRACE BRAND
SYLVIA SHERWOOD
KATHY ROSS

Broccoli Supreme

1-1/2 pounds fresh or frozen broccoli, chopped (24 ounces)
2 eggs
1 cup cottage cheese
2 tablespoons minced onion
1/2 teaspoon salt
1/4 teaspoon pepper
1 teaspoon Worcestershire sauce
3 tablespoons cheddar cheese, grated
1/2 cup melted butter
1/2 cup butter
1/4 cup bread crumbs

Preheat oven to 350 degrees. Cook broccoli in salted water just until tender. Arrange broccoli in buttered casserole dish. Mix together eggs, cottage cheese, minced onion, salt, pepper, Worcestershire sauce, cheddar cheese and butter and pour over broccoli. Melt the last 1/2 cup of butter and combine with bread crumbs. Pour on top of casserole. Bake for 30 minutes until golden on top and a slight crust has formed. (6 servings)

BARBARA RICHARDS

Fried Cabbage

8 slices bacon, diced
1 onion, chopped
1 cabbage, shredded
Salt and pepper to taste

Fry bacon and onion in a large skillet. Add cabbage, salt and pepper. Fry until tender and serve.

MARY WASKERWITZ

Brandied Carrots

24 small carrots
1 tablespoon butter
3 tablespoons Chambord (raspberry liqueur)
Juice of 1 lemon
1/4 cup brandy
1/4 cup honey
2 tablespoons parsley, finely chopped

Preheat oven to 350 degrees. In a large pot cook the carrots in salted water until tender. Drain and arrange in buttered casserole. Make syrup of Chambord, lemon juice, brandy and honey. Pour over carrots. Sprinkle parsley on top and bake for 15-20 minutes. (4 servings)

JANET GILSDORF

Cauliflower Pulau

1-1/2 cups long grain rice
1/2 cup butter
1 (10-ounce) package cauliflower frozen (or 1 medium cut into 1/2-inch pieces)
2 teaspoons salt
1/2 teaspoon black pepper
1/2 teaspoon red pepper powder
2 medium onions, chopped
12 cloves garlic, finely minced
2 crushed cardamom
1 stick cinnamon
6 cloves
1/2 teaspoon fresh ginger, grated
2-3 green chilies
1 teaspoon salt
1 teaspoon cumin seeds
1/2 teaspoon coriander powder
2-1/2 to 3 cups water
5 tablespoons sour cream

Wash rice and soak in water for half hour. Heat butter in a large skillet. Fry cauliflower with 1 teaspoon salt, black and red pepper until it is half-cooked. Remove cauliflower from pan and fry onion and garlic in the same butter. Add cardamom, cinnamon, cloves and rice and fry a few more minutes. Add fried cauliflower pieces, grated ginger, green chilies, salt, cumin seeds and coriander powder. Fry for 5 more minutes on low heat. Add water and sour cream. Bring to boil. Cover and cook on low heat until all water evaporates. Pour the mixture in a greased metallic or Pyrex pan and bake at 300 degrees for 20 minutes. (6 servings)

VASANTHA PADMANABHAN

VEGETABLES

Mixed Vegetable Curry

3 tablespoons vegetable oil
2 teaspoons ground coriander
1/2 teaspon chili powder
1/4 teaspoon turmeric
1/4 teaspoon fresh ginger, chopped
2 cloves garlic, minced
3 tablespoons grated unsweetened coconut
1 cup cauliflower, cut up
2 small raw potatoes, peeled and cubed
1 cup green peas
2 carrots, peeled and sliced
1 medium onion, thinly sliced
2 large tomatoes, chopped
1/4 to 1/2 dried or fresh green or red chili, finely chopped (or to taste)
1 teaspoon salt
1/4 cup water

Heat vegetable oil in a large skillet and fry coriander, chili powder, turmeric, ginger, garlic and coconut 2-3 minutes. Add cauliflower, potatoes, green peas and carrots. Fry for 5 minutes. Add onions, tomatoes, green chili, salt and water. Simmer until all vegetables are tender, adding water if it gets too dry.

DIANE SCHWARTZ

Vegetable Kabobs

3 cups broccoli flowerets
2 cups summer squash, diagonally sliced
2 large sweet red peppers, cut into 2-inch pieces
2 medium red onions, cut into wedges

MARINADE:
1/2 cup vegetable oil
1/4 cup red wine vinegar
1 tablespoon soy sauce
2 teaspoons red pepper flakes
1 teaspoon ground ginger
1/2 teaspoon garlic salt

In a large bowl combine broccoli, squash, red pepper and onion; set aside. In a small bowl mix together remaining ingredients; pour over vegetables. Marinate at room temperature for 1-2 hours, tossing occasionally. Prepare outdoor grill for barbecuing. Thread vegetables alternately onto long skewers. Place kabobs on cooking grid over medium coals. Grill for 5-7 minutes turning and basting with remaining marinade.

ANNE MENDE

166

Creamed Corn

2 (20-ounce) packages frozen whole kernel corn
1 cup whipping cream
1 cup milk
2 tablespoons sugar
1 teaspoon salt
1/4 teaspoon MSG (optional)
Pinch of white pepper
2 tablespoons soft butter
2 tablespoons all-purpose flour
Parmesan cheese

Combine corn, whipping cream, milk, sugar, salt, MSG and pepper in a large saucepan. Bring to boil, reduce heat and simmer 5 minutes. Blend together butter and flour. Stir into corn. Cook and stir until thickened. Pour into buttered 2-1/2 quart casserole. Sprinkle cheese over top. Brown under broiler.

MARY ELLEN BOTSFORD

Eggplant and Rice

1 eggplant (cut in 1-inch cubes)
4 tablespoons olive oil
1 cup onion, chopped
1 green pepper, chopped in large pieces
2 garlic cloves, minced
1 teaspoon thyme
1 bay leaf
1 (1-pound) can stewed tomatoes
1 cup rice
3-3/4 cups chicken broth
1/4 cup grated Parmesan cheese
Salt and pepper to taste

Preheat oven to 375 degrees. In a large saucepan saute eggplant in oil. Add onion, green pepper, garlic, thyme, bay leaf and stir. Add tomatoes and simmer 5 minutes. Stir in rice, broth, salt and pepper. Spoon into greased baking dish and top with cheese. Bake uncovered for 1 hour.

MARY WASKERWITZ

Eggplant Souffle

1 large eggplant (pared and cut into 1/2-inch cubes)
2 eggs, beaten
1/2 cup milk
1/2 cup bread crumbs
1 onion (chopped and sauteed)
Salt and pepper to taste
3/4 cup Velveeta cheese, cubed

Preheat oven to 350 degrees. In a large saucepan cook eggplant in salted water for 15 minutes. Drain and mash. Add rest of ingredients. Place in greased casserole and bake 40 minutes.

MARY WASKERWITZ

Fourth Street Burger

1/2 cup lentils
1 cup boiling water
1/4 cup dry cracked wheat
1/3 cup boiling water
1/3 cup rolled oats
1/3 cup boiling water
7/8 cup cooked brown rice
1/3 cup whole wheat flour
1/8 cup cornmeal
1/3 cup sesame seeds
1/4 cup sunflower seeds
1/3 cup chopped onions
1 tablespoon oil
1 teaspoon tamari
1/4 teaspoon ground coriander
Pinch of cayenne
1-1/2 teaspoons dill weed
1/4 teaspoon garlic powder
1-1/2 tablespoons tamari
1/2 teaspoon salt (optional)
1/2 teaspoon thyme
1-1/2 tablespoons dry parsley

Soak lentils until soft in 1 cup boiling water. Mash. Soak cracked wheat until soft in 1/3 cup boiled water. Preheat oven to 350 degrees. Place oats, brown rice, wheat flour, cornmeal, sesame and sunflower seeds on baking sheet and bake for 20 minutes. Saute onions in oil or water with tamari. Mix last eight spice ingredients together in a large bowl. Mix everything together thoroughly. Bake patties on lightly oiled baking sheet for 25 minutes. Before serving, brown each side briefly in hot skillet. (Makes 5-7 burgers)

JAN WESTBY

Okra and Tomatoes

2-3 strips bacon
1 medium onion, finely chopped
1 pound fresh okra
1 (28-ounce) can of tomatoes (or 5-6 fresh peeled tomatoes)
Salt and pepper to taste
Worcestershire sauce to taste
Cooked rice

Cut bacon into small pieces and gently fry in a skillet with finely chopped
onion. Dice the okra into 1/2-inch pieces and stir into bacon to lightly fry. Add
the tomatoes. Stir, adding salt, pepper and Worcestershire sauce to taste.
Simmer for several hours over medium heat. Serve hot over cooked rice.
(4-6 servings)

MACDONALD DICK

Mama Iannotti's Peppers and Tomatoes

12 sweet bell peppers (4 each green, red and yellow)
1/4 cup vegetable oil
3 tablespoons olive oil
4-6 garlic cloves, coarsely chopped
1 (28-ounce) can whole peeled tomatoes, drained

Slice peppers in half. Remove seeds and membranes and slice into quarter-inch
slices. Heat vegetable oil in a large skillet over medium-high heat. Saute half of
sliced peppers until they become soft and begin to turn black. Remove from oil
and drain on paper towels. Cook second half in similar manner and drain.
Discard remaining oil. Add olive oil to pan, heat and add garlic. After a few
seconds add tomatoes, squashing them in your hand as you put in pan. Cook
until mixture becomes thick, about 10 minutes. Add peppers and mix.
Refrigerate and serve cold. (8-12 servings) *"Authentic Neopolitan dish."*

PAMELA AND FAUSTO IANNOTTI

Zwiebelkuchen
(Onion Pie)

4 cups sliced onions
1 cup sour cream
1 beaten egg
1 teaspoon salt
1/4 teaspoon pepper
3 teaspoons caraway seeds
1 (9-inch) unbaked pie shell
6 slices bacon, cooked and crumbled

Preheat oven to 375 degrees. Cover and steam onions until soft. Remove from heat. Place half of the steamed onions in the pie shell. Mix sour cream with beaten egg, salt, pepper and caraway seeds. Pour half of this mixture on top. Repeat layers of onions and egg mixture. Sprinkle bacon on top of pie. Bake for 35-40 minutes or until brown on top. Serve hot in wedges. *"A good side-dish for a buffet."*

COOK'S TIP: To save time, you may cook bacon in microwave on high 4-5 minutes and onions on high 5-6 minutes.

ELIZABETH STONE

Sweet Potato Pie

5 medium yams or sweet potatoes
3/4 cup butter
2-1/2 cups sugar
1 tablespoon vanilla
1 tablespoon mace or nutmeg
1 teaspoon cinnamon
6 eggs
1 (12-ounce) can evaporated milk
3 (9-inch) unbaked pie shells

Preheat oven to 325 degrees. Peel yams and cook in covered boiler until soft. Drain off water in a colander. After fully drained put yams in a mixing bowl while still hot and add butter and sugar and mash with a potato masher or mixer until smooth. After smooth add vanilla, mace and cinnamon and mix well. Add eggs; mix thoroughly and add milk gradually using a folding motion. Pour into pie shells. Bake for 1 hour. (Makes 3 pies)

LORENE HAYNES

Au Gratin Potatoes

1-1/2 cups half-and-half cream
1 (12-ounce) package frozen hash brown potatoes
4 tablespoons butter
Salt and pepper to taste
1 tablespoon Parmesan cheese
1 tablespoon melted butter

Carefully bring cream to boil in a saucepan. Add potatoes, butter, salt and pepper. Simmer slowly until it thickens. Pour into greased broiler-safe casserole dish. Sprinkle with Parmesan cheese and melted butter. Place under broiler to brown lightly. (Note: You may increase the recipe to serve a large group.) (4 servings)

JERI KELCH

Southern Yam Custard

1 cup half-and-half cream
1 tablespoon butter
2 eggs, slightly beaten
1/2 cup sugar
1/4 teaspoon salt
1/4 teaspoon cinnamon
1/4 teaspoon ginger
Pinch of nutmeg
1/2 teaspoon vanilla
1 (17-ounce) can packed yams

Preheat oven to 350 degrees. Heat cream with butter in a small saucepan until butter melts. Stir eggs, sugar, salt, spices and vanilla in a bowl and blend until smooth. Mash or puree yams in warm cream. Stir into egg mixture. Pour yam mixture into well-buttered 1-1/2 quart casserole.

TOPPING:
(can be doubled for added richness)
1/3 cup light brown sugar
2 tablespoons all-purpose flour
2 tablespoons butter
1/3 cup chopped pecans
1/3 cup flaked coconut

Mix all topping ingredients together and sprinkle over yam mixture. Put casserole into a slightly larger pan and fill with boiling water to come up to within 1 inch of the casserole. Bake 60 minutes or until knife comes out clean.

SUE HENDERSON

171

Potato Curry (Fried Potatoes)

4 large potatoes
5 tablespoons oil
1/4 teaspoon mustard seeds
6 tablespoons onion, chopped
3/4 teaspoon salt (or to taste)
1/2 teaspoon red chili powder or red pepper (or to taste)

Pare the potatoes and cut them into 1/2-inch pieces. In a skillet, heat oil with mustard seed. When mustard seeds crack, add onion. When onion turns golden brown, add cut potatoes, salt and chili powder. Stir fry on low heat until potato turns golden brown and is cooked. Serve hot. (6 servings)

VASANTHA PADMANABHAN

Stuffed Baked Potatoes

4 medium baking potatoes
1/4 cup butter
1/4 cup milk
1 teaspoon salt
1/8 teaspoon pepper
1/4 cup grated cheddar cheese
1/4 cup crumbled cooked bacon
1/4 cup green onions, chopped
Paprika

Bake potatoes until soft, about 50 minutes. Cut a thin slice lengthwise off the top of each potato. Scoop out pulp, reserving potato shells. Mash pulp. Add butter, milk, salt, and pepper and mix well. Spoon back into potato shells. Scatter cheese, bacon and onions over top. Sprinkle a dash of paprika over tops. Cover with plastic wrap and refrigerate for 6-8 hours or overnight. Preheat oven to 425 degrees. Bake until heated through and tops are brown, about 30-40 minutes. (4 servings)   CHARLOTTE BETZ

Potatoes Royale

1 (2-pound) package hash brown potatoes
1 (10-3/4 ounce) can cream of chicken soup
6-8 ounces grated Kraft cracker barrel sharp cheese
1 (8-ounce) carton sour cream
1/2 cup chopped onion
1 teaspoon salt and dash of pepper
1/4 pound melted butter

Defrost potatoes enough to break up. Preheat oven to 325 degrees. Place all ingredients into a 9 x 13-inch glass casserole dish. Mix well and bake for 40-50 minutes. (6 servings)   KIRK DZENKO

Mashed Potato Casserole

1 onion, chopped
1/2 pound mushrooms, chopped
4 tablespoons margarine
8 medium potatoes, boiled and mashed
1/2 cup sour cream
Salt and pepper
Grated Parmesan cheese

Preheat oven to 400 degrees. In a skillet saute onion and mushrooms in 2 tablespoons margarine. Combine potatoes, onions, mushrooms, sour cream, and seasonings in a bowl. Pat into greased 9 x 9-inch pan. Sprinkle with cheese and dot with 2 tablespoons margarine. Bake for 1/2 hour.

MARY WASKERWITZ

Potato Casserole Supreme

9 medium baking potatoes
1/2 cup margarine or butter
1-1/2 teaspoons salt
1/4 teaspoon pepper
2/3 cup warm milk
1-1/2 cups cheddar cheese, grated
1 cup heavy cream, whipped

Preheat oven to 350 degrees. Peel and boil potatoes in a saucepan until tender. Drain and beat in large bowl with mixer until fluffy, adding butter, seasonings and milk. Pour into buttered shallow casserole dish. Fold cheese into whipped cream and spread over top. Bake for 25 minutes or until golden brown. May be prepared ahead of time and baked when needed.

CAROL MESZAROS

Spinach-Cheese Pie

1 (3-ounce) package cream cheese, softened
1 cup grated cheddar cheese
6 eggs, slightly beaten
1 (10-ounce) package frozen chopped spinach (cooked and drained)
2 teaspoons parsley
2 tablespoons minced onion
Salt and pepper to taste
1 (9-inch) unbaked pie shell
2 tablespoons Parmesan cheese

Preheat oven to 400 degrees. Mix all ingredients except cheese, thoroughly in a bowl. Pour into 9-inch pie shell and sprinkle top with Parmesan cheese. Bake for 25 minutes. Let stand 10 minutes before cutting. (Serves 6)

JERRY REED

Spinach Torte

3 (10-ounce) packages frozen chopped spinach, thawed and drained
2 cups Progresso bread crumbs
1-1/2 cups grated sharp cheese
1-1/2 cups olive oil (may use less)
10 eggs
1 cup chopped fresh parsley
2 onions, chopped
2 cloves garlic, minced
1-1/2 teaspoons Italian seasoning
2 teaspoons salt
2 teaspoons pepper
Dash of Tabasco sauce

Preheat oven to 325 degrees. Mix all ingredients together in a large bowl. Bake in a shallow pan, 16 x 11 inches, for 40 minutes. Cut into squares and serve. Can also be used hot or cold for appetizers.

POLLY COMSTOCK

Cheese-Spinach Casserole

1 (6-ounce) package Uncle Ben's long grain and wild rice
1 (4-ounce) can sliced mushrooms, drained
2 teaspoons prepared mustard
1/2 teaspoon salt
2-1/4 cups water
1 (10-ounce) package frozen chopped or leaf spinach
3/4 cup chopped onion
1 tablespoon butter or margarine
1 (8-ounce) package cream cheese, cubed

Preheat oven to 375 degrees. Place contents of rice and seasoning packets, mushrooms, mustard and salt in a 2-quart casserole. In a large saucepan, combine water, spinach, onion and butter or margarine. Bring to a boil. Pour over rice mixture and stir. Cover tightly and bake 30 minutes. Stir in cream cheese. Bake, uncovered, for 10-15 minutes. (6-8 servings)

CATHY MAZZOLINI

Spaghetti Squash, Straw and Hay

1/4 cup butter or margarine
6 cups or 1 large spaghetti squash, cooked (save shell)
3/4 cup sliced and cooked ham, cut in strips
1/2 cup cooked peas
1 (4-ounce) jar of sliced mushrooms, drained
2 egg yolks, beaten
1 cup whipping cream
1 cup grated Parmesan cheese
Spaghetti squash shell

In a large bowl, stir butter or margarine into hot squash until melted. Fold in ham, peas and mushrooms. In a small bowl, whisk egg yolks and cream until foamy. Slowly add cream mixture to squash mixture and mix well. Stir in half of the cheese. Drain the juice from baking dish used to cook the squash. Put squash mixture back into the shells and cover with vented plastic wrap and microwave at full power for 4-6 minutes or until heated through and the sauce has thickened. Toss twice and top with remaining cheese.

SHELLY ROBBINS

Aunt Jane's Squash Casserole

2 pounds yellow summer squash, sliced
Salt and pepper to taste
1 (2-ounce) jar chopped pimento
1 onion, chopped
1/3 cup sour cream
1 (10-3/4 ounce) can cream of chicken soup
3 carrots, grated
6 ounces Pepperidge Farm cornbread stuffing, crushed

Preheat oven to 350 degrees. Steam squash. Drain and mash. Season. Stir in remaining ingredients, reserving 3 ounces of stuffing. Line flat greased casserole baking dish with 2 ounces of stuffing. Pat in squash mixture, sprinkle remaining stuffing on top. Bake for 1/2 hour.

MARY WASKERWITZ

Fried Zucchini

1 pound thinly sliced zucchini
1 onion, chopped
3 tablespoons peanut oil
2 tablespoons sesame seeds
2 tablespoons soy sauce
Salt and pepper to taste

In a large skillet fry zucchini and onion in hot oil until crisp. Stir in remaining ingredients.

MARY WASKERWITZ

175

Stuffed Zucchini

6 medium zucchini
1 (3-ounce) package cream cheese
2 tablespoons finely chopped onion
1/2 teaspoon salt
1/4 teaspoon pepper
1 cup sour cream
Paprika

Place whole unpeeled zucchini in boiling water to cover. Reduce heat and simmer till nearly tender (5-10 minutes). Cool until you can handle. Preheat oven to 325 degrees. Cut in half lengthwise and scoop out pulp and seeds into a bowl. Mix pulp and seeds with cream cheese, onion, salt and pepper. Stuff mixture back into zucchini halves. Arrange them in buttered baking dish. Spoon sour cream over top. Sprinkle with paprika. Bake for 10 minutes. (Can be prepared up to 3 hours in advance before baking.)

JERI KELCH

Zucchini Pancakes

1 cup all-purpose flour
1 teaspoon salt
3/4 teaspoon baking powder
1/2 teaspoon garlic powder
Dash of pepper
5 eggs
3 cups grated zucchini
2/3 cup milk
Sour cream
Grated Parmesan cheese

In a large bowl mix ingredients except sour cream and cheese. Fry like pancakes in hot margarine or oil. Spread with sour cream and sprinkle with Parmesan cheese to serve.

MARY WASKERWITZ

Desserts

Cookies
Candies
Cakes
Pies
Desserts

DESSERTS

Anise Butter Cookies

1 cup butter
3/4 cup sugar
1/4 teaspoon salt
1 teaspoon anise seed (crushed)
2-1/4 cups sifted all-purpose flour
Sugar (confectioners' or regular)
Candied cherry halves

Preheat oven to 375 degrees. Cream butter and sugar together in a mixing bowl. Add salt and anise seeds. Mix well. Blend in flour mixing thoroughly. Form dough into small balls using about 2 teaspoons for each and roll or press in additional sugar. Place on ungreased cookie sheets, flatten to 1/4-inch thickness with bottom of a glass. Press a cherry half on each cookie. Bake for 15 minutes. (Makes 3 dozen cookies) *"Makes a very good Christmas cookie."*

KATHERINE KERSEY

Molasses Cookies

3/4 cup butter or margarine (or combination)
1 cup sugar
Generous 1/4 cup molasses
1 egg
1-3/4 cups all-purpose flour
1/2 teaspoon ground cloves
1/2 teaspoon ground ginger (or use more for added spice)
1 teaspoon ground cinnamon
1/2 teaspoon salt
1/2 teaspoon baking soda

Preheat oven to 350 degrees. Melt butter or margarine in a saucepan. Add sugar and molasses and mix. Pour into mixing bowl and add lightly beaten egg. Add sifted dry ingredients. Mix. (Batter will be wet.) Lay a sheet of aluminum foil on cookie sheet. Drop tablespoons of batter on foil 2 inches apart. Bake 8-10 minutes or until cookies begin to darken, but are still soft. Remove from oven. Remove foil sheets. Set aside to cool before removing cookies from foil. *"This is a soft, spicy, very chewy cookie."*

SUSAN HURWITZ

179

Oatmeal Coconut Crispies

1 cup shortening
1 cup brown sugar
1 cup sugar
2 eggs
1 teaspoon vanilla
1-1/2 cups sifted all-purpose flour
1 teaspoon salt
1 teaspoon soda
1 teaspoon cinnamon
1/2 teaspoon nutmeg
1-1/2 cups three-minute brand oats
1-1/2 cups flaked coconut
3/4 cup chopped nuts

Preheat oven to 350 degrees. Cream shortening and sugars in a mixing bowl. Add eggs and vanilla and mix well. Sift flour, salt, soda, cinnamon and nutmeg. Fold into the creamed mixture. Blend in oats, coconut and nuts. Drop by spoonful onto a greased baking sheet. Bake for 8-10 minutes.

JANICE CHAPMAN

Oatmeal-Raisin Cookies

3/4 cup butter or margarine (or combination)
1-1/3 cups dark brown sugar
2 large eggs
1 teaspoon vanilla
1 cup all-purpose flour
3/4 teaspoon baking soda
1/2 teaspoon salt
1/4 teaspoon nutmeg (freshly grated, if possible)
1/4 teaspoon cloves
1 teaspoon cinnamon
2-1/2 cups regular oats (not quick-cooking)
1 cup raisins
1 cup bran, not bran cereal (optional)

Preheat oven to 350 degrees. Cream butter and sugar. Add eggs and vanilla. Mix well. Add sifted dry ingredients (save oats, raisins and bran). Then mix in oats, raisins and bran. Drop by large teaspoonful on foil-covered cookie sheets. Bake 12-15 minutes or until they begin to brown and get firm. Remove foil sheets by picking up whole sheet at opposite corners. Cool before removing cookies from foil. (Makes 30-40 cookies)

SUSAN HURWITZ

Butterscotch Cookies

6 cups all-purpose flour
1 tablespoon baking soda
1 tablespoon cream of tartar
1 teaspoon nutmeg
1/2 teaspoon salt
4 cups brown sugar
4 eggs
1 cup melted shortening
Chopped nuts (optional)

Mix together flour, soda, tartar, nutmeg and salt in a large bowl. Mix brown sugar, eggs and melted shortening and add to the dry mixture. Add nuts if desired. Make into a roll and let stand in refrigerator overnight. (May be frozen and sliced and baked when needed.) Slice and bake at 350 degrees for 15 minutes.

KAY MOLER

Scotchie Cookies

1/2 cup shortening
1 cup brown sugar
1 egg
1 cup all-purpose flour
1/2 teaspoon soda
1/2 teaspoon salt
1 teaspoon vanilla
1 cup regular oats
1/2 cup pecans, finely chopped
1 cup grated coconut

Preheat oven to 375 degrees. Cream together shortening, brown sugar and egg. Mix together flour, soda, salt and add to above mixture. Add vanilla. Then add oats, pecans and coconut. Mix well after adding each. Roll into 1 tablespoon-size balls or drops. Bake on ungreased cookie sheet for 12-15 minutes. (Makes 3 dozen cookies)

KATHERINE KERSEY

181

COOKIES

Applesauce Date Cookies

2 cups all-purpose flour, sifted
1/4 teaspoon ground cloves
1 teaspoon ground cinnamon
1/4 teaspoon ground nutmeg
1/2 teaspoon baking powder
1 teaspoon baking soda
1/2 teaspoon salt
1 cup nuts, chopped
1/2 cup dates, chopped
1/2 cup shortening
1 cup sugar
1 egg
1 cup thick canned applesauce

FROSTING:
1 cup confectioners' sugar
4 teaspoons water
Few drops food coloring (optional)

Preheat oven to 350 degrees. Sift dry ingredients together and use 1/2 cup of mixture to mix with nuts and dates, coating well. Cream shortening until light and gradually stir in sugar, then beat until fluffy. Add egg, beat thoroughly. Add rest of the dry ingredients alternately with applesauce, blending well after each addition. Stir in floured fruit-nut mixture. Drop by tablespoon 2 inches apart on a greased cookie sheet. Frost with confectioners' sugar, water and food coloring of your choice. Dab frosting in center of cooled cookies. Bake for 15-20 minutes.

HAZEL CHARTERS

Great Orange Cashew Cookies

1 cup butter
1/2 cup brown sugar
1/2 cup sugar
1 egg
1/2 cup chopped cashew nuts
2-3/4 cups all-purpose flour, sifted once
1/2 teaspoon soda
2 tablespoons orange juice
1 tablespoon orange rind, grated
Maraschino cherries

Cream butter, sugars and egg in a large mixing bowl. Add nuts. Add flour and soda alternating with juice and rind. Shape into rolls 1-1/2 inches thick (use wax paper). Chill. Preheat oven to 350 degrees. Slice thin. Put a piece of maraschino cherry in the center of each cookie. Bake for 10 minutes.

JEAN WIETING

Gumdrop Cookies

4 eggs
2 cups brown sugar
1 tablespoon cold water
2 cups all-purpose flour
4 teaspoons salt
1/4 teaspoon cinnamon
1 cup gumdrops, chopped (or use the small ones whole)
1/2 cup chopped pecans

Preheat oven to 325 degrees. Beat eggs in a large mixing bowl; add sugar a little at a time. Add water. Sift flour, salt and cinnamon together. Add part of it to gumdrops and nuts. Add flour and rest of gumdrop mixture. Spread on cookie sheet as thin as possible. Bake for 30 minutes.

FROSTING:
1 tablespoon butter
2 cups confectioners' sugar
3 tablespoons orange juice

Mix frosting ingredients together till smooth. Spread this mixture on cookies while still warm and cut while warm.

JEAN WIETING

Cookies With Mints

1 cup sugar
1/2 cup brown sugar
1 cup butter or margarine
2 eggs
1 tablespoon water
3 cups sifted all-purpose flour
1 teaspoon soda
1/2 teaspoon salt
1 package small mint patties

Cream sugars and butter together in a large bowl. Add eggs and water. Mix until well-blended. Add rest of ingredients, blend well. Refrigerate 2 hours. Take a teaspoon of dough, flatten between palms. Preheat oven to 375 degrees. Insert mint patty and press or bend dough around patty. Place on cookie sheet about two inches apart. Bake for 10-12 minutes. (Makes 3 dozen)

SHARON LAUGHLIN

Chocolate Chip Cookies

First we put in eggs and then we stir them. Then put in milk and flour and not sugar because me and Mommy are on a diet. Then we put in chocolate chips and then we bake them.

BRANDON
AGE 9

Thumbprints

1/2 cup Crisco
1/2 cup butter
1/2 cup brown sugar
2 eggs, separated
1 teaspoon vanilla
2 cups all-purpose flour
1/2 teaspoon salt
Walnuts or pecans
Chocolate or vanilla frosting

Preheat oven to 375 degrees. Mix above ingredients well except egg whites, nuts and frosting. Beat 2 egg whites and set aside. Roll dough into small balls, then dip in egg whites and roll in crushed nuts (walnuts or pecans). Place on ungreased cookie sheet and bake for 5 minutes. Remove from oven, make a thumbprint in middle of cookie. Return to oven, bake for 5-8 minutes longer until lightly golden. Cool, then place dab of frosting in center of each cookie (chocolate frosting is best).

KATHY DUNN

Ginger Cookies

1 cup sugar
2 cups all-purpose flour
2 teaspoons soda
1 teaspoon salt
1 teaspoon ginger
1 teaspoon cinnamon
1 teaspoon cloves
1/4 cup molasses
1/2 cup butter
1 egg
Sugar

Preheat oven to 350 degrees. Combine all dry ingredients in a large mixing bowl. Blend in the molasses, butter and egg. Roll into balls and roll into sugar. Bake for 10-12 minutes.   JO ZEISLER

Sugar Cookies

1 cup margarine
1 cup sugar
1 egg, separated
2 cups all-purpose flour
1 teaspoon cinnamon
1 tablespoon water
Chopped walnuts

Cream margarine and sugar in a bowl. Add egg yolk, flour and cinnamon. Form into 2 rolls, chill. Slice into 1/4-inch cookies. Preheat oven to 325 degrees. Beat egg white with water. Brush onto each cookie, top with nuts. Bake 13 minutes.   MARY WASKERWITZ

Velvet Cookies

2-1/2 cups all-purpose flour
1 cup plus 2 teaspoons butter, softened
1/4 teaspoon salt
2 eggs, separated
1 cup confectioners' sugar
Apricot jam

Preheat oven to 350 degrees. Mix the first 4 ingredients together in a large bowl. If the mixture is too crumbly, add a little milk. Roll the dough thin and cut out 2-inch circles. Mix by hand egg whites with confectioners' sugar until white. Spread on circles. Place circles on greased cookie sheet. Bake for 20 minutes or until just pink. Cool. Put two circles together with jam. (Makes 30 cookies)   LUBA CHAPELSKY

Chocolate Chip Cookies - Philly Style

1 (8-ounce) package cream cheese
1/2 cup unsalted butter
1/2 cup margarine
3/4 cup sugar
3/4 cup brown sugar, packed
1 large egg
1 teaspoon vanilla
2-1/2 cups all-purpose flour
1 teaspoon baking powder
1/2 teaspoon salt
1 (12-ounce) package semisweet chocolate chips
1 cup pecans or walnuts, chopped

Preheat oven to 375 degrees. In a large bowl, combine cream cheese, butter, margarine and both sugars. Mix until well-blended. Add egg and vanilla. In a separate bowl, combine flour, baking powder and salt. Gradually add to the batter and combine well. Stir in chips and nuts. Drop by teaspoon onto ungreased baking sheet. Bake for 11 minutes or just until tops and edges start to brown. (Makes 4 dozen cookies)

NANCY COLLINS

Forgotten Cookies

2 egg whites
3/4 cup sugar
1 cup broken nutmeats
1 (6-ounce) package chocolate chips

Preheat oven to 350 degrees. Beat egg whites until stiff. Slowly add sugar and beat until stiff. Fold in nutmeats and chocolate chips. Drop by spoonful on wax paper on a cookie sheet. Place in oven and turn off heat. Leave in oven overnight.

SHELLY ROBBINS

Michigan Cookies

1 cup brown sugar, firmly packed
1/2 cup butter or margarine
1 egg, well beaten
2 (1-ounce) squares melted unsweetened chocolate
1-3/4 cups all-purpose flour, sifted
1/4 teaspoon baking soda
1 teaspoon baking powder
1/2 teaspoon salt
1/2 cup milk
1/2 cup nuts, chopped

Preheat oven to 325 degrees. Cream sugar and shortening in a bowl; add egg, beat until creamy and fluffy. Add chocolate and blend well. Sift together dry ingredients and add alternately with milk to shortening mixture. Add nuts. Drop by teaspoon 3 inches apart on oiled baking sheet for 8-10 minutes. Remove from oven. May frost. (Makes 5 dozen 1-1/2 inch cookies)

ETHEL JOHNSTON

Chocolate Cheese Drop Cookies

2 (1-ounce) squares unsweetened chocolate
1/2 cup butter
1/2 cup shortening
1 (3-ounce) package cream cheese
1 egg
1/2 teaspoon salt
1-1/2 cup sugar
2 tablespoons milk
1 teaspoon vanilla
2-1/4 cups all-purpose flour
1-1/2 teaspoons baking powder
1/2 cup chopped nuts (optional)

Preheat oven to 350 degrees. Melt chocolate in a double boiler over hot water. Cream together butter, shortening, cream cheese, egg, salt, sugar, milk and vanilla. Stir in chocolate. Add flour and baking powder. Add chopped nuts, if desired. Drop by teaspoonful onto greased baking sheet. Bake 10-15 minutes, depending on size of cookies. (Makes 5 dozen cookies) *These cookies are best if slightly underbaked. They will firm up when cooled. They freeze well, that is, if there are any left!*

MOLLY GATES

Chocolate Cut-Out Cookies

2 (1-ounce) squares unsweetened chocolate
1-1/2 cups sifted all-purpose flour
1 teaspoon baking powder
1/4 teaspoon salt
1/16 teaspoon baking soda
1/4 teaspoon mace (optional)
1/2 cup sweet butter
1/2 teaspoon vanilla
1 cup sugar
1 egg
Sugar (optional)

Place the chocolate in the top of a small double boiler over hot water on moderate heat. Cover until partially melted, then uncover and stir until completely melted. Set aside to cool. Sift together the flour, baking powder, salt, baking soda and mace and set aside. In the large bowl of an electric mixer, cream the butter. Add the vanilla and sugar and beat to mix well. Beat in the egg and then chocolate. On low speed gradually add the sifted dry ingredients. Stir only until everything is blended in. Transfer the dough to wax paper, flatten slightly, wrap airtight and refrigerate a few hours. Preheat oven to 375 degrees. Line cookie sheets with foil. On lightly floured surface, roll half of the dough to 1/8-inch thick. Cut the dough with cookie cutters and if desired sprinkle tops with granulated sugar. Bake 2 sheets at a time for about 15 minutes or until cookies feel semi-firm. Reverse sheets on shelves to insure even baking.

SHEILA HAUSBECK

Chocolate Cerise Cookies

1 large jar cherries (drained and marinated with brandy or kirsch for 8 hours)
1 cup sifted all-purpose flour
1/3 cup brown sugar
1/3 cup butter
1/3 cup chopped nuts
Semisweet chocolate

Preheat oven to 350 degrees. Combine flour and brown sugar in a bowl. Cut in butter and nuts. Press into 8-inch square pan. Bake for 15-20 minutes. Cool; cut into small squares. Melt semisweet chocolate in the top of double boiler until smooth. Dip marinated cherries into melted chocolate and place on toffee base. Hold briefly until it sets. Store in flat container in cool place.

JEAN WIETING

Super Quick and Easy Chocolate Bars

1/2 cup butter
1/2 cup brown sugar
1-1/4 cups all-purpose flour
Pinch of salt
1 (6-ounce) package of chocolate chips*
Topping: Nuts, coconut, granola (optional)

Preheat oven to 350 degrees. Cream softened butter and brown sugar in a large mixing bowl. Add flour and salt, mix well until crumbly. Press into a 13 x 9-inch pan. Bake until lightly browned, about 10-12 minutes. Remove from oven and sprinkle chocolate chips onto crust immediately. Return the pan to the oven with the heat off just long enough to soften the chips. Remove and spread chocolate evenly over the crust. Sprinkle with your choice of topping. Cool.
*COOK'S TIP: Imitation chocolate chips will not spread well.

MARY ANNE MULARONI

Deluxe Chocolate Peanut Butter Bars

1/4 cup brown sugar
1/2 cup Karo syrup
Dash of salt
1 teaspoon vanilla (optional)
1 cup peanut butter
1 cup chocolate chips
3 cups crisp rice cereal

Butter a 9 x 9-inch pan. Place brown sugar, syrup and salt in a saucepan and bring to a boil, stirring constantly. Remove from heat. Add vanilla, peanut butter, chocolate and cereal. Mix well and press into pan. Refrigerate and cut.

STEPHANIE MINERATH

189

Magic Bars

1/2 cup butter or margarine
2 cups crushed graham crackers
1 (6-ounce) package chocolate chips
1 (6-ounce) package butterscotch chips
1 cup flaked coconut
1 cup nutmeats
1 (14-ounce) can sweetened condensed milk

Preheat oven to 350 degrees. Melt one stick of butter in a 9 x 13-inch pan. Sprinkle crushed graham cracker crumbs over butter. Mix and press over bottom of pan. Sprinkle chocolate chips, butterscotch chips, coconut and nutmeats over above. Pour can of condensed milk on top. Bake for 25-30 minutes. Cut while warm. (Makes 36-40 bars)

JOANNE LEITH

Oatmeal Fudge Bars

1 cup margarine (at room temperature)
2 cups firmly packed light brown sugar
2 eggs
3 cups Quaker rolled oats (not instant)
2-1/2 cups all-purpose flour
2 teaspoons vanilla
1 teaspoon baking soda
1 teaspoon salt
1 cup chopped walnuts
1 (14-ounce) can sweetened condensed milk
1 (12-ounce) package semisweet chocolate chips
1-1/2 cups chopped walnuts
2 tablespoons margarine
2 teaspoons vanilla
1/2 teaspoon salt

Preheat oven to 350 degrees. Generously grease a 10 x 15-inch baking pan. Cream margarine with sugar in a large bowl. Add eggs one at a time, beating well after each addition. Mix in oats, flour, vanilla, baking soda and salt. Stir in walnuts. Set aside. Combine milk and chocolate in top of double boiler set over hot water and stir until chocolate melts. (This step can also be done in a glass bowl placed in microwave for 3-4 minutes on high.) Add remaining ingredients and blend well. Spoon half of oat mixture into prepared pan, compacting with fork. Spread chocolate mixture over top. Crumble remaining oat mixture over chocolate and spread with fork trying to completely cover chocolate. Bake until golden, about 30 minutes. Cool. Cut into 1-1/2 inch bars. (Makes 4 dozen bars)

NANCY COLLINS

Brownies I

4 (1-ounce) squares baking chocolate
1 cup butter
1 cup all-purpose flour
1 teaspoon baking powder
4 eggs
2 cups sugar
2 teaspoons vanilla
2 cups chopped walnuts

Preheat oven to 350 degrees (if using a Pyrex pan, reduce heat slightly). In a double boiler melt the chocolate and the butter. Let mixture cool. Mix flour and baking powder. Beat eggs well; gradually beat in sugar. Blend in chocolate-butter mixture and vanilla. Add flour-baking powder mixture, then add nuts. Pour into buttered 9 x 13-inch pan. Bake for 25 minutes.

COOK'S TIP: These brownies look undercooked at 25 minutes, do not worry. If you put them, pan and all, in the refrigerator after they are out of the oven for 10-15 minutes, they will have a more fudgy consistency.

MARCIA LEONARD

Brownies II

1/2 cup butter or margarine
2 (1-ounce) squares bitter chocolate
1 cup sugar
2 eggs, beaten with fork
2/3 cup all-purpose flour
1/2 cup chopped nuts
Pinch of salt
1 teaspoon vanilla

Preheat oven to 350 degrees. Melt margarine and bitter chocolate in a double broiler. Add sugar and mix well. Add eggs and mix well. Add flour, mix and add remaining ingredients. Pour into greased and floured 8 x 8 x 2-inch pan. Bake for 25-30 minutes. When cool, frost with chocolate frosting or dust with confectioners' sugar. *"If you double this recipe, bake in a 13 x 9-inch pan. Delicious, easy, and uses just one pan for mixing!"*

MARY ELLEN BOTSFORD

Brownies III

1 cup Crisco shortening
4 tablespoons margarine
3/4 cup cocoa
2 cups sugar
2 teaspoons vanilla
4 eggs, beaten
1-1/2 cups all-purpose flour
1 teaspoon baking powder
1/2 teaspoon salt
1/2 cup raisins

Preheat oven to 350 degrees. Melt Crisco and margarine in a saucepan over low heat. Add cocoa to mixture and turn off heat. Add sugar, vanilla and eggs. Beat mixture until smooth. Sift flour, baking powder and salt together. Add flour mixture to cocoa, sugar, egg mixture and blend well. Add raisins. Pour into a 9 x 13-inch lightly greased pan and bake for 20-25 minutes. Cool.

ICING:
1/2 cup margarine, melted
1/4 cup cocoa
6 tablespoons evaporated milk
1 (16-ounce) box confectioners' sugar
1 teaspoon vanilla
1 cup chopped nuts

In a small saucepan heat the margarine, cocoa and evaporated milk to near boiling. Remove from heat and add one box of sifted confectioners' sugar, vanilla and nuts and blend well. Spread over brownies. Let set a few minutes and then cut. CATHY MAZZOLINI

Brownies IV

4 (1-ounce) squares unsweetened chocolate
1/2 cup butter
1-1/4 cups plus 3 tablespoons sugar
1 teaspoon vanilla
3 large eggs
3/4 cup all-purpose flour
Confectioners' sugar (optional)

Preheat oven to 350 degrees. Grease an 8-inch square pan. In a double boiler, melt chocolate and butter. Set aside to cool. Beat chocolate mixture and sugar until completely combined. Add vanilla and eggs and mix only until combined. Add the flour and beat just until mixture is totally blended. Spread batter evenly into pan and bake 20-25 minutes, until knife inserted in center comes out barely clean. Cool thoroughly before cutting. Sprinkle with confectioners' sugar if desired. (Makes 16 bars) KATHY JOY

Brownies V

2 (1-ounce) squares of unsweetened chocolate
1/2 cup butter or margarine
1 cup sugar
2 eggs
1 teaspoon vanilla
1/2 cup sifted all-purpose flour
1/2 cup chopped nuts (optional)

Preheat oven to 325 degrees. Melt chocolate over hot water in a double boiler. Set melted chocolate aside to cool. Cream butter and sugar; add eggs and beat well. Blend in chocolate, vanilla and flour. Mix nuts into batter or sprinkle over the top of the batter once in pan. Pour batter into greased 8 x 8 x 2-inch pan and bake for 35 minutes. Frost if desired. (Makes 12 brownies)

PEANUT MARBLE BROWNIES (Optional Filling)
1/2 cup crunchy peanut butter
4 tablespoons margarine
3/4 cup sugar
2 eggs
6 tablespoons all-purpose flour

Beat together the peanut butter, margarine and sugar in a mixing bowl. Then gradually add the eggs and flour. Prepare brownie recipe. (If using recipe above, double for 9 x 13-inch pan). Spread half of the brownie recipe in greased pan, spoon on filling, then add remaining batter. Marbleize with knife. Bake at 350 degrees for 40-45 minutes. Frost, if desired.

KATHY DUNN

Graham Cracker Toffee Bars

24 graham cracker squares
1-1/4 cups margarine
1-1/4 cups firmly packed brown sugar
1-1/4 cups finely chopped pecans or walnuts

Preheat oven to 350 degrees. In a foil-lined 15 x 10-inch baking sheet, arrange graham crackers close together, in a single layer. Combine margarine and brown sugar in a small saucepan. Cook and stir over low heat until well-blended. (I use a microwave.) Add nuts and spread mixture over crackers. Bake for 10 minutes until bubbly. Cool 10 minutes. Cut each in half and serve when cool. (Makes 48 bars) *"A favorite at church coffee hours."*

CAROL COLBY

Brownies VI

2 cups sugar
2 cups all-purpose flour
1 cup water
1/2 cup margarine
1/2 cup shortening
3-1/2 tablespoons cocoa
2 eggs
1/2 cup buttermilk
1 teaspoon baking soda

Preheat oven to 375 degrees. In a large bowl mix sugar and flour and set aside. In a saucepan, mix water, margarine, shortening, cocoa, and bring to a boil and add to sugar and flour mixture. To this, add eggs, buttermilk and soda and mix all well. Pour into a large (17 x 11-inch) cookie sheet with sides. Bake for 20 minutes or until done. (Makes 20 bars)

CHOCOLATE FROSTING:
1/2 cup margarine
1/3 cup milk
3 tablespoons cocoa
1 (1-pound) box confectioners' sugar
1 teaspoon vanilla
1 cup walnuts or pecans, chopped

About 5 minutes before cake is done, place in a saucepan the margarine, milk and cocoa and bring to a boil. Remove from heat and add confectioners' sugar, vanilla and nuts and pour over cake as it comes from oven.

JOYCE TREPPA

Coconut-Honey Bars

1/3 cup margarine
2 cups quick-cook oats
1 cup flaked coconut
1 cup peanut butter chips or chocolate chips
1/2 cup raisins (optional)
1/3 cup packed brown sugar
1/2 teaspoon vanilla
1/3 cup honey

Preheat oven to 400 degrees. In a saucepan, melt the margarine. Remove from heat, cool slightly and add oats, coconut, peanut butter chips, raisins, brown sugar, honey and vanilla. Press into greased 8-inch square pan. Bake for 20 minutes until golden. Cool and cut into bars. (Makes 24 bars)

LAURA MURPHY

Mint Brownies

3 (1-ounce) squares unsweetened chocolate
3/4 cup butter or margarine
3 eggs
Pinch of salt
3/4 teaspoon vanilla
1-1/2 cups light brown sugar
3/4 cup sifted all-purpose flour
3/4 cup coarsely chopped walnuts (optional)

Preheat oven to 350 degrees. Butter a 13 x 9-inch pan. Melt chocolate and butter over low heat. Stir until smooth. Set aside to cool completely. Beat eggs until foamy. Add salt, vanilla and sugar. Add chocolate mixture. Mix. On low speed add flour. Stir in nuts. Pour in pan and bake 25 minutes or until barely done. Better to under-bake brownies rather than over-bake. Cool on rack. (Makes 32-36 brownies)

ICING:
4 tablespoons butter (at room temperature)
2 cups sifted confectioners' sugar
2 tablespoons heavy cream
1 teaspoon peppermint extract

Place all icing ingredients in bowl and mix well. Should be spreadable. Spread over brownies evenly. Refrigerate 5 minutes.

GLAZE:
2 (1-ounce) squares unsweetened chocolate
2 tablespoons butter

Melt chocolate and butter. Stir until smooth. Pour hot glaze over icing, turning pan quickly to cover icing. Refrigerate 30 minutes and cut.

SUSAN HURWITZ

Prize-Winning Brownies

1/2 cup butter or margarine, softened
1 cup sugar
2 eggs
1 teaspoon vanilla
1-1/4 cups all-purpose flour
1/4 cup unsweetened cocoa
1/4 teaspoon baking soda
Dash of salt
3/4 cup chocolate syrup
1/2 cup semisweet chocolate chips
1/2 cup milk chocolate chips
1/2 cup chopped German sweet chocolate
1 cup chopped pecans

Preheat oven to 350 degrees. In a large bowl of electric mixer, cream butter and sugar; add eggs, one at a time and vanilla and beat until fluffy. Sift together flour, cocoa, baking soda and salt. Add flour mixture and chocolate syrup to creamed mixture. Stir in chocolate chips, sweet chocolate and pecans. Spread in greased 9 x 13-inch baking pan and bake for 35-40 minutes until mixture pulls away from sides of pan. Remove from oven and cool on wire rack. When cool, spread with frosting. Cut into squares. (Makes 2 dozen bars)

CHOCOLATE FROSTING:
8 ounces confectioners' sugar (1/2 box)
1/4 cup unsweetened cocoa
1/4 cup butter or margarine (4 tablespoons)
3 tablespoons milk
1/2 teaspoon vanilla
Dash of salt

Place all ingredients in top of double boiler. Stir until smooth over simmering water. Remove from heat and stir briskly until mixture is proper spreading consistency. Makes about 1-1/2 cups of frosting. Recipe may be doubled for cake frosting.

NANCY COLLINS

Ritz-Lemon Bars

LEMON FILLING:
1 dozen eggs, beaten
4 cups sugar
1 cup butter
3/4 cup lemon juice
2 tablespoons lemon rind, grated

CRUMB MIXTURE:
6 cups Ritz cracker crumbs
2 cups all-purpose flour
2 cups butter
2 cups sugar

Combine filling ingredients in a saucepan and cook until thickened, stirring constantly. Set aside to cool. Preheat oven to 375 degrees. Combine crumb ingredients in a large bowl and mix well. Press half of mixture into 12 x 18-inch ungreased jelly roll pan. Pour Lemon Filling over top and cover with remainder of crumbs. Bake for 40 minutes. Cut into bars.
(Makes 9 dozen 2-inch bars)

JOANNE LEITH

Lemon Bars

CRUST:
2 cups all-purpose flour
1/2 cup confectioners' sugar
1 cup butter or margarine

TOPPING:
2 cups sugar
4 tablespoons all-purpose flour
1/2 teaspoon baking powder
4 eggs, beaten well
6 tablespoons concentrated lemon juice
Confectioners' sugar

Preheat oven to 350 degrees. To make the crust mix flour, confectioners' sugar and butter or margarine like a pie crust and press into a well-greased 9 x 13-inch pan. Bake for 20-25 minutes. Mix dry topping ingredients together. Fold into beaten eggs with lemon juice. Spread this mixture over the baked bottom layer. Bake additional 25 minutes. Sprinkle with confectioners' sugar. Cut into oblongs or squares. (Makes 40 bars)

CAROL COLBY

197

Apricot Bars

3/4 cup chopped dried apricots
1/2 cup water
1/2 cup margarine
1/4 cup sugar
1 cup all-purpose flour
Additional 1/3 cup all-purpose flour
1/2 teaspoon baking powder
2 eggs, beaten
1 cup brown sugar
1 teaspoon vanilla
1/2 cup chopped nuts
Apricots

Preheat oven to 350 degrees. In a medium saucepan simmer the dried apricots and water for 10 minutes. Cool. Combine in a mixing bowl the margarine, sugar and 1 cup of flour and blend until crumbly. Pack firmly into a 9 x 9-inch pan. Bake for 15 minutes. Sift together the 1/3 cup of flour and baking powder. Beat the eggs and brown sugar together and add them to the flour mixture. Add the vanilla and chopped nuts and apricots to above. Spread over baked crust and put back into oven for 25 minutes.

KATHY CLARK

Sugarless Spicy Raisin Bars

1/3 cup shortening, melted
1/3 cup molasses
2 eggs, well-beaten
3/4 cup all-purpose flour
1/2 teaspoon cinnamon
1/2 teaspoon nutmeg
1/4 teaspoon cloves
1 cup chopped walnuts
1 cup raisins

Preheat oven to 350 degrees. Combine shortening, molasses and eggs in a bowl. Add flour sifted with spices. Beat thoroughly using a wire whisk. Stir in nuts and raisins. Spread in a greased 11 x 7 x 2-inch pan. Bake for 25 minutes. Cut into bars when cool. (Makes 24 bars)

BARBARA MAY

Chewy Peanut Squares

2 cups sifted all-purpose flour
1/2 teaspoon baking powder
1 teaspoon salt
2/3 cup oil
1 cup peanut butter (crunchy)
1 cup brown sugar
2 cups sugar
4 eggs
2 teaspoons vanilla

Preheat oven to 350 degrees. Combine everything in order above in a large bowl and mix until blended. (Use a spoon not a mixer.) Spread into a 15 x 10 x 1-inch pan. Bake for 25-30 minutes. Only bake until golden brown to keep bars chewy. (Makes 5 dozen bars)

KATHY DUNN

Buckeye Candy

1/2 cup butter
1 cup peanut butter
3 cups confectioners' sugar
1 tablespoon vanilla
1 cup semisweet chocolate bits
1/4 bar Parowax

Mix first four ingredients in a large bowl and roll into balls about the size of a small walnut. Melt chocolate bits and Parowax in top of a double boiler; keep mixture hot. Using toothpicks, dip balls in chocolate mixture. Cover about 3/4 of ball with chocolate. Place on waxed paper until cool. *"When finished, candy should look like a buckeye, being dark on the bottom. Be sure to double recipe, they disappear quickly. Especially nice to serve on OSU-Michigan football game day!"*

CAROL MESZAROS

Chocolate Marble Candy

1 (14-ounce) can sweetened condensed milk
1 (1-pound) box confectioners' sugar
1 (14-ounce) package flaked coconut
2 cups pecans, walnuts or almonds, chopped fine
2 (1-ounce) squares semisweet chocolate
1 tablespoon shortening

Mix milk, sugar, coconut and nuts together in a large bowl. Chill for three hours or longer. Roll into balls. Chill and cover eight hours or longer. Melt chocolate and shortening in a double boiler. Drop balls in chocolate to coat completely. Refrigerate.

SUE HENDERSON

Butter Nut Crunch

1 cup sugar
1/2 teaspoon salt
1/4 cup water
1/2 cup butter or margarine
1-1/2 cups walnuts, chopped
2 (6-ounce) packages semisweet chocolate pieces, melted

Combine sugar, salt, water and butter in a medium saucepan; heat to boiling. Cook to light crack stage (285 degrees). Add 1/2 cup nuts. Pour onto well-greased cookie sheet. Cool. Spread half of chocolate mixture over top and sprinkle with 1/2 cup nuts. Cool. Spread remaining chocolate and sprinkle with remaining nuts. Cool. Break into pieces to serve.
(Makes 2 dozen pieces)

MARGARET BEEBE

Buttery Peanut Brittle

2 cups sugar
1 cup light corn syrup
1/2 cup water
1 cup butter or margarine
2 cups peanuts, chopped
1 teaspoon baking soda

In a 3-quart saucepan, heat and stir sugar, syrup and water until sugar dissolves. While syrup boils, blend in butter. Checking with a candy thermometer, stir often after 230 degrees. Add nuts at 280 degrees. Stir constantly to hard-crack stage (305 degrees). Remove from heat. Quickly stir in soda, mixing well. Pour onto 2 buttered cookie sheets. Stretch them by lifting and pulling from edges with forks. Loosen from pans as soon as possible. (Makes 2-1/2 pounds)

JULIE SCHIEBOLD

Peanut Butter Fudge

2 cups sugar
1/2 cup milk
3 tablespoons cocoa
2 cups peanut butter
1 teaspoon vanilla

In a saucepan bring sugar, milk and cocoa to a bubbly boil. Remove from heat. Add peanut butter and vanilla. Stir in well. Pour into greased cake pan. Cool. Let set and refrigerate.

SUE HENDERSON

Praline Popcorn Crunch

1-1/2 cups whole pecans
1/2 cup slivered almonds
10 cups popped corn
1-1/3 cups sugar
1 cup butter
1/4 cup praline liqueur
1/4 cup light corn syrup
Additional 1 tablespoon praline liqueur
1/4 teaspoon salt

Heat oven to 325 degrees. Butter baking sheet and large bowl. Toast pecans and almonds until light brown, about 12-15 minutes. Mix popped corn and nuts in large bowl. Combine sugar, butter, 1/4 cup praline liqueur and corn syrup in heavy 2-quart saucepan. Cook over medium-high heat, stirring occasionally to 275 degrees or until small amount dropped into very cold water reaches soft crack stage (separates into hard, but not brittle threads). Remove from heat, quickly stir in one tablespoon of praline liqueur and salt. Pour over popped corn and nuts, mixing until evenly coated. Immediately spread mixture on baking sheet. Let stand about one hour. Break into bite-size pieces.

MARLYN BEECHIE

$250.00 Red Velvet Cake

2 teaspoons red food coloring
2 tablespoons cocoa
1-1/2 cups sugar
1/2 cup butter
2 unbeaten eggs
1/2 teaspoon salt
2-1/2 cups sifted all-purpose flour
1 cup buttermilk
1-2 teaspoons vanilla
2 teaspoons baking soda
1 tablespoon vinegar

Preheat oven to 350 degrees. Mix red food coloring with cocoa and let stand until ready. Cream sugar and butter together until it peaks, add eggs. Sift salt and flour together and add alternately with buttermilk to creamed mix. Add vanilla, color mix, soda and vinegar. Bake in four 9-inch pans until done, 15 minutes or so; batter is not thick and will cook fast. Cool cake before frosting.

ICING:
1 cup milk
6 level teaspoons all-purpose flour
1 cup butter
1 cup sugar
1 cup chopped pecans
1 (3-1/2 ounce) can coconut

Cook milk and flour in a saucepan until thick. Cool. Cream butter and sugar until it peaks. Add just cooled mix and beat 15 minutes. Add nuts and coconut. Spread on cooled cake. THOMAS SHOPE

Cinnamon Flop

1 cup sugar
1 cup milk
2 cups all-purpose flour
Dash of salt
2 tablespoons butter
2-1/2 teaspoons vanilla
2 teaspoons baking powder
1/2 cup sugar
2 teaspoons cinnamon
2 tablespoons butter

Preheat oven to 325 degrees. Mix first 7 ingredients in a large bowl and pour into two greased and floured 8-inch round cake pans. Sprinkle top with sugar and cinnamon. Dot with small pieces of butter. Bake for 25 minutes. Good warm or cold. *"Eggless!"* JILL FLYNN

203

7-Up Cake

1 (18-1/2 ounce) package lemon supreme cake mix
1 (3-1/2 ounce) package pineapple instant pudding
4 eggs
3/4 cup Wesson oil
1 (10-ounce) bottle 7-Up

Preheat oven to 325 degrees. Mix all cake ingredients together in a large mixing bowl and pour into a greased and floured 9 x 12-inch cake pan. Bake for 30 minutes. Cool and frost with pineapple frosting.

PINEAPPLE FROSTING:
1 (13-ounce) can crushed pineapple, drained
1/2 cup margarine
1-1/2 cups sugar
2 eggs
3 tablespoons all-purpose flour
1 (3-1/2 ounce) can angel flake coconut

Mix ingredients for frosting except coconut in a medium saucepan and cook over low heat until thick. Fold in coconut.

PEG GRIFFIN

Old-Fashioned Pound Cake

2 cups butter
2-1/4 cups sugar
1 tablespoon vanilla
10 eggs
4-1/4 cups sifted cake flour
3/4 teaspoon salt
1/2 teaspoon ground mace

Preheat oven to 325 degrees. Cream butter with sugar and vanilla in a mixing bowl until light and fluffy. Add eggs, one at a time, beating vigorously after each addition. Add sifted dry ingredients in fourths, beating until smooth after each addition. Finally, beat only until batter is smooth. Do not overbeat. Turn batter into two greased 9-1/2 x 5-1/4-inch loaf pans. Bake for 1-1/4 hours. Cool 10 minutes before removing from pans to cooling racks.
(Makes two 9 x 5-inch cakes)

KATHERINE KERSEY

The Very Best Poundcake

2 cups unsalted butter (at room temperature)
3 cups sugar
6 large eggs
1 cup milk
2 teaspoons vanilla extract
2 tablespoons lemon juice
4 cups sifted all-purpose flour
1 teaspoon baking powder
1/2 teaspoon salt
Pinch of freshly grated nutmeg

Preheat oven to 300 degrees. Butter and flour a 10-inch tube pan. Cream butter until very light and fluffy. Add sugar gradually, beating constantly. Add eggs, beating after each addition just enough to mix. Combine milk and flavoring. Add sifted dry ingredients alternately with milk, beginning and ending with dry ingredients. Pour into pan (to within 2-inches of top). Bake 1 hour and 20 minutes or until gentle finger indentation vanishes slowly. *"This can be served with fresh fruit or ice cream. The cake has a smooth, velvety texture and sugary, crunchy top."*

SUSAN HURWITZ

Walnut Glory Cake

3/4 cup all-purpose flour
2 teaspoons cinnamon
1 teaspoon salt
9 eggs, separated
1-1/2 cups sugar
2 teaspoons vanilla
2 cups finely chopped walnuts
1 pint whipping cream, whipped
Chocolate shavings
Maraschino cherries

Preheat oven to 350 degrees. Sift flour, cinnamon and salt in a bowl. Set aside. Beat egg whites (1-1/2 cups) in large mixing bowl until soft mounds form. Gradually add 3/4 cup sugar. Continue beating until stiff peaks form. (Do not under-beat.) Set aside. Combine egg yolks, 3/4 cup sugar and vanilla. Beat until lemon-colored. Stir in dry ingredients. Fold batter gently into egg whites using wire whip or spatula. Fold in walnuts. Turn into ungreased 10-inch tube pan. Bake for 55-60 minutes. Invert immediately. Cool completely. Frost with whipped cream (1 pint). Decorate with chocolate shavings or masaschino cherries or both. (20 servings)

HELGA JUBIN

205

Grandma's Hickory Nut Cake

1/2 cup shortening
1-1/2 cups sugar
2 cups all-purpose flour
3 teaspoons baking powder
3/4 cup milk
1 teaspoon vanilla
4 egg whites
1 cup hickory nuts, finely chopped
1 cup grated coconut

Preheat oven to 350 degrees. Cream shortening and sugar in a mixing bowl. Mix flour and baking powder . Mix milk and vanilla and blend with the flour mixture. Beat egg whites till stiff and fold in. Add nuts and coconut last. Pour into a greased and floured 9 x 13-inch pan. Bake for 25-30 minutes. Cool.
HICKORY NUT FROSTING:
1 tablespoon butter
3 egg yolks
1 cup sugar
2 tablespoons milk
1/2 cup hickory nuts, finely chopped

Melt butter. Add yolks, sugar and milk. Cook until thick. Add nuts and beat.
ANN BETZ

Rum Cake

1 (18-1/2 ounce) package yellow cake mix
1 (3-1/2 ounce) package instant vanilla pudding mix
4 eggs
1/2 cup rum
1/2 cup oil
1/2 cup water
1 cup chopped nuts

Preheat oven to 325 degrees. Grease and flour Bundt pan. Mix all cake ingredients except nuts thoroughly. Line Bundt pan with chopped nuts. Pour ingredients into pan. Bake for 50-60 minutes. Allow to cool for 25 minutes.
RUM SAUCE:
1/4 cup rum
1/2 cup water
1 cup sugar
1/2 cup butter

Combine all sauce ingredients in a small saucepan. Boil for 2 minutes. Pour sauce over cake slowly. Allow to absorb and cool, then unmold onto plate and continue to cool. (10-12 servings) (If the cake gets stuck, heat in the oven until sauce becomes liquid again.)
PRUE ROSENTHAL

Baba Au Rhum

3 packages dry yeast
2/3 cup lukewarm milk
1 teaspoon sugar
3 cups all-purpose flour
1/2 teaspoon salt
12 whole eggs
1 cup butter
1/2 cup sugar
1/2 teaspoon cardamom
1 lemon rind, grated
Fine bread crumbs

Dissolve yeast in milk with the sugar and 2/3 cup flour. Beat until well-blended and let rise in warm place for 15 minutes. Add salt to eggs and beat until thick. Cream butter, add remaining sugar gradually. Add beaten eggs, cardamom and lemon rind. Add remaining flour and beat for 10 minutes with electric mixer. Cover, let rise until double in bulk, about one hour. Punch down, let rise again until double in bulk. Butter tube pan generously, dust with fine bread crumbs. Preheat oven to 350 degrees. Pour in batter, let rise in warm place for half hour. Bake for 50 minutes. Remove from pan and pour Rum Sauce over top and sides.

RUM SAUCE:
1/2 cup sugar
3/4 cup apricot juice (or 1/2 cup water)
1 teaspoon lemon juice
1/2 cup rum

Cook sugar with fruit juice or water for 5 minutes. Add lemon juice and pour over top and sides of Baba. Spoon the rum over this. Serve warm with whipped cream.

BLANCHE EHRENKREUTZ

207

Oatmeal Cake

1-1/4 cups boiling water
1 cup quick-cook oatmeal
1/2 cup shortening
1 cup brown sugar
1 cup sugar
2 eggs
1 teaspoon vanilla
1-1/3 cups all-purpose flour
1 teaspoon baking soda
1/2 teaspoon cinnamon
1/2 teaspoon nutmeg
1/2 teaspoon salt

Preheat oven to 350 degrees. Pour water over oatmeal in a bowl and let sit. Cream shortening, brown sugar, sugar, eggs and vanilla. Stir oatmeal mixture and add to creamed mixture. Sift flour, soda, cinnamon, nutmeg and salt into mixture. Pour into 13 x 8 x 2-inch pan and bake for 25 minutes. (24 servings)

TOPPING:
1 cup brown sugar
1 (3-1/2 ounce) can angel flake coconut
1 cup chopped nuts
1/4 pound butter, melted
1 egg

Mix topping ingredients together and spread over cake. Bake cake 15 minutes more or until brown. (24 servings) *"This cake is very moist, not dry and airy."*

ROBIN MACLEOD
MARY ELLEN BOTSFORD

Dump Cake

1 (18-1/2 ounce) package Duncan Hines deluxe yellow cake mix
1 (20-ounce) can crushed pineapple in syrup, undrained
1 (21-ounce) can cherry pie filling
1 cup chopped pecans
1/2 cup butter or margarine, cut in thin slices

Preheat oven to 350 degrees. Grease a 9 x 13-inch cake pan. Dump undrained pineapple into pan. Spread evenly. Dump in pie filling and spread into even layer. Dump dry cake mix onto cherry layer. Spread evenly. Sprinkle pecans over cake mix. Put butter over top. Bake for 45-55 minutes. Serve warm or cool. (12-16 servings) *"Easy and delicious."*

JUDY CASTAGNA
NIKKI WOODROW-RUSH

Italian Cream Cake

1 cup buttermilk
1 teaspoon baking soda
5 eggs, separated
2 cups sugar
1/2 cup butter or margarine
1/2 cup shortening
2 cups sifted all-purpose flour
1 teaspoon vanilla
1 cup chopped pecans
1 (3-1/2 ounce) can coconut flakes

Preheat oven to 325 degrees. Mix buttermilk and soda together and let stand. Beat egg whites until stiff. Cream together sugar, butter, shortening and egg yolks. Add buttermilk mixture to sugar mixture alternately with flour and vanilla. Fold in egg whites, pecans and coconut. Bake in three 9-inch round pans for 25 minutes. Cool on racks.

CREAM CHEESE FROSTING:
1 (8-ounce) package cream cheese
1/2 cup butter
1 (1-pound) box confectioners' sugar
Pinch of salt
1 teaspoon vanilla
1 cup chopped pecans

Cream the cream cheese and butter. Combine with remaining ingredients and mix well. Ice the layers (just the tops, not the sides; same as you do for German chocolate cake). Keep cake refrigerated. (Makes one 3-layer cake) *"Exquisite!"*

STEPHANIE MINERATH

Angel Delight

1 (3-1/2 ounce) package vanilla instant pudding
1 pint whipping cream
1 (20-ounce) can crushed pineapple (drained)
1 prepared angel food cake, split into thirds

Make pudding according to package directions. Whip the cream. Blend pudding and pineapple together. Fold in whipped cream. Spread between cake layers and on top of baked and cooled cake. *"This is a fast, easy and very good dessert."*

ANN BETZ

209

Lane Cake

3 cups all-purpose flour, sifted
1 tablespoon baking powder
8 egg whites
1/4 teaspoon salt
2 cups sugar, divided
1 cup butter or margarine, softened
1 teaspoon vanilla
1 cup milk
1 can dried fruit (optional)

Preheat oven to 350 degrees. Stir together flour and baking powder. Beat egg whites and salt until foamy; gradually add 1/2 cup sugar and beat until stiff. Cream butter, the remaining 1-1/2 cups sugar and vanilla until light; stir in flour mixture alternately with milk until well blended. Fold in egg white mixture gently but thoroughly. Divide batter among 3 greased and floured 9-inch layer cake pans. Bake for 20-25 minutes or until golden brown. Cool pans on racks 5 minutes, then invert on racks and turn layers top side up. Cool thoroughly.

FILLING:
8 egg yolks
1 cup sugar
1 cup raisins
1 cup fresh or canned grated coconut
1/2 cup butter or margarine, softened
1/4 cup bourbon or blended whiskey

Combine egg yolks, sugar, raisins, coconut and butter in top of double boiler. Cook and stir until thick and mixture mounds when dropped from spoon, 15-20 minutes. Remove from heat and stir in bourbon. Cool. Spread filling between layers.

BOILED FROSTING:
1/2 cup sugar
1/2 teaspoon cream of tartar
1/8 teaspoon salt
1/2 cup hot water
4 egg whites
Candied fruit (optional)

Combine first four ingredients in a small saucepan. Cook rapidly without stirring to softball stage, 240 degrees on candy thermometer, 6-8 minutes. Beat egg whites in a large bowl until stiff but not dry. Pour hot syrup in thin stream into egg whites beating constantly at high speed, until frosting holds stiff peaks, is shiny and smooth. Frost top and sides with boiled frosting. Add candied fruit if desired.

DOROTHY LAMERSON

Spice Nut Cake With Maple Fluff Frosting

2 cups sifted all-purpose flour
1 cup sugar
1 teaspoon baking powder
1 teaspoon salt
3/4 teaspoon baking soda
3/4 teaspoon ground cloves
3/4 teaspoon ground cinnamon
2/3 cup shortening
3/4 cup brown sugar
1 cup buttermilk or sour milk
3 eggs
1/2 cup finely chopped walnuts

Preheat oven to 350 degrees. Sift together first 7 ingredients. Add shortening, brown sugar and buttermilk. Mix until all flour is moistened. Beat 2 minutes at medium speed on electric mixer. Add eggs, beat 2 minutes more. Stir in nuts. Bake in 2 greased and lightly floured 9 x 1-1/2-inch round pans for 30-35 minutes or until done. Cool 10 minutes, remove from pans. Cool completely.

MAPLE FLUFF FROSTING:
1 cup maple-flavored syrup
3 egg whites

In a 1-quart saucepan, boil the syrup over medium heat for 5 minutes. Gradually pour hot syrup over stiffly beaten egg whites, beating constantly until frosting forms soft peaks. Frost tops and sides of two 9-inch layers.

JOYCE LONDON

Poppyseed Cake

1 cup Crisco shortening
1-1/2 cups sugar
2-1/2 cups all-purpose flour
1 teaspoon baking soda
1 teaspoon salt
1 (2-1/8 ounce) tin poppyseeds
1 tablespoon vanilla
1 cup sour cream
4 eggs, separated
Confectioners' sugar

Preheat oven to 350 degrees. Cream together the shortening and sugar. In separate bowl, sift together flour, soda and salt. Combine wet and dry ingredients along with poppyseeds, vanilla, sour cream and egg yolks. Fold in stiffly beaten egg whites last. Bake 40-50 minutes in greased Bundt pan. Sprinkle confectioners' sugar on baked warm cake. *"Delicious alone or with a scoop of good vanilla ice cream."*

ANN BETZ

Babka

1/2 cup soft butter
1/2 cup sugar
4 egg yolks
1 teaspoon salt
1 package dry yeast
1/4 cup lukewarm water
Grated rind of 1 lemon
1/2 teaspoon cinnamon
4 cups all-purpose flour
1 cup milk, scalded
1 cup white raisins
Fine bread crumbs
1 egg yolk, beaten
2 tablespoons water
1/4 cup chopped almonds

Mix butter and sugar in a large mixing bowl. Add salt to egg yolks and beat until thick. Add to sugar and butter mixture. Add yeast softened in lukewarm water. Add lemon rind and cinnamon. Add flour alternately with milk and beat well to make smooth batter. Add raisins and knead with your hand until batter leaves the fingers. Let rise in warm place until double in bulk (about 1-1/2 hours). Punch down and let rise again until double in bulk. Preheat oven to 350 degrees. Butter fluted tube pan generously, sprinkle with fine bread crumbs and fill with dough. Brush with mixture made by beating 1 egg yolk with 2 tablespoons water. Sprinkle with almonds, let rise and bake 30 minutes.

BLANCHE EHRENKREUTZ

Apple Cake I

1 cup brown sugar
1 cup sugar
1-1/2 cups oil
2 eggs
3 cups all-purpose flour
1 teaspoon cinnamon
1 teaspoon baking soda
1/4 teaspoon salt
2 teaspoons vanilla
3 cups chopped apples
1 cup chopped nuts

Preheat oven to 350 degrees. Beat sugars and oil in a large mixing bowl. Add eggs one at a time. Combine dry ingredients. Add rest of ingredients. Pour batter into ungreased pan, 9 x 13 inches. Bake for 50-60 minutes. *"No need for frosting this moist cake. A crust forms on top . Delicious when served warm from oven."*

CAROL COLBY

Apple Cake II

1-1/2 cups Crisco Oil
2 cups sugar
3 eggs, beaten
2 cups all-purpose flour
1 teaspoon baking soda
1 teaspoon salt
1 teaspoon cinnamon
1 teaspoon vanilla
1 teaspoon lemon extract
3 cups apples, unpeeled and chopped (McIntosh, Jonathan or any tart apple)
1 cup chopped nuts

Preheat oven to 300 degrees. In a large mixing bowl, combine oil and sugar. Blend in beaten eggs. Combine flour, baking soda , salt and cinnamon in a separate bowl. Add to oil and sugar mixture. Add vanilla and lemon extract. Add apples and nuts. Pour into a greased 9 x 13-inch pan and bake 1 hour and 20 minutes.

LEMON GLAZE:
1 cup confectioners' sugar
Juice of 2 lemons

Blend confectioners' sugar with lemon juice. While cake is still warm, cover the surface with glaze.

AGNES BUBACK

Applesauce Cake

1/2 cup butter or margarine
1/2 cup sugar
1 egg
1-1/2 teaspoons vanilla
1 cup dates, sliced fine
1-1/2 cups applesauce
1 cup nuts, chopped
1 cup raisins, chopped
3/4 teaspoon cinnamon
2 cups all-purpose flour
2 teaspoons baking soda

Preheat oven to 350 degrees. Cream butter and sugar together in a mixing bowl. Add well-beaten egg and vanilla. Combine the other ingredients and add to the first. Mix all well. Turn into a well-buttered loaf pan. Bake for one hour.

RACHEL HARRISON

213

Banana Spice Cake

2 cups all-purpose flour
1/2 teaspoon baking powder
3/4 teaspoon baking soda
1/2 teaspoon salt
1-1/2 teaspoons cinnamon
1/2 teaspoon nutmeg
1/8 teaspoon ground cloves
1 cup mashed ripe bananas (about 3)
1 teaspoon vanilla
1/4 cup sour milk (or fresh milk with squirt of lemon juice)
1/2 cup butter or margarine
1-1/2 cups sugar
2 eggs

Preheat oven to 350 degrees. Sift dry ingredients together. In separate bowl combine bananas, vanilla and milk. Cream butter and sugar. Beat in the eggs. Continue to beat until color lightens. Add flour mixture alternately with banana mixture, stirring until smooth after each addition. Turn into 2 greased 9-inch layer pans. Bake for about 30 minutes or until done. Cool on racks and ice with buttercream frosting. (*Kay won a prize at the Michigan State Fair for this recipe about 10 years ago.*)

KAY SHAW

Easy Banana Sour Cream Cake

1 (18-1/2 ounce) package yellow cake mix (not pudding type)
1 (3-1/2 ounce) package vanilla pudding mix
4 eggs
1 cup sour cream
1/2 cup salad oil
2 bananas, sliced
1/2 teaspoon ground mace
Confectioners' sugar (optional)

Preheat oven to 350 degrees. In a large bowl combine all ingredients, stir to blend. Beat at medium speed 5 minutes. Pour into greased and floured 10-inch tube or Bundt pan. Bake until done. Remove from pan when cool. If desired, dust with confectioners' sugar.

NANCY MORIN

Carrot Cake I

1-1/4 cups salad oil
4 eggs
2 cups sugar
2 teaspoons cinnamon
1 teaspoon salt
3 cups grated raw carrots
2 cups all-purpose flour
1 teaspoon baking soda
2 teaspoons baking powder
1 cup chopped pecans

Preheat oven to 325 degrees. In a large bowl blend oil, eggs, sugar, cinnamon and salt together. Add carrots. In another bowl sift together the flour, soda and baking powder. Mix dry flour mixture with carrot mixture. Stir in pecans. Pour into 2 greased and floured 8 or 9-inch round pans. Bake for about 1 hour. (12 servings)

CREAM CHEESE ICING:
4 tablespoons butter (at room temperature)
1 (8-ounce) package cream cheese (at room temperature)
2 cups sifted confectioners' sugar
1 teaspoon vanilla
1/2 cup grated coconut (optional)
1/2 cup chopped pecans*

Blend butter and cream cheese together. Slowly add confectioners' sugar. Add vanilla, coconut and pecans. Ice only middle and top of cake.

*Pecans may be reserved from the icing and sprinkled on top of cake instead.

KATHY KAHERL

215

Carrot Cake II

1 cup corn oil
3 eggs, slightly beaten
2 cups shredded carrots
1 (13-ounce) can crushed pineapple with the juice
2 teaspoons vanilla
2 cups all-purpose flour
2 cups sugar
2 teaspoons cinnamon
2 teaspoons baking soda
1 teaspoon salt
1-1/2 cups flaked coconut
1 cup chopped nuts

Preheat oven to 375 degrees. Mix corn oil, eggs, carrots, pineapple and vanilla together. Do not use a mixer. In separate bowl, combine flour, sugar, cinnamon, soda, salt, coconut and nuts together. Alternate mixing dry ingredients with wet. Pour into greased and floured 9 x 13-inch pan. Bake for 50-60 minutes. Cool.

CREAM CHEESE FROSTING:
1 (8-ounce) package cream cheese
1/2 cup butter
1 teaspoon vanilla
2 cups confectioners' sugar

Cream the cream cheese, butter and vanilla until fluffy. Add confectioners' sugar. Beat again until light and frost the cooled cake. *"This cake is always a hit!"*

ANN BETZ

Quick Fluffy Frosting

1 egg white
1/2 cup Karo syrup
1/2 teaspoon vanilla

Put all ingredients in small bowl of electric mixer. Beat until mixture holds firm peaks and is of spreading consistency. This is enough to cover top and sides of an 8 or 9-inch layer cake.

MARY ARBOUR

Carrot Cake III

2 cups all-purpose flour
1-1/2 cups sugar
1-1/2 teaspoons baking powder
1 teaspoon baking soda
1 teaspoon cinnamon
1 teaspoon nutmeg
1-1/4 cups Crisco oil
2 cups mashed cooked carrot
1/2 cup raisins
1 cup nuts
3 eggs, beaten
1 teaspoon vanilla extract

Preheat oven to 350 degrees. Blend all dry ingredients. Add oil, carrots, raisins, nuts, eggs and vanilla. Mix at medium speed of mixer until blended. Bake in two greased 9-inch pans (round) for 45 minutes. Cool. (12 servings)

CREAM CHEESE FROSTING:
1 (8-ounce) package cream cheese
1 tablespoon butter
1 teaspoon vanilla extract
1 (16-ounce) box confectioners' sugar
Milk

In a mixing bowl, beat cream cheese until softened. Add butter and beat until softened. Add vanilla extract and beat till light. Gradually add confectioners' sugar. Beat till fluffy. Add milk to make a spreading consistency and frost cooled cake.

GISELE ZANGARI

Cocoa Frosting

1/2 cup margarine
3 tablespoons cocoa powder
3/4 box confectioners' sugar
2-1/2 ounces evaporated milk
1 teaspoon vanilla
1/2 teaspoon salt

Cream margarine and cocoa together in a large mixing bowl. Add sugar, milk, vanilla and salt. Beat until fluffy.

MARY WASKERWITZ

Lemon Delite

FIRST LAYER:
1 cup margarine
1 cup chopped nuts
2 cups all-purpose flour

SECOND LAYER:
1 (8-ounce) package cream cheese
1 cup confectioners' sugar
1 cup Cool Whip

THIRD LAYER:
3 cups milk
2 (3-1/2 ounce) packages instant lemon pudding

FOURTH LAYER:
1 (12-ounce) container Cool Whip

Preheat oven to 350 degrees. Combine margarine, nuts and flour. Press into 9 x 13-inch pan. Bake until golden, about 20-22 minutes. Watch closely. Cool. Mix cream cheese, confectioners' sugar and Cool Whip together. Place on top of cooled crust. Blend milk and two boxes of dry pudding mix together in a bowl. Add on top of third layer. Frost with Cool Whip. Refrigerate until serving time. (12 servings)

STEPHANIE MINERATH

Lemon Bundt Cake

1 (18-1/2 ounce) package Duncan Hines lemon cake mix
1/2 cup sugar
1 cup apricot nectar
3/4 cup oil
4 eggs

Preheat oven to 350 degrees. Oil and flour a 10-inch Bundt pan. Mix cake ingredients in a bowl and beat for 2 minutes. Bake for 55 minutes. Let cake cool 20 minutes, then invert on cake plate.

LEMON GLAZE:
Juice of 2 lemons
1-1/2 cups confectioners' sugar

Mix glaze ingredients until smooth and consistency of cream. Drizzle glaze on warm cake. It will absorb the glaze to make a moist and tasty cake. (12 servings) *"A simple, dependable and delicious cake."*

NANCY LIVERMORE

Honey Cake

1 orange or lemon, whole
2 eggs
1 pound honey
1 cup sugar
1 cup strong coffee
1/2 cup oil
4 cups all-purpose flour
4 teaspoons baking powder
1 teaspoon baking soda
1/2 teaspoon allspice
1 teaspoon cinnamon
1 teaspoon salt (or less)
Nuts, dates, ginger, nutmeg (optional)

Preheat oven to 350 degrees. Cut orange into eighths or quarters and remove seeds. Pour into a blender the eggs, honey, sugar, coffee, orange or lemon and oil. Blend till smooth. Pour into bowl. Add remaining ingredients. Stir until just mixed. Add nuts, dates, ginger, nutmeg, as you wish. Pour into 2 greased loaf pans and bake for 45 minutes. Can line pan with aluminum foil and wrap and freeze as soon as baked. (Makes 2 loaves) *Easy to make. Makes a marvelously tasteful base for Trifle, page 247."*

MARILYN LINDENAUER

Five-Minute Dark Chocolate Cake

1-3/4 cups unsifted all-purpose flour
2 cups sugar
3/4 cup cocoa
1-1/2 teaspoons baking soda
1-1/2 teaspoons baking powder
1 teaspoon salt
2 eggs
1 cup milk
1/2 cup vegetable oil
2 teaspoons vanilla
1 cup boiling water

Preheat oven to 350 degrees. Combine dry ingredients in a large mixing bowl. Add remaining ingredients except boiling water; beat at medium speed 2 minutes. Remove from mixer; stir in boiling water. (Batter will be thin.) Pour into two greased and floured 9-inch or three 8-inch layer pans or one 9 x 13-inch pan. Bake for 30-35 minutes for layers or 35-40 minutes for 9 x 13-inch pan. Cool 10 minutes on rack. Remove from pans. Cool completely. Top with your favorite frosting.

JOYCE LONDON

Judy's Chocolate Cake

2 cups all-purpose flour
2 cups sugar
1 teaspoon baking soda
4 tablespoons cocoa
1 cup water
1/2 cup margarine
1/2 cup Crisco
1/2 cup buttermilk
2 eggs
1 teaspoon vanilla

Preheat oven to 400 degrees. Sift flour, sugar and soda together in a large bowl. In a medium saucepan, mix cocoa, water, margarine and Crisco. Bring just to a boil, but do not allow to boil. Add buttermilk to cocoa mixture and then eggs and vanilla. Combine both mixtures. Bake for 20 minutes in a greased and floured pan (9 x 13 inches).

FROSTING:
1/2 cup margarine
4 tablespoons cocoa
6 tablespoons milk
1 teaspoon vanilla
2-1/2 cups confectioners' sugar (sifted)

In a saucepan heat the margarine, cocoa, milk and vanilla together. Add the confectioners' sugar and ice the cake while both are hot. *"For chocolate lovers."*
JUDY MOYER

Chocolate Chip Zucchini Cake

2 eggs
2 cups sugar
1-1/2 cups oil
3 cups peeled and grated zucchini (1 zucchini = 1 cup)
2 cups all-purpose flour
3 teaspoons cinnamon
2 teaspoons baking soda
1 teaspoon salt
1 cup walnuts or pecans, chopped
1 (6-ounce) package chocolate chips

Preheat oven to 350 degrees. Beat eggs in a large mixing bowl. Add sugar, oil and zucchini. Add dry ingredients, nuts and chocolate chips. Bake in greased 9 x 13-inch pan for 50 minutes. Frost when cool. *"I recommend cream cheese frosting."*
KAREN EPSTEIN

Black Bottom Cupcakes

1 (8-ounce) package cream cheese (at room temperature)
1 egg
1/3 cup sugar
1/8 teaspoon salt
1 cup semisweet chocolate chips
1-1/2 cups all-purpose flour
1 cup sugar
1/4 cup cocoa
1 teaspoon baking soda
1/2 teaspoon salt
1 cup water
1/3 cup vegetable oil
1 tablespoon white vinegar
1 teaspoon vanilla

Preheat oven to 375 degrees. Line muffin tins with cupcake papers. Using a wooden spoon, blend cream cheese, egg, sugar and salt in a mixing bowl. Carefully fold in chocolate chips. Set aside. Combine dry ingredients in another bowl and mix well. Add remaining ingredients and blend thoroughly. Fill cupcake papers about three-fourths full with batter. Drop a heaping tablespoon of cream cheese mixture into center of each. Bake until done, about 35-40 minutes. (Makes 1-1/2 dozen cupcakes)

JOANNE LEITH

Chocolate Wine Cake

1 (18-1/2 ounce) package yellow cake mix
1 (3-1/2 ounce) package instant chocolate pudding
4 eggs
3/4 cup sherry wine
3/4 cup Wesson oil

Preheat oven to 350 degrees. Mix all ingredients together in a large bowl for 4 minutes at medium speed. Bake for 45 minutes in a Bundt pan.

GLAZE:
1/3 cup sherry wine
2 cups confectioners' sugar

Heat wine and sugar together in a saucepan. Glaze while warm.

SYLVIA SHERWOOD

221

Chocolate Lovers Delite

1 (18-1/2 ounce) package devil's food cake mix (2-layer)
1 (3-1/2 ounce) package instant chocolate pudding mix
2 eggs
1-3/4 cups milk
1 (12-ounce) package semisweet chocolate chips

Preheat oven to 350 degrees. Mix everything in a bowl for 2 minutes or until well-mixed. Pour into greased and floured Bundt cake pan. Bake for 1 hour or until it springs back. *"Yum!"*

PHYLLIS ASKEW

Chocolate Angel Food Cake

1 cup sifted cake flour
4 tablespoons cocoa
1 cup sugar
1-1/2 cups egg whites (12 eggs)
1/2 teaspoon salt
1 teaspoon cream of tartar
1 teaspoon vanilla
1/4 teaspoon black walnut extract
Additional 3/4 cup sugar

Preheat oven to 350 degrees. Measure flour, cocoa, and sugar into sifter and sift 3 times. Combine egg whites, salt, cream of tartar and flavorings in a large mixing bowl; beat until foamy. Add 3/4 cup of sugar gradually and continue beating until mixture holds stiff peaks. Sift flour mixture in small amounts over beaten eggs and fold in gently. Do not stir. Continue folding only until flour mixture disappears. Pour into ungreased 10-inch tube pan. Bake for 45-50 minutes or until done. Invert and cool. Cut the cake into three layers. (12-16 servings)

CHOCOLATE WHIPPED CREAM TOPPING:
5 tablespoons sugar
5 tablespoons cocoa
1/8 teaspoon salt
3 cups whipping cream
Blanched almonds (optional)

Combine first four ingredients in a mixing bowl and whip until stiff and chill for one hour. Spread the chocolate whipped cream mixture between the layers, top and sides. Chill. If desired, can also sprinkle with blanched whole salted buttered almonds.

BARBARA STRONG

My Mom's Black Forest Torte

1-3/4 cups all-purpose flour
1-3/4 cups sugar
1-1/4 teaspoons baking soda
1 teaspoon salt
1/4 teaspoon baking powder
2/3 cup soft margarine
4 (1-ounce) squares unsweetened chocolate*
1-1/4 cups water
1 teaspoon vanilla
3 eggs
2 bars German sweet chocolate
3/4 cup soft margarine
1/2 cup chopped toasted almonds (optional)
2 cups whipping cream (1 pint)
1 tablespoon sugar
1 teaspoon vanilla

Heat oven to 350 degrees. Brush sides and bottom of four 9-inch round layer pans with soft margarine and flour. Line pans with wax paper, cut to fit. Bake only 2 layers at a time, if desired. Measure into large mixer bowl: flour, sugar, soda, salt, baking powder, soft margarine and unsweetened chocolate melted and cooled, water and vanilla. Beat at low speed to blend. Then beat 2 minutes at medium speed, scraping sides and bottom of bowl frequently. Add eggs. Beat 2 minutes more. Pour 1/4 of the batter (about 1 cup) into each pan. (Layers will be thin.) Bake 15-18 minutes or until done. Cool slightly and remove from pan. Cool completely.

CHOCOLATE FILLING: Melt 1-1/2 bars (4 ounce each) German sweet chocolate (may substitute 6-8 ounces of chocolate chips) over hot water. Cool. Blend in the soft margarine. Stir in chopped toasted almonds.

CREAM FILLING: Beat whipping cream with sugar and vanilla. Whip until stiff; do not overbeat.

TO FINISH TORTE: Place bottom layer of cake on serving plate. Spread with 1/2 of chocolate filling. Next layer, with 1/2 of cream filling. Repeat layers, having cream filling on top. Do not frost sides. Make chocolate curls with remaining 1/2 bar of chocolate. Decorate top completely. Wrap with Saran Wrap. Refrigerate until ready to serve. (12 servings)

*May substitute 12 tablespoons cocoa and 4 tablespoons margarine for 4 squares of chocolate.

JANICE CHAPMAN

Choc-Oat Nut Cake

1-1/2 cups all-purpose flour
1/2 teaspoon salt
1 teaspoon baking soda
1 tablespoon unsweetened cocoa powder
1 cup rolled oats (not instant)
1-1/2 cups boiling water
1/2 cup softened butter or margarine
1 cup packed light brown sugar
1 cup sugar
3 eggs
1 (12-ounce) package chocolate chips
3/4 cup chopped walnuts

Preheat oven to 350 degrees. Stir together flour, salt, soda and cocoa in a large mixing bowl and set aside. Combine oatmeal and boiling water. Let stand 10 minutes. Stir in butter and sugars. Add eggs. Mix well. Beat in flour mixture, mix well. Fold in half the chocolate chips and nuts. Spread in a greased and floured 13 x 9-inch pan. Sprinkle remaining chips and nuts on top. Bake approximately 45-50 minutes. Serve in squares. Can also use a Bundt pan. (12-16 servings)

PAMELA OLTON

Chocolate Mousse Cake

1/2 cup unsalted butter
3 cups chocolate wafer crumbs (Nabisco Famous chocolate wafers, 2 boxes)
1 (12-ounce) package Nestles' semisweet morsels
4 (1-ounce) squares Baker's German sweet chocolate
2 eggs
4 eggs, separated
2 cups whipping cream
6 tablespoons confectioners' sugar
Garnish: Chocolate shavings

Melt butter in a small saucepan. Mix in wafer crumbs. Press onto bottom and up sides of large-size spring pan. Refrigerate about 1/2 hour. Melt chocolate (Nestles' and Baker's) in double boiler and cool slightly. Mix melted chocolate, 2 eggs and 4 egg yolks. Whip the whipping cream until soft peaks form. Add confectioners' sugar. Beat remaining egg whites. Add small amount of egg whites and whipping cream to chocolate mixture, gently but thoroughly. Fold in remainder of egg whites and whipped cream to chocolate. Pour into crust and refrigerate for at least six hours. Garnish with chocolate shavings. Do not remove from spring pan until serving time. (10-12 servings) *"Rich and delicious."*

M.A. SANGEORZAN

Chocolate Marble Chiffon Cake

1/4 cup cocoa
1/4 cup sugar
1/4 cup boiling water
1/4 teaspoon red food coloring (optional)
2-1/4 cups cake flour
1-1/2 cups sugar
3 teaspoons baking powder
1 teaspoon salt
1/2 cup salad oil
5 unbeaten egg yolks
3/4 cup cold water
2 teaspoons vanilla
1 cup egg whites
1/2 teaspoon cream of tartar

Preheat oven to 325 degrees. Stir cocoa, sugar, boiling water and food coloring together in a bowl until cool and smooth. Measure and sift cake flour, sugar, baking powder and salt together in a large mixing bowl. Make a well and add in order, the salad oil, egg yolks, cold water and vanilla. Beat with a spoon until smooth. Measure egg whites and cream of tartar into a large mixing bowl. Whip until whites form very stiff peaks. (They should be much stiffer than for an angel food cake. Do not under-beat.) Pour egg yolk mixture gradually over egg whites, gently folding just until blended. Do not stir. Place half of the batter in another bowl. Pour cocoa mixture gradually over it, gently folding until blended. Immediately pour alternate layers of dark and light batter into ungreased tube pan. Bake in 10-inch tube pan in 325 degree oven for 55 minutes, then 350 degrees for 10-15 minutes. Invert pan while cooling, may place on bottle. Frost when cool. *"Good with either chocolate or white boiled frosting."*

STEPHANIE MINERATH

225

The League's Chocolate Cake

3-1/4 cups sugar
1/2 cup butter
1/2 cup vegetable shortening
1/2 teaspoon salt
1 teaspoon vanilla
1 whole egg
1 egg yolk
2 cups buttermilk
4 cups all-purpose flour
1 tablespoon baking soda
2 (1-ounce) squares melted bitter chocolate

Preheat oven to 350 degrees. Cream lightly together the sugar, butter, shortening, salt and vanilla for about 3 minutes. Add the eggs and mix lightly. Add the buttermilk alternately with the flour and baking soda sifted together twice. Lastly, add the chocolate. Bake for 40-50 minutes or until done. (Makes two 8-1/2 inch squares)

THE MICHIGAN LEAGUE

Chocolate Bundt Cake

1 (18-1/2 ounce) package chocolate cake mix
1 (3-1/2 ounce) package instant chocolate fudge pudding
1 cup sour cream
3/4 cup water
3/4 cup oil
4 eggs
1 (6-ounce) package chocolate chips

Preheat oven to 350 degrees. Beat everything together in a deep bowl except the chocolate chips for 5 minutes at medium speed. Fold in chips. Pour into a large, well-greased and floured Bundt pan. Bake for 40 minutes.

CHOCOLATE FROSTING:
1 (1-ounce) square baking chocolate
2 tablespoons butter
2 tablespoons water
1/4 teaspoon vanilla
1 cup confectioners' sugar

In the top of a double boiler, heat baking chocolate, butter and water together just until melted. Add vanilla. Cool until lukewarm. Then add the confectioners' sugar. Beat until spreading consistency, adding a little warm water if necessary. Frost the cooled cake by drizzling frosting over top and down sides. Alternative is to sprinkle confectioners' sugar over top of cake rather than frost. *"Frosting is also excellent on brownies and other cakes."*

STEPHANIE MINERATH

226

My Mother's Mother's Fudge Cake

3 cups sugar
3/4 cup soft butter
6 eggs
1-1/2 cups cake flour
4-1/2 tablespoons cocoa
Pinch of salt
1-1/2 teaspoons vanilla
1 cup ground pecans

Preheat oven to 300 degrees. Grease a 9 x 12" cake pan with butter and then dust with flour. Cream sugar with the soft butter. Beat the eggs one or two at a time and stir into sugar/butter mixture. Sift the cake flour with the cocoa and salt. Stir flour mixture into butter mixture. Stir in the vanilla and the ground pecans. Pour batter into greased and floured pans. Bake for 40-45 minutes. Cut into pieces when warm, but do not remove from pan until cool. (48 pieces)

MACDONALD DICK

Cinnamon Bundt Coffee Cake

1 cup margarine
2 cups sugar
4 eggs
2 teaspoons vanilla
1 cup yogurt (or sour cream)
3 cups unsifted all-purpose flour
2 teaspoons baking soda
2-1/2 teaspoons baking powder
Dash of salt

TOPPING:
2/3 to 1 cup sugar
2 teaspoons cinnamon
1 cup chopped nuts

Preheat oven to 350 degrees. Cream together the margarine and sugar in a mixing bowl. Add the eggs and vanilla and cream until fluffy. Add the yogurt or sour cream, flour, soda, baking powder and salt. Prepare the topping in a separate bowl by combining the sugar, cinnamon and nuts. Grease and flour a Bundt pan. Sprinkle with some topping mixture, then batter, then topping for the middle. End with a batter layer. Bake for 55-60 minutes.

STEPHANIE MINERATH
NICK KOLOKITHAS
KATHY DUNN

Carol's Pecan Cream Pie

2 cups milk
2 eggs, beaten
1/2 cup sugar
1 heaping tablespoon cornstarch
Pinch of salt
2 teaspoons vanilla
1 cup chopped pecans
1 (8-inch) baked pie shell

Heat milk in top of double boiler. Combine eggs, sugar, cornstarch, salt and vanilla. Pour into milk and cook, stirring constantly until thickened. Allow to cool and stir in chopped pecans. Turn into baked pie shell.

TOPPING:
1/2 pint whipping cream
1 tablespoon sugar
1/2 teaspoon vanilla
1 tablespoon chopped pecans

Whip cream until fluffy. Add sugar and vanilla. Refrigerate; then spread on top of thoroughly cooled pie. Sprinkle with chopped pecans.

CAROL MESZAROS

Damson Pie

3 eggs
1 cup sugar
1/2 cup margarine, melted
1/2 cup damson jelly
1 teaspoon vanilla
1 (9-inch) unbaked pie shell

Preheat oven to 325 degrees. Beat eggs in a large bowl or use mixer. Add other ingredients. Beat until well-blended. Pour into pie shell. Bake for 30-45 minutes. Let cool before cutting. (Serves 6-8) *"Pie actually tastes like a pecan pie without the pecans, so the name is misleading!"*

EVELYN KINNARD

Ritz Whipped Cream Pie

3 egg whites
1/2 teaspoon cream of tartar
1 cup sugar
1 teaspoon vanilla
23 Ritz crackers, crushed fine
1 cup chopped walnuts
2 tablespoons sweetened cocoa, like Swiss Miss (optional)
1 cup Cool Whip or Dream Whip
Chocolate bits (optional)

Preheat oven to 350 degrees. Beat egg whites and cream of tartar in a mixing bowl until frothy. Add sugar slowly, 2 tablespoons at a time, until stiff. Add vanilla. Fold in cracker crumbs and nuts. Spoon into well-greased 9-inch pie pan. Bake for 20 minutes. Cool well. Combine cocoa and Cool Whip; spread on pie, sprinkle with chocolate bits.

SUSAN HUBBARD

Ten-Minute German Sweet Chocolate Cream Pie

4 (1-ounce) squares Baker's German Sweet Chocolate
1/3 cup milk
2 tablespoons sugar
1 (3-ounce) package cream cheese, softened
1 (8-ounce) container Cool Whip
1 (8-inch) graham cracker or Oreo crumb crust
Chocolate curls (optional)

Heat chocolate and 2 tablespoons of milk in saucepan over low heat, stirring until chocolate is melted. Beat sugar into cream cheese; add remaining milk and chocolate mixture and beat until smooth. Fold in whipped topping blending until smooth. Spoon into crust. Freeze until firm, about 4 hours. Garnish with chocolate curls, if desired. Store any leftover pie in freezer.

MARIE BAZIL

Fudge Pie

2 (1-ounce) squares unsweetened chocolate squares
1/4 cup butter
1-1/2 cups sugar
1 (5.3-ounce) can evaporated milk
2 eggs, slightly beaten
1 teaspoon vanilla
1 (9-inch) unbaked deep-dish pie shell

Preheat oven to 350 degrees. Melt chocolate squares and butter together in a double boiler. Mix sugar, evaporated milk, eggs and vanilla together and add to chocolate mixture. Blend well. Pour into unbaked deep-dish pie shell. Bake for 30 minutes or until just set.

MARY ELLEN BOTSFORD

Chocolate Pie

CRUST:
4 ounces Oreo Cookies, crushed
2-1/3 tablespoons melted butter

Preheat oven to 350 degrees. Blend all crust ingredients together and press into pie plate. Bake a few minutes to set. Cool.

FILLING:
5-1/3 cups Cool Whip
1/3 pound (5-1/3 ounce) instant hot cocoa mix
2 teaspoons vanilla extract
3/4 cup miniature marshmallows
1/3 cup coarsely chopped walnuts
Shaved chocolate

Fold all filling ingredients together and add to crust. Top with shaved chocolate. *"Everyone will ask for this recipe!"*

POLLY COMSTOCK

Peanut Butter Pie

CRUST:
1 (6-ounce) package chocolate pieces (semisweet or milk chocolate)
1/2 cup butter
2-1/2 cups Rice Krispies

Melt chocolate pieces and butter in a medium saucepan. Mix in Rice Krispies and pat into 9-inch pie pan. Refrigerate for 30 minutes.

FILLING:
1 (8-ounce) package cream cheese
3/4 cup peanut butter
1 (14-ounce) can sweetened condensed milk
3 tablespoons lemon juice
1 teaspoon vanilla
1 cup Cool Whip
1 tablespoon chocolate sauce

Beat cream cheese until light. Beat in peanut butter and milk. Mix in lemon juice and vanilla. Fold in Cool Whip. Pour into crust. Drizzle chocolate sauce over top and swirl. Refrigerate 4-6 hours. (6-8 servings) *"Very rich and yummy."*

FLORENCE NEZAMIS

Peanut Butter Banana Pie

CRUST:
3 cups miniature marshmallows
1/2 cup smooth peanut butter
1/4 cup butter
4 cups cornflakes

Melt first three crust ingredients together in a large saucepan. Stir until blended. Remove from heat and add cornflakes. Pat into pie plate.

FILLING:
3 cups prepared vanilla pudding
1-1/2 cups miniature marshmallows
1 cup whipped topping
3 sliced bananas

Mix all filling ingredients together and pour into crust. Chill.

POLLY COMSTOCK

231

Fresh Fruit Cheese Pie

1 (8-ounce) package cream cheese, softened
1 (14-ounce) can Eagle Brand sweetened condensed milk
1/3 cup real lemon juice
1 teaspoon vanilla extract
1 (9-inch) baked pie shell
Fresh fruit
White corn syrup (optional)

In a large bowl, beat cheese until fluffy. Gradually beat in milk until smooth. Stir in lemon juice and vanilla. Pour into prepared pie shell. Chill 3 hours or until set. Arrange fruit on top of pie. Just before serving, brush with corn syrup if desired. Refrigerate leftovers.　　SUE HENDERSON

The League's Lemon Chiffon Pie

1/4 cup lemon juice
Grated rind of 1 lemon
3 egg yolks
1/2 cup sugar
Pinch of salt
1 packet Knox unflavored gelatin
1/4 cup cold water
3 egg whites
1/2 cup sugar
1 (9-inch) baked pie shell
Whipped cream

Cook the lemon juice and rind, egg yolks, sugar and salt in a double boiler until of custard consistency. Soak gelatin in the cold water until softened and add to the hot custard. Cool. Beat egg whites stiffly with sugar and fold into cool custard. Pile into baked pie shell. Top with whipped cream.
　　THE MICHIGAN LEAGUE

Peach Cream Pie

1 (9-inch) unbaked deep-dish pie shell
Peaches, about 2 pounds (may use canned drained peaches)
1 cup sugar
3 tablespoons all-purpose flour
1/2 pint whipping cream (do not use half-and-half cream)
1 teaspoon vanilla

Preheat oven to 350 degrees. Slice peaches into pie shell until half full. In a bowl combine sugar and flour. Add whipping cream and vanilla mixing well. Pour half of this mixture over peaches. Slice peaches into pie shell until full. Pour remaining cream mixture over peaches. Bake for 45 minutes.
　　SHARON GREEN

Peach Streusel Pie

1 (10-inch) unbaked pie shell
1 egg white
2/3 cup brown sugar
3 tablespoons all-purpose flour
1 teaspoon cinnamon
1/4 cup cold butter, cut in small pieces
3 pounds peaches
1 tablespoon lemon juice

Preheat oven to 425 degrees. Line pie crust with foil. Fill with beans or rice to weigh down foil. Bake for 15 minutes. Remove from oven and remove beans and foil and bake 15 minutes more. Remove from oven and brush with egg white. Let cool. Turn oven down to 375 degrees. Combine sugar, flour, cinnamon and butter and cut with pastry blender until mix resembles coarse meal. Sprinkle a third of this streusel into bottom of cooled pie shell. Blanch peaches in boiling water for 1 minute. Remove and peel, quarter and slice. Arrange half of the peaches over streusel. Top with a third of the remaining streusel, then rest of peaches. Drizzle with lemon juice and sprinkle remaining streusel evenly over peaches. Bake for 45-55 minutes until filling is bubbly and peaches are tender. (Crust will become golden brown and begin to darken.) *"Serve with vanilla ice cream or plain. It is wonderful!"*

SUSAN HURWITZ

Joyce's Pumpkin Pie

1 (30-ounce) can pumpkin (3 cups)
1 cup brown sugar
1 teaspoon salt
1 tablespoon ginger
1/2 teaspoon cinnamon
3 eggs
1 cup whipping cream
1/2 cup milk
2 (9-inch) unbaked pie shells

Preheat oven to 450 degrees. Mix all pie ingredients well and divide into 2 unbaked pie shells. Bake 10 minutes. Lower oven temperature to 350 degrees and bake until knife comes out clean (about 50 minutes). (Makes 2 pies)

CAROLINE BLANE

233

Pumpkin Ice Cream Pie

CRUST:
2 cups sifted all-purpose flour
1 teaspoon salt
1 tablespoon sugar
3/4 cup shortening
1/4 cup ice water

Preheat oven to 375 degrees. Mix pie crust ingredients, except water, in a large bowl; mix until crumbly. Add water. Roll out for 2 pies and place in pie plates. Bake for 10-15 minutes. Cool.

FILLING:
1 quart vanilla ice cream
1 cup pumpkin, canned
1/2 cup sugar
Pinch of salt
3/4 teaspoon pumpkin pie spice
1 cup heavy cream

Soften ice cream and spread in shell. Place in freezer until hard. Blend together pumpkin, sugar, salt and spice. Whip cream and fold into pumpkin mixture. Spoon over ice cream. Replace in freezer. Serve with whipped cream if desired. (Can be made ahead of time and kept in freezer for several weeks.) (Makes 2 pies)

GLORIA PROCHOWNIK

Rhubarb Pie

2 eggs
1-1/4 cups sugar
2 tablespoons all-purpose flour
2 tablespoons butter
4 cups rhubarb, cut into 1/2-inch pieces
Pastry for 2-crust (9-inch) pie, unbaked
Sugar

Preheat oven to 400 degrees. Beat eggs well in a large mixing bowl. Add sugar, flour, and butter to beaten eggs. Stir well. Add rhubarb and stir. Let set for a short time. Spoon into unbaked pie shell. Cover pie with lattice top. Sprinkle lightly with sugar. Bake for 15 minutes, then 350 degrees till brown on top.

DEBRA HAAS

"Big Boy" Strawberry Pie

3/4 cup sugar
2 tablespoons cornstarch
1-1/2 cups water
1 (3-ounce) package strawberry gelatin
1 quart fresh strawberries, hulled and sliced
1 (8-9 inch) baked pie shell

Mix first 3 ingredients in a saucepan over medium heat, stirring constantly until thick and clear (approximately 10-12 minutes). Remove from heat and add package of strawberry gelatin; stir until dissolved. Cool in the refrigerator about 10 minutes but do not let thicken. Place prepared strawberries in pie shell. Pour mixture over berries and let it set.

SHELLY ROBBINS

Fresh Strawberry Pie

CRUST:
1 cup all-purpose flour
3-1/2 tablespoons confectioners' sugar
1/2 cup margarine

Preheat oven to 350 degrees. Prepare crust. Mix all ingredients together in a large bowl and pat into a 9-inch pie pan or springform pan. Bake for 20 minutes and cool. (6 servings)

FILLING:
2/3 quart fresh strawberries

Clean and slice fruit. Fill crust with fruit. Refrigerate.

GLAZE:
1 cup sugar
1 cup water
3 tablespoons cornstarch
3 tablespoons dry strawberry gelatin

In a saucepan combine sugar, water and cornstarch. Cook at low heat until clear. Add gelatin. Stir until uniform color. Pour hot glaze over fruit and refrigerate. Serve in about 2 hours. (Can also be made with peaches, raspberries, or blueberries using the appropriate gelatin.) *"From the kitchen of my mom, Lyn Fink."*

PAULA FINK

Fresh Fruit Pie

CRUST:
2-1/4 cups all-purpose flour
1/2 cup Mazola oil
3 tablespoons milk
1/2 teaspoon salt
3 tablespoons sugar

Preheat oven to 400 degrees. Blend all crust ingredients with fork. Press into 10-inch pie pan. Bake 10-15 minutes. Cool.

FILLING:
1 cup sugar
3 tablespoons cornstarch
1/8 teaspoon salt
3 tablespoons white corn syrup
1 cup water
3 tablespoons dry strawberry gelatin (or peach gelatin)
1 quart strawberries (or sliced peaches*)

Combine sugar, cornstarch, salt, corn syrup and water in a saucepan. Cook until thickened (5 minutes). Add gelatin and cook until clear and thick. Slice fruit into bottom of pie shell. Spoon filling over fruit. Chill.

*COOK'S TIP: For peach pie add 1-2 tablespoons lemon juice.

JERI KELCH

Buttery Pie Crust (for Food Processor)

2 cups all-purpose flour
1 tablespoon sugar
1/4 teaspoon salt
8 tablespoons butter, sliced into 8 pieces
3 tablespoons Crisco
5-6 tablespoons ice water

Place flour, sugar, salt, butter and Crisco in food processor and blend until mixture resembles coarse meal (about 15-20 seconds). With processor running, drizzle in only enough ice water so that mixture forms a solid ball. Remove from processor and roll out quickly to fit 10-inch pie plate.

SUSAN HURWITZ

Danish Puff

PASTRY DOUGH:
1/2 cup butter
1 cup sifted all-purpose flour
2 tablespoons cold water

Cut butter into flour in a mixing bowl. Add cold water. Mix well. Roll in rectangle. Place in greased 13 x 9-inch pan.

FILLING:
1/2 cup butter
1 cup water
1 teaspoon almond extract
1 cup sifted all-purpose flour
3 eggs

Preheat oven to 400 degrees. Bring the butter and water to a boil in a saucepan. Remove from heat. Add the almond extract and flour. Add eggs separately. Beat well after each addition. Spread over dough. Bake for 35 minutes. (12 servings)

TOPPING:
2 cups sifted confectioners' sugar
1 teaspoon butter
3 tablespoons heated cream or milk
1 teaspoon vanilla
1/8 teaspoon salt
1/4 cup chopped nuts

Mix all topping ingredients together in a bowl except the nuts and spread mixture onto warm cake. Sprinkle nuts on top.

TONIE LEEDS
CATHERINE ANDREA

Rugelach

PASTRY:
8 tablespoons margarine, softened
1 cup all-purpose flour
2/3 cup sour cream

FILLING:
1/2 cup white raisins
1 tablespoon sugar
1/2 teaspoon cinnamon
Confectioners' sugar (to sprinkle on filling)

Rub margarine into flour. Add the sour cream and mix to form dough. Chill. For the filling combine raisins, sugar and cinnamon. Roll out half the pastry at a time into a circle and cut pie wedge-shaped triangles. Place a small amount of filling in the center of each triangle and roll, starting from wide end of piece. Place on greased tin. Bake at 425 degrees for 10 minutes. Sprinkle with confectioners' sugar. (Makes 2 dozen servings)

WANDA BRODERICK

Nora's Double Decker Pastry

5 cups all-purpose flour
1 cup sugar
4 teaspoons baking powder
2 teaspoons baking soda
Pinch of salt
2 tablespoons Crisco
1/2 pound butter
4 egg yolks
1/2 pint sour cream
1 teaspoon vanilla
2-1/2 cups ground walnuts
1/2 cup sugar
Jam (raspberry, apricot or any flavor)

Preheat oven to 350 degrees. Sift together flour, sugar, baking powder, baking soda and salt in a large bowl. Add Crisco and butter; add egg yolks, sour cream and vanilla. Divide dough into three portions. Roll out first layer as for pie; place in bottom of large cookie sheet; spread nuts and sugar mixture on first layer. Roll out second layer; place over nuts. Spread this layer with jam; sprinkle a little of nut and sugar mixture over jam. Roll out third layer; cut into strips and place on top to form lattice work. Bake for 25 minutes. *"Delicious served warm with ice cream."*

CAROL MESZAROS

Easy Refrigerator Twinkie Dessert

6 Twinkies, split lengthwise (crust trimmed slightly)
1 (6-ounce) package semisweet chocolate chips (1 cup)
2 tablespoons hot water
4 eggs, separated
1 (8-ounce) container Cool Whip
Nuts, chopped

Place split Twinkies in buttered 8 x 8-inch pan. Melt chocolate chips and water. Cool slightly. Beat 4 egg yolks. Gradually add to chocolate mixture and then cool. Whip 4 egg whites until stiff. Fold into cooled chocolate mixture. Add 1 cup Cool Whip to chocolate mixture. Let thicken slightly and pour over Twinkies. Refrigerate until stiff and sprinkle with chopped nuts. (8 servings)

Optional Variation: Add a layer of sliced banana before adding Cool Whip top.

CHARLOTTE BETZ

Heath Bar Dessert

2 cups Ritz crackers
1/3 cup butter or margarine (add more if needed)
1 (3-1/2 ounce) package butterscotch instant pudding
1 (3-1/2 ounce) package French vanilla instant pudding
1 cup milk
1 pint butter pecan ice cream, softened
1 (12-ounce) container Cool Whip
2 Heath bars

Crumble Ritz crackers with a rolling pin. Melt butter or margarine in a saucepan and add cracker crumbs. When crumbs are moist, spread them into a 9 x 13-inch baking dish. Set aside. In a large mixing bowl, combine both pudding mixes, milk and fold in ice cream. Stir until well-mixed and creamy. Pour ingredients onto cracker crumbs. Let this sit in refrigerator or until it is firm. Then pour Cool Whip on top. Add Heath Bar shavings on top of this. (9 servings)

LYNN FRENCH

Mini Pecan Tarts

CRUST:
1 (3-ounce) package cream cheese
1/2 cup butter (at room temperature)
1 cup all-purpose flour

In a bowl cream together the cream cheese and butter until smooth. Stir in the flour and mix well. Refrigerate the dough for 1 hour. Preheat oven to 350 degrees. Shape the dough into 24 small or 12 regular balls, depending on your pan size. Press mixture into muffin or tart tins. Bake for 20 minutes. (Makes 24 small tarts or 12 regular tarts)

FILLING:
1 tablespoon butter
3/4 cup brown sugar
1 egg, beaten
1 teaspoon vanilla
2/3 cup chopped pecans

Prepare the filling by melting the butter in a saucepan. Stir in the sugar and egg and blend thoroughly. Stir in vanilla and pecans. Fill each pastry shell with 1 teaspoon of the filling. Bake the tarts for 20-25 minutes.

MARY DOYLE

Blue Ribbon Cheesecake

1-1/2 cups graham cracker crumbs
1/2 cup melted butter or margarine
3 tablespoons sugar
3 (8-ounce) packages cream cheese
1 cup sugar
3 eggs
1/2 cup melted butter or margarine
1/2 teaspoon orange extract (or 1 teaspoon lemon juice)

Combine cracker crumbs, butter and sugar in a large bowl. Press evenly onto bottom and about 3/4 inches up sides of 9-inch springform pan. Preheat oven to 450 degrees. Beat together cream cheese and sugar until light and fluffy. (May use food processor.) Add eggs one at a time, beating after each addition. Blend in 1/2 cup melted butter and extract. Turn mixture into springform pan. Place pan on cookie sheet to catch drippings. Bake for only 15 minutes. Cool. Refrigerate at least 12 hours before serving. (10-12 generous servings) *"Bakes only 15 minutes. I have made this up to one month in advance, frozen it and then thawed in the refrigerator."*

SANDRA MERKEL

Cherry Delight

BASE:
2 cups all-purpose flour
1 cup ground nuts
1/2 cup brown sugar
1 cup soft butter

Preheat oven to 400 degrees. Mix all base ingredients together and spread into a 9 x 13-inch pan. Bake 15 minutes. Cool. Crumble and pat back into pan.

MIDDLE LAYER:
1 (8-ounce) package cream cheese
1 cup confectioners' sugar
1 teaspoon vanilla
2 packages Dream Whip

Combine cream cheese, confectioners' sugar and vanilla in a large bowl and mix well. Prepare Dream Whip according to package directions. Mix Dream Whip with cream cheese mixture. Spread over crumb mixture.

TOP LAYER:
1 large can cherry pie filling

Spread pie filling on top of cheese mixture. Chill for 12 hours.

CAROL COLBY

241

Easy Cheesecake

1-1/4 cups crushed graham crackers
2 tablespoons sugar
1/4 cup melted margarine
2 eggs
1/2 cup sugar
1 (8-ounce) and 1 (3-ounce) package cream cheese (at room temperature)
1 teaspoon vanilla
1 cup sour cream
2 tablespoons sugar
1/2 teaspoon vanilla

Preheat oven to 350 degrees. Combine graham crackers, sugar and melted margarine in a large mixing bowl. Press into 9-inch pie pan and bake for about 6 minutes. Cool. Beat eggs. Add sugar until fluffy. Beat in cheese. Add vanilla. Pour into crust. Bake 20-25 minutes at 375 degrees. Let cool 15-20 minutes. Combine sour cream, sugar and vanilla and spread on cake. Bake at 475 degrees for 5 minutes. (6 servings)

STEPHANIE MINERATH

Gooey Butter Cheesecake

CRUST:
1 Duncan Hines cake mix (white or chocolate*)
1 egg, slightly beaten
6 tablespoons butter or margarine

Mix all crust ingredients well in a large mixing bowl, until crumbly. Pat into a greased 9 x 13-inch pan. Preheat oven to 350 degrees.

FILLING:
2 (8-ounce) package cream cheese
1 (1-pound) box confectioners' sugar
2 eggs, slightly beaten

Beat cream cheese until fluffy. Add confectioners' sugar a little at a time. Add eggs and mix well. Pour over crust. Bake for 1 hour or until golden brown.

*COOK'S TIP: Chocolate cake mix makes it taste like a cream cheese brownie.

FLORENCE NEZAMIS

Strawberry-Glazed Cheesecake

CRUST:
16 slices (4 ounces) Zwieback (or 1-3/4 cups crumbs)
1/3 cup confectioners' sugar
1 teaspoon grated lemon peel
1/3 cup butter

Lightly butter bottom and sides of a 7-inch springform pan. Crush Zwieback and combine with confectioners' sugar and lemon peel. Using a fork or pastry blender, blend in the softened butter. With fingers or back of spoon, press crumb mixture very firmly into an even layer on bottom of pan and up around sides to the rim. Set aside.

FILLING:
4 (8-ounce) packages cream cheese
1 teaspoon grated lemon peel
1/2 teaspoon vanilla extract
1 cup plus 6 tablespoons sugar
2 tablespoons plus 1 teaspoon all-purpose flour
4 eggs plus 1 egg yolk, beaten
3-1/2 tablespoons heavy cream

Preheat oven to 250 degrees. Beat together cream cheese, lemon peel and vanilla extract in a large mixing bowl. Gradually beat in the sugar and flour. Blend in thoroughly the eggs and heavy cream. Turn into pan and spread evenly. Bake for 70-75 minutes. Turn off heat. Let stand in oven 1 hour longer. Remove to cooling rack to cool completely 4-6 hours. Chill several hours or overnight.

GLAZE:
1 quart fresh ripe strawberries
1/2 cup sugar
1 tablespoon cornstarch
1/4 cup water
2 teaspoons butter or margarine
8 drops red food coloring (optional)
Strawberries for garnish

When cheesecake is thoroughly chilled, sort, rinse, drain and hull the strawberries. Crush enough berries to make 1/2 cup crushed. Set remaining strawberries in refrigerator to chill. Mix in a saucepan sugar and cornstarch. Add gradually, stirring until blended, the crushed berries and 1/4 cup water. Stirring constantly, bring rapidly to boiling. Continue stirring and boil about 2 minutes. Remove from heat and stir in butter and red food coloring. Strain the glaze and set aside to cool slightly. Meanwhile, carefully arrange the strawberries on the cheesecake. Spoon the cooled glaze carefully over the berries. Chill in refrigerator. (12-16 servings)

RUTH LUM

Royal Marble Cheesecake

3/4 cup all-purpose flour
2 tablespoons sugar
1/4 teaspoon salt
1/4 cup butter or margarine
1 (6-ounce) package semisweet chocolate pieces, melted

Heat oven to 400 degrees. In a small mixing bowl, combine flour, sugar and salt. Cut in butter or margarine until particles are fine. Stir in 2 tablespoons melted chocolate pieces. Press onto bottom of 9 to 10-inch springform pan. Bake for 10 minutes.

FILLING:
3 (8-ounce) packages cream cheese, softened
1 cup sugar
1/4 cup all-purpose flour
2 teaspoons vanilla
6 eggs
1 cup dairy sour cream

In a large mixer bowl, beat cream cheese with sugar at medium speed until smooth and creamy. Blend in flour and vanilla. Add eggs one at a time, beating well after each. Blend in sour cream. Blend 1-3/4 cups of filling with the remaining melted chocolate pieces. Pour remainder of filling over baked crust. Top with chocolate mixture. Cut through batter (but not crust) to marbleize. Place in 400 degree oven; immediately reduce setting to 300 degrees. Bake 1 hour. Turn off oven; leave in closed oven 1 hour. Cool away from drafts until completely cooled. Chill at least 8 hours before serving. (16 servings)

THOMAS SHOPE

Chocolate Fondue

1 (6-ounce) package chocolate chips
1/2 cup sugar
1/2 cup milk
1/2 cup chunky peanut butter
Condiments for dipping

Melt the chocolate chips, sugar and milk in a fondue pot; then add peanut butter. Serve with pineapple chunks, bananas, apples, marshmallows, pecans, maraschino cherries, angel food cake pieces. *"A quick and easy dessert."*

CAROL MESZAROS

Four Seasons Fruit Flan

FLAN SHELL:
1/4 cup soft butter
2 tablespoons sugar
3 tablespoons almond paste
1/2 teaspoon grated lemon peel
1 egg white
3/4 cup sifted all-purpose flour

Preheat oven to 300 degrees. Grease and flour an 8-inch round cake pan. In a large mixing bowl beat butter, sugar, almond paste and lemon peel at medium speed until well combined. Add egg white; beat on high speed until smooth. Gradually beat in flour. Press evenly onto bottom and side of pan. Refrigerate 1 hour. Bake shell 50 minutes or until golden. Cool 15 minutes. Gently turn out on rack; cool.

PASTRY CREAM:
1 (3-1/2 ounce) package vanilla pudding and pie filling
1-1/2 cups milk
1 teaspoon vanilla
4 ladyfingers, split
2 teaspoons kirsch or fruit liqueur

In a saucepan, combine pudding and milk; cook as package directs, then remove from heat. Turn into bowl and add vanilla. Place waxed paper on surface of filling and chill. About 1 hour before serving, spread half of pastry cream over bottom of shell. Arrange ladyfingers over surface. Sprinkle with kirsch. Cover with rest of cream.

APRICOT GLAZE:
1/2 cup apricot preserves
2 tablespoons water
Approximately 13 (1/8-inch thick) banana slices
1/3 cup fresh raspberries
1/3 cup seedless green grapes
8 fresh strawberries, halved
1/4 cup fresh blueberries

In a small saucepan heat preserves with water until melted. Strain and cool. Arrange fruit over surface of flan in whatever attractive pattern you wish. Brush fruit with glaze. Refrigerate. *"This dessert is not only delicious, but beautiful. You may substitute fruits if desired, such as seeded dark grapes for blueberries and kiwi fruit for green grapes. Just use a variety of colors of fruits for an impressive look."*

ELIZABETH STONE

DESSERTS

Fermented Fruit

In a 1-gallon ceramic container, place **1 cup sugar** and **1 cup of fruit** in season cut into small pieces. Every two weeks add another cup of sugar and another cup of different fresh fruit. Never let container become less than 1-1/2 cups. Never refrigerate. Keep at room temperature. Never put lid on tightly. *"Excellent served on top of ice cream or pound cake. Also may serve as an accompaniment to pork, veal or chops."*

ANN BETZ

Oven-Glazed Fruit

1/2 (1-pound) can pineapple slices
6-8 peach halves
6-8 pear halves
12-15 maraschino cherries, sliced
1/4 cup butter or margarine
3/4 cup packed brown sugar
1 teaspoon curry

Drain fruit well. Mix butter, sugar, curry and melt together in a small saucepan. Arrange fruit in casserole. Pour melted mixture over fruit. Bake at 350 degrees for 45 minutes to 1 hour.

GERALDINE CROWLEY

Apple Crisp

8 large golden delicious apples (peeled and sliced)
2/3 cup sugar (more if apples are tart)
1 teaspoon cinnamon
1 tablespoon all-purpose flour
1 tablespoon lemon juice
1/3 cup water
1/2 cup margarine
3/4 cup brown sugar
3/4 cup rolled oats
3/4 cup all-purpose flour
1/2 teaspoon baking powder
1/2 teaspoon baking soda
1/4 teaspoon salt

Preheat oven to 350 degrees. Mix apples, sugar, cinnamon, flour and lemon juice together in a bowl and put in a 9 x 13-inch buttered pan. Pour 1/3 cup water over apples. Mix margarine, brown sugar, oatmeal, flour, baking powder, soda and salt together until crumbly and sprinkle over the apples. Bake for 45 minutes. (10-12 servings)

CHARLOTTE BETZ

Apfelkuchen

PASTRY DOUGH:
3-l/2 to 4 cups all-purpose flour
1 cup sugar
Pinch of salt
1-1/2 teaspoons baking powder
1 egg
1-1/2 cups margarine
Few drops of almond flavoring

FILLING:
12-14 apples (peeled, sliced and slightly cooked)
1 cup raisins
2 tablespoons cinnamon
3/4 cup sugar

TOPPING:
Confectioners' sugar
Lemon juice

Preheat oven to 375 degrees. Mix all ingredients together for the dough in a bowl until smooth and forms a good ball. Roll out half the dough and place in pan approximately 12 x 15 inches. The dough should go up on the pan sides. Bake about 15 minutes until lightly browned. Combine filling ingredients. Spread the filling over the cooked dough. Roll out the second half and lay over the apple mixture. Dough may have to be patched. Brush milk or cream over the top and bake until brown. Spread the topping over. Cut into squares.

HANS HENNING BODE

Trifle

Sponge cake or honey cake* (store bought or home-made), cut in 1/2-inch cubes
Whipped cream (1 tub of prepared or 1 pint homemade)
2 pounds fresh strawberries
1-1/2 pounds fresh blueberries
Fresh pineapple, chunks
1/2 cup brandy or kirsch

Using a 9 x 13-inch glass cake pan or a large glass bowl, layer whipped cream on top of cake pieces, then layer strawberries, then layer of blueberries, then layer of pineapple with a layer of cake on top. Pour 1/4 cup of kirsch or brandy over all. Repeat layers. Pour remaining 1/4 cup brandy over all. Finish off with whipped cream on top. Garnish with fresh fruit. Refrigerate. *"Can be prepared early in day. Prettiest if arranged in large glass bowl."*

*See Honey Cake recipe page 219.

MARILYN LINDENAUER

Blueberry Ginger Crisp

1 cup unbleached all-purpose flour
1/8 teaspoon baking powder
2 tablespoons powdered ginger
1/4 cup sugar
1/4 cup brown sugar
2 tablespoons crystallized ginger, finely chopped
1/2 cup butter (at room temperature)
4 cups blueberries, frozen or fresh

Preheat oven to 375 degrees. Combine the first five ingredients together in a mixing bowl. Cut the crystallized ginger and butter into flour mixture until crumbly. Place blueberries in buttered 8 x 8-inch pan. Sprinkle the mixed ingredients on the top. Bake for 40 minutes. (Serves 6) *"Can be served with ice cream."*

KATHY CLARK

Cherry-Cheese Dessert Pizza

Pastry for 2-crust (9-inch) pie
1 (8-ounce) package cream cheese, softened
1/2 cup sugar
2 eggs
1/3 cup chopped walnuts
1 teaspoon vanilla
2 (1 pound 5-ounce) cans cherry pie filling*
Whipped cream or whipped cream cheese for topping

Preheat oven to 350 degrees. On lightly floured surface, roll pastry to 14-inch circle. Place in 12-inch pizza pan. Flute edges; prick crust. Bake for 15 minutes. Blend cream cheese and sugar in a mixing bowl. Add eggs and beat well. Add nuts and vanilla. Pour into partially baked crust and bake for 10 minutes more. Cool. Spread cherry pie filling over cheese layer. Chill. Top chilled pie with dollops of whipped cream cheese or whipped cream. To serve, cut into wedges. (Serves 10-12)

*Can also use blueberry pie filling with same delicious results.

AL MARTIN

Cherry Torte

2 cups red tart pitted cherries (drain and save juice)
1 cup all-purpose flour
1 tablespoon melted butter
1 teaspoon vanilla (or rum)
1-1/4 cups sugar
1 teaspoon baking soda
1 egg, beaten
1/2 cup chopped pecans
Dash of salt

Preheat oven to 350 degrees. Blend all ingredients together in a mixing bowl. Pour into greased springform pan. Bake for 40-50 minutes. Cool and remove from pan. Cut in wedges and serve with whipped cream or ice cream and top with cherry sauce. (8-10 servings)

CHERRY SAUCE:
1 cup drained cherry juice
1/2 cup sugar
1 tablespoon cornstarch
1 tablespoon butter
Red food coloring (optional)

Mix all ingredients together in a saucepan. Heat until sugar dissolves. Cool and serve with cake. (Serve same day as it is made.)

MARILYN LINDENAUER

Frozen Lemon Torte

MERINGUES:
5 egg whites (at room temperature)
3/4 cup sugar
Additional 1/2 cup sugar

Preheat oven to 250 degrees. In a mixing bowl beat egg whites with 3/4 cup sugar for 5-8 minutes until dull. Add additional 1/2 cup sugar. Make three 8-inch circles on parchment paper or greased and floured pans. Pipe the mixture into the pans and spread evenly with a pastry tube. Put in oven and bake 15 minutes. Turn off the heat, but allow it to remain in the oven for 4-5 hours or overnight.

LEMON CURD:
10 egg yolks
1/2 cup sugar
Juice of 4 lemons (3/4 cup)
1/2 cup butter
2 cups whipping cream, whipped

In a heavy (not aluminum) saucepan, put the egg yolks, sugar and lemon juice. Cook over medium heat, stirring constantly until it starts to boil. Then remove from heat. Add the stick of butter cut into pieces and stir until melted. Chill. Whip the heavy cream. Fold into chilled lemon curd. In a 9-inch springform pan, place 1 meringue. Put almost half of lemon curd on top. Spread. Place second meringue and rest of the cream. Press down slightly but do not break meringue. Add third meringue and put 3/4 of remaining cream mixture on top. If runny, chill for 30 minutes and try again. Spread over edges.
(Makes an 8-inch cake)

TOP:
White chocolate
Semisweet chocolate

Before completely set, scrape off feather of white chocolate and semisweet chocolate and completely cover cake top and sides. Freeze in plastic bag. Can be done weeks ahead. Take from freeezer about 1 hour before serving. *"A real favorite!"*

ARLENE ROCCHINI

Pear Tart

CRUST:
1-1/4 cups all-purpose flour
1/2 cup well-chilled butter
3 tablespoons heavy cream
1 tablespoon brown sugar
1/2 teaspoon ginger
1/4 teaspoon nutmeg
1/4 teaspoon salt
2 tablespoons brown sugar

Preheat oven to 375 degrees. Butter tart pan with removable bottom. Place all crust ingredients except last 2 tablespoons brown sugar, in food processor. Blend using on/off button for 30 seconds. Transfer 1/2 cup plus 2 tablespoons to small bowl for sprinkling on very top. Mix 2 tablespoons of brown sugar into remaining dough. Press rest of mixture into bottom and sides of pan. Bake 20 minutes.

FILLING:
3/4 cup sugar
1/3 cup cream
1/4 cup all-purpose flour
3 egg yolks
1 teaspoon lemon juice
3 large ripe pears (peeled and sliced in 1/4-inch pieces)

Combine filling ingredients, excluding pears, in food processor for 5-10 seconds. Pour custard into crust. Arrange pear slices over custard. Sprinkle with reserved crumb mixture. Bake 40 minutes or more until custard is set. May take longer if pears are very juicy. *"This should be served warm and is great with vanilla ice cream on top."*

SUSAN HURWITZ

DESSERTS

Raspberry Souffle and Sherry Custard Sauce

3/4 cup fresh raspberries
1 tablespoon lemon juice
Few grains of salt
2 tablespoons sugar
3 egg whites, beaten stiff
1 teaspoon butter
1 tablespoon sugar

Preheat oven to 325 degrees. Mix first 4 ingredients in food processor. Fold in egg whites. Butter 5-1/2 inch souffle dish and coat with sugar. Pour mixture into souffle dish and bake for 25 minutes. (2 servings)

SHERRY CUSTARD SAUCE:
1 cup Bird's Imported English Dessert Mix*
2 tablespoons sherry

Make dessert mix as directed on can and add sherry at end. Serve souffle with sauce separately.

*Bird's Sauce available at specialty stores such as Big 10 in Ann Arbor.

CAROLINE BLANE

Raspberry Torte

PASTRY DOUGH:
1/2 cup all-purpose flour
1/4 cup sugar
2 cups ground pecans or almonds or hazelnuts
1/2 cup margarine
1 egg white
1 teaspoon almond flavoring
1-2 tablespoons water

FILLING:
Raspberry jam

TOPPING:
1 (12-ounce) container Cool Whip

Preheat oven to 350 degrees. Combine dough ingredients sequentially in food processor or with a fork. Add 1-2 tablespoons of water until it makes a ball. (Reserve enough dough for lattice top.) Place in a pie pan or a quiche pan. Place a layer of raspberry jam. Decorate top with strips of dough. Add more jam between strips. (May use yellow or green jam for color.) Bake for 30 minutes. Serve cold with Cool Whip. (8 servings)

INTA ERTEL

*Bird's Sauce available at specialty stores such as Big 10 in Ann Arbor.

Preheat oven to 350 degrees. Combine dough ingredients sequentially in food processor or with a fork. Add 1-2 tablespoons of water until it makes a ball. (Reserve enough dough for lattice top.) Place in a pie pan or a quiche pan. Place a layer of raspberry jam. Decorate top with strips of dough. Add more jam between strips. (May use yellow or green jam for color.) Bake for 30 minutes. Serve cold with Cool Whip. (8 servings)

INTA ERTEL

Sour Cream Strawberry Shortcake

2 cups all-purpose flour
3 teaspoons baking powder
3/4 teaspoon salt
1/4 cup sugar
2 tablespoons butter
1 (3-ounce) package cream cheese, softened
1 egg, beaten
1/2 cup milk
1 quart fresh strawberries (washed, hulled and sliced)
1 cup sour cream (sweetened with 1/2 cup brown sugar) for top

Preheat oven to 450 degrees. Sift flour, baking powder, salt and sugar in a large mixing bowl. Add butter and cream cheese and blend until mixture is like coarse cornmeal. Pour beaten egg into measuring cup and add enough milk to make 3/4 cup. Stir into flour mixture. Knead about 20 seconds. Pat half of the dough into greased round 8-inch cake pan. Brush surface with 1-2 tablespoons melted butter. Pat remaining dough over the top. Bake for 20 minutes. Cool on rack. Split the layers. Place one on a plate. Spoon strawberries between layers of shortcake and on top. Sweeten sour cream with brown sugar and dollop!   SALLY JOHNSTON

Hot Fudge Sundae Cake

CRUST:
Half of 13-ounce package graham cracker crumbs
1/4 pound butter, melted

Pour cracker crumbs into a 9 x 13-inch pan. Add melted butter and mix well. Set aside 1/3 to 1/2 cup of this mixture for the topping. Pat crumb mixture over bottom of pan and bake 5 minutes at 350 degrees.

HOT FUDGE LAYER:
3 (1-ounce) squares unsweetened chocolate
1/2 cup butter or margarine
2 cups confectioners' sugar
3 eggs, beaten
1 teaspoon vanilla
1/2 cup broken walnuts (optional)
1/2 gallon vanilla ice cream, softened

In a double boiler melt the chocolate and butter over low heat, stirring constantly until mixture begins to boil. Remove from heat, add sugar and eggs, stir and let cool. Stir in vanilla and walnuts and pour over the crust. Spread softened ice cream over the hot fudge layer and add remaining crumbs to garnish. Freeze. Take out of the freezer when you serve dinner so it has thawed enough to cut. Best if made a day ahead of time. *"Easy and delicious. We make it often for large parties."*   BOB AND PATTI FORMAN

Amaretto Mousse

5 eggs, separated
1/2 cup sugar
Pinch of salt
1 teaspoon vanilla
1 cup milk
1 envelope unflavored gelatin
2 tablespoons cold water
1 pint heavy cream, whipped
4 ounces Amaretto liqueur
Additional tablespoon of Amaretto
Whipped cream
Toasted almonds

In a large mixing bowl beat the egg yolks and sugar until light and lemon-colored. Add salt and beat briefly. In a saucepan bring the vanilla and milk just to a boil; cool slightly. Dissolve gelatin in cold water. Add to milk mixture and strain, if necessary. Add milk mixture to beaten egg yolk and heat over low heat, stirring constantly. Do not boil. Mixture may begin to thicken. Cool mixture, preferably by placing a pan in a bowl of ice. When cooled, fold in whipped cream and then fold in egg whites, stiffly beaten. Add about 4 ounces of Amaretto. Chill in a pretty serving bowl or individual glasses. When ready to serve this, float a tablespoon or so of Amaretto on top, a little whipped cream and a sprinkling of toasted almonds. (6-8 servings) *"The most delicious dessert you have ever tasted."*

CAROL WILLIAMS

Colorado Strawberry Mousse

1/2 cup butter
1/4 cup brown sugar, packed
1/2 cup chopped nuts
1 cup all-purpose flour
2 egg whites
3/4 cup white sugar
2 tablespoons fresh lemon juice
1 (10-ounce) package frozen strawberries, slightly thawed
4 ounces Cool Whip

Preheat oven to 350 degrees. Melt butter in 9 x 13-inch pan in warm oven. Remove from oven and add brown sugar, nuts and flour. Mix well and spread evenly in pan. Return to oven and bake for 20 minutes. Stir occasionally to make crumbs. Cool. Beat egg whites at low speed until thick. Add white sugar, lemon juice, frozen strawberries and beat at high speed until stiff peaks form (about 10-12 minutes). Mix in Cool Whip. Pat 2/3 cup of the crumb mixture in bottom of the pan. Pour in mousse. Sprinkle with remaining crumbs. Freeze overnight. Keep uneaten portion frozen.

DIANE BAKER

Amaretto/Chocolate Mousse Cake
(Adapted from Amaretto di Saronno Company)

1 (6-ounce) package semisweet chocolate morsels
20 whole blanched almonds
1/2 cup Amaretto di Saronno
2 envelopes unflavored gelatin
1/4 cup water (may substitute Amaretto for water)
4 egg yolks (5 if small)
1/3 cup sugar
2 cups milk
4 egg whites, stiffly beaten (5 if small)
2 cups heavy cream, whipped
Shaved French bittersweet chocolate
2 (3-ounce) packages ladyfingers, split

Melt chocolate morsels in top of a double boiler. Stir until chocolate is melted. Dip bottom half of almonds into chocolate and place on wax paper. Chill until firm. (I freeze a large supply of these and use them as needed). Gradually stir Amaretto into remaining melted chocolate which you have removed from the stove. Set this aside. In a saucepan, combine gelatin and water (this is where I substitute more Amaretto). Stir in the egg yolks, sugar and milk. Stir over low heat until mixture thickens slightly (it will stick to a metal spoon). Stir in the chocolate mixture. Chill until mixture mounds (I cheat and put in the freezer for about 8 minutes before putting in the refrigerator). Fold in egg whites. Remove 1 cup of the whipped cream and set aside for decorating the top. Fold remaining cream into chocolate mixture. Add shaved French bittersweet chocolate. Chill until mixture mounds. Line the bottom and sides of an ungreased 9-inch springform pan with split ladyfingers. Gently pour in the chocolate mixture. Chill until firm, usually 6 hours minimum. Decorate top with the remaining whipped cream and the chocolate almonds. Remove sides from pan and serve. (Makes a 9-inch cake)

NIKKI WOODROW-RUSH

New Orleans Bread Pudding With Whiskey Sauce

1 loaf French Bread, torn into pieces
1 quart milk
3 eggs
2 cups sugar
2 tablespoons vanilla
1 cup raisins
3 tablespoons butter, melted

Preheat oven to 300 degrees. Soak bread in milk; crush with hands until well mixed. Then add eggs, sugar, vanilla and raisins and stir well. Pour butter into bottom of 9 x 13-inch pan and add pudding mixture; bake until very firm, about 1 hour. Let cool.

WHISKEY SAUCE:
1 cup sugar
1 egg
1/2 cup butter
1/2 cup whiskey (or to taste)

Cream sugar and egg until well mixed. Pour into small saucepan and add melted butter and continue to dissolve over low heat. Cool slightly. Add whiskey to taste which should make the sauce creamy smooth. When ready to serve, pour some sauce on the top of baked pudding and heat under broiler. Serve with remaining Whiskey Sauce on the side.

ANN BETZ

Almond and Rice Flour Custard

2 cups half-and-half cream
2 cups milk
1 cup blanched almonds, pulverized
3/4 cup sugar
1/2 teaspoon almond extract
1/4 cup rice flour
1/4 cup sliced almonds

In a large saucepan combine the cream, 1-1/2 cups milk, almonds, sugar and almond extract. Bring to boil, remove from heat, cover and let almonds steep for 20 minutes. Return almond-flavored liquid to saucepan. Dissolve rice flour in remaining 1/2 cup milk, stir it into the liquid and set over low heat. Simmer for 15 minutes, stirring frequently until custard thickens. Spoon into individual dessert bowls. Chill about 1 hour. Toast almonds in oven or in cast iron frying pan until lightly browned. Garnish custard with toasted almonds. (6 servings)

JANET GILSDORF

Carrot Pudding

1 cup grated suet
1/2 cup shortening, scant
1 cup brown sugar
1 cup raw carrots, grated
1 cup raw potatoes, grated
1 egg
1-1/2 cups all-purpose flour (plus possibly 2 tablespoons more)
1-1/2 teaspoons baking soda
1/2 teaspoon cinnamon
1/4 teaspoon cloves
1/2 teaspoon nutmeg
1 teaspoon salt
1 cup raisins
1 cup currants
1 cup mixed peel
1 teaspoon lemon extract
Nuts (optional)

Mix suet, shortening, brown sugar, carrots, potatoes and egg in a bowl. Add flour sifted with soda and spices and salt. Add fruits and lemon extract last. Steam in a mold or make 10 individual molds, about 3 hours for large mold, less for small ones.

ETHEL JOHNSTON

Doctored Chocolate Pudding

1 (5-1/8 ounce) package royal chocolate pudding
1 (13-ounce) can evaporated milk
Homogenized milk
2 eggs
1 teaspoon vanilla
Cool Whip

Pour the pudding mix in a saucepan. Combine the evaporated milk and regular milk to equal 3 cups. Add to pudding mix with the eggs. Cook over medium heat, stirring constantly until it boils. Stir in vanilla. Cool and layer in dessert dishes with Cool Whip. (4 servings)

MARY ELLEN BOTSFORD

257

Strawberry Bavarian Cream

2 envelopes unflavored gelatin
1/4 cup cold water or milk
1 (10-ounce) package frozen strawberries (or 1 pint fresh)
1/4 cup sugar
2 eggs
1 heaping cup crushed ice
1 cup heavy cream
Fresh strawberries

Soften gelatin in milk or water. Defrost frozen strawberries. (If using fresh, slice, hull, sprinkle with sugar and let sit for 1/2 hour.) Separate strawberries and juice. Add enough water to make 1/2 cup of liquid. Heat juice to simmering in a saucepan. Pour into blender with water and milk and gelatin. Blend 40 seconds. Add sugar and eggs. Blend 5 seconds. Add ice and cream. Blend 20 seconds. Pour into a pretty dish. Chill several hours. Garnish with fresh strawberries.

SALLY JOHNSTON

Zabaglione

9 egg yolks
3 tablespoons sugar
1/3 cup marsala wine
Strawberries
Ladyfingers (optional)
Light wafers (optional)

Beat egg yolks with sugar in a bowl until blended well. Put into double boiler and beat constantly while adding wine. Remove from heat as soon as the eggs coddle and the mixture still light and fluffy. (Do not overcook.) Top each portion with a slice of strawberry for color. Serve warm or very cold with ladyfingers or other light wafers. (6 servings)

TONIE LEEDS

Lemon Pudding

1 (3-ounce) package lemon gelatin
1-1/2 cups hot water
1 cup sugar
Rind and juice of 1 lemon
1 (12-ounce) can evaporated milk*
1/4 teaspoon salt
1 cup graham cracker crumbs

In a bowl combine the package of lemon gelatin, hot water and sugar. Let cool until it begins to congeal. Add grated lemon rind and juice. Whip the evaporated milk with salt until it forms a peak. Then put in the gelatin mixture and beat until it almost peaks. Have casserole dish lightly greased with butter. Dust with a small amount of graham cracker crumbs. Pour in pudding mixture and sprinkle 1 cup of cracker crumbs over all. Refrigerate. Can be cut out in squares to serve. (Serves 12) *"This delicious dessert, perfect in hot weather, was given to me by my grandmother, Zelma Douglass."*

*COOK'S TIP: 1/4 teaspoon salt added to milk will give a better flavor.

MARIGIM THOENE

Sauces and Dressings

SAUCES AND DRESSINGS

263-272

Heavenly Hot Fudge Sauce

1/2 cup butter or margarine
4 (1-ounce) squares unsweetened chocolate, melted
3 cups sugar
1 (14-1/2 ounce) can evaporated milk
1/2 teaspoon salt

Melt butter and chocolate in top of double boiler over simmering water. Add sugar, milk and salt and cook over low heat, stirring frequently for 20 minutes. (Makes 1 quart)

JAMES SKINNER

Helen's Chocolate Syrup

1 cup sugar
3 heaping tablespoons cocoa
3/4 cup milk
1 teaspoon vanilla

Mix first three ingredients well in a saucepan and bring to a boil, stirring constantly. Add vanilla and remove from heat in about one minute.

THOMAS SHOPE

Incredible Hot Fudge Sauce

1 cup heavy cream
3/4 cup butter
1-1/3 cups dark brown sugar (or more to taste)
1/3 cup sugar
1/2 cup plus 2 tablespoons light corn syrup
1 tablespoon vanilla
1 cup cocoa
1-2 tablespoons rum
Pinch of salt
1-2 squares unsweetened chocolate

Heat cream in a saucepan. Add butter and melt. Add sugars and stir to dissolve. Add corn syrup, vanilla and then strained cocoa. Stir in rum, salt and unsweetened chocolate. Simmer at low temperature until syrup reaches desired consistency. The longer it simmers, the thicker and gooier it becomes.

SUSAN HURWITZ

Chocolate Sauce

1/2 cup semisweet chocolate morsels
1 (5.3-ounce) can evaporated milk
1 cup sifted confectioners' sugar
1/4 cup butter

Combine all ingredients in a saucepan. Cook on low heat, stirring occasionally. Cool completely. Good on ice cream.

ANNA KELLY

Tangy Lemon Sauce

1/2 cup sugar
1 tablespoon cornstarch
1 cup water
Grated rind of 1 lemon
2 tablespoons lemon juice
2 tablespoons butter or margarine

Combine sugar and cornstarch in a medium-size saucepan; gradually add water, stirring until blended. Cook over medium heat, stirring constantly, until mixture thickens and boils 1 minute; remove from heat. Stir in lemon rind and juice and butter or margarine; cool.

ETHEL JOHNSTON

Sauce for Plum Pudding

1 cup sugar
1/2 cup butter
4 egg yolks, well-beaten
1 wine glass of wine or brandy
Pinch of salt
1 cup cream or rich milk

Cream together the sugar and butter. When light and creamy, add the well beaten egg yolks. Stir into the wine or brandy, salt and hot cream or milk. Beat this mixture well; place it in a saucepan over the fire, stir it until it cooks sufficiently to thicken like cream. (Be sure not to let it boil.)

MRS. W.F. CUENY

Dressing for Fruit

1 cup plain yogurt
1 tablespoon honey
1/4 cup flaked coconut
1 tablespoon sunflower seeds or chopped nuts

Combine all ingredients in a small bowl and serve with fruit of your choice. *"This dressing is also good combined with granola and eaten for a quick breakfast."*

ANN BETZ

Thousand Island Dressing

1 cup mayonnaise
1 teaspoon paprika
1/4 cup chili sauce
2 tablespoons vinegar
1/2 cup finely chopped celery
1/2 cup chopped green olives
2 tablespoons fresh parsley
3 chopped hard-boiled eggs

Blend all ingredients well and chill.

MARY WASKERWITZ
MARY ELLEN BOTSFORD

Easy Versatile Tomato Sauce

1/4 cup olive oil
1 large onion, finely chopped
1 clove garlic, finely minced
1 quart peeled, seeded and chopped fresh tomatoes
1 (6-ounce) can tomato paste
Salt and freshly ground pepper to taste
1 bay leaf
1 teaspoon basil, dried (or 1 tablespoon fresh, chopped)
1/2 teaspoon thyme
1/2 teaspoon oregano

Heat oil in a large saute pan. Saute onion and garlic in oil until tender. Add tomatoes, tomato paste, salt, pepper, bay leaf and basil. Bring to a boil and let simmer 20 minutes. Add thyme and oregano and simmer 5 minutes longer. *"Use as is over pasta or freeze for use as spaghetti sauce base at a later date. This is a great way to use extra tomatoes in the summer."*

SUSAN HURWITZ

Barbecue Sauce

1 medium onion, finely chopped
2 tablespoons butter or margarine
2 tablespoons vinegar
2 tablespoons dark brown sugar
1/4 cup lemon juice
1 cup ketchup
3 tablespoons Worcestershire sauce
1/2 tablespoon prepared mustard
1/2 cup water
1/2 cup chopped parsley

Cook onion in butter in a skillet until wilted. Add vinegar, brown sugar, lemon juice, ketchup, Worcestershire, mustard, water and parsley. Simmer 30 minutes or until sauce is thick. (Makes 1-1/2 to 2 cups) *"Use with chicken or spareribs. This is a great, tangy sauce without a fake smokey flavor."*

SUSAN HURWITZ

Best-Ever Barbecue Sauce

1 (12-ounce) can beer
2 (14-ounce) bottles ketchup
1 (12-ounce) bottle chili sauce
1/3 cup prepared mustard
1 tablespoon dry mustard
1-1/2 cups packed brown sugar
1 cup fresh lemon juice
1/2 cup bottled thick steak sauce
Dash of Tabasco sauce
1/4 cup Worcestershire sauce
1 tablespoon soy sauce
2 tablespoons salad oil
Minced garlic

Open can of beer about an hour before preparing to allow it to go flat. Mix all of the ingredients well in a large bowl and it is ready to serve. This also freezes well. (Makes 3 quarts)

ELEANOR MATTIS

Denver Barbecue Sauce

1 large onion (sliced thin, in rings)
1 cup chopped celery (large pieces)
2 tablespoons margarine (or oil)
1 cup ketchup
1 cup water
1 (8-ounce) can tomato sauce
1/8 teaspoon Tabasco sauce
2 tablespoons Worcestershire sauce
2 tablespoons brown sugar

In a large saucepan saute onion and celery in margarine or oil. Stir in remaining ingredients and simmer 10 minutes.

MARY WASKERWITZ

Marinade I

1-1/2 cups salad oil
3/4 cup soy sauce
1/4 cup Worcestershire sauce
2 tablespoons dry mustard
2-1/4 teaspoons salt
1 tablespoon coarse ground black pepper
1/2 cup wine vinegar
1-1/2 teaspoons dried parsley flakes
2 cloves garlic, minced
1/3 cup lemon juice

Combine all ingredients and mix well. Use to marinate chicken, beef or venison. Especially works well with a chuck roast. Marinate 4-8 hours, then barbeque. Store in covered jar in refrigerator. Keeps 3-4 months. (Makes 3-1/2 cups)

SANDRA MERKEL

Marinade II

3/4 cup oil
1/4 cup soy sauce
1/4 cup honey
2 tablespoons vinegar
2 tablespoons chopped green onion
1 clove garlic, minced
1-1/2 teaspoons ginger

Mix all ingredients together in a bowl. Marinate meat for several hours or overnight. Then grill or broil the meat. *"Great marinade for flank steak."*

PHYLLIS ASKEW

267

Marinade for London Broil

2 teaspoons salad oil
1 teaspoon wine vinegar
1/2 onion, chopped
1 clove garlic, minced
1/4 teaspoon rosemary
1/4 teaspoon basil
1/2 teaspoon black pepper
1 teaspoon salt
1-1/2 to 2 pounds flank steak

Combine oil, vinegar and seasonings in a shallow pan. Let steak stand in mixture for at least 2 hours. Broil for 5 minutes, turn and brush with remaining marinade and broil another 4 minutes. Slice steak diagonally across the grain as thin as possible. Spoon pan juices over meat. (4-6 servings)

ROSWITHA BIRD

Marinade for Flank Steak

1 cup consomme
1/3 cup soy sauce
1-1/2 teaspoons Accent
1/4 cup green onions, chopped
1 clove garlic, minced
3 tablespoons lemon juice
2 tablespoons brown sugar
2 pounds flank steak

Combine all ingredients for marinade in a mixing bowl. Place flank steak in pan and pour marinade over it. Marinate overnight and cook over hot coals or broil. Heat marinade and serve as sauce. (4 servings)

JUDY MOYER

Mustard Sauce

1 cup brown sugar
1 tablespoon all-purpose flour
3 eggs
1/4 cup dry mustard
1/2 cup vinegar
1 beef bouillon cube

Heat sugar, flour, eggs and mustard in a medium saucepan. Add vinegar; stir slow until thick. Dissolve beef bouillon cube in a little hot water and add to sauce. Use less mustard and vinegar if you don't want it too hot. *"Excellent accompaniment to any kind of meat."*

LIL JOHNSTON

Jezebel Sauce

1 (18-ounce) jar pineapple preserves
1 (18-ounce) jar apple jelly
1 (2-ounce) can dry mustard
1 (5-ounce) jar horseradish

In a large bowl mix all the ingredients together well. Divide the sauce in jars and refrigerate. Serve the sauce as an accompaniment to ham, pork, roast beef or as an appetizer over Philadelphia cream cheese. (Makes 1 quart)

ANN BETZ

Tomato Pudding

1 (12-ounce) can tomato puree
1/3 cup boiling water
1 cup light brown sugar
1/4 teaspoon salt
2 cups fresh white 1-inch square bread cubes
1/4 pound butter, melted

Preheat oven to 325 degrees. In a saucepan bring tomato puree, boiling water, sugar and salt to boil. Reduce heat and simmer 5 minutes. Place bread cubes in 1-1/2 quart casserole. Pour melted butter over cubes and lightly toss. Pour hot tomato mixture over the bread cubes and toss again. Bake, covered, for 45 minutes. *"A good side-dish for roast beef or other meats."*

ELIZABETH STONE

Pear-Ginger Conserve for Roast Pork

1 tablespoon fresh ginger, finely minced
Zest of 1 orange, shredded
Zest of 1 lemon, shredded
1/3 cup dry white wine
3/4 cup honey
Juice of 1 lemon
Juice of 1 orange
4 firm pears (peeled, cored and coarsely chopped)
1/3 cup pecan or black walnut meats, chopped

In a medium saucepan combine ginger, orange, lemon zest and wine. Cook for 5 minutes until peel is tender. Add honey and fruit juices and stir. Add pears and cook until tender (not mushy), about 10 minutes. Add nutmeats. Store in refrigerator or pour into half-pint jars and process in boiling water bath for 10 minutes. (Makes 2 pints)

JANET GILSDORF

Native American Cranberry Sauce

1-1/2 cups pure maple syrup
1/2 cup water
1 teaspoon fresh ginger, peeled and minced
4 cups fresh cranberries

Bring syrup, water and ginger to boil in a heavy, 2-1/2 quart saucepan over medium heat. Stir in cranberries. Simmer until berries begin to pop, about 5 minutes, stirring occasionally. Turn into bowl and let cool. May be refrigerated up to 3 days. (Makes 4 cups) *"Serve with baked turkey or duck."*

JANET GILSDORF

Chunky Chutney

1-1/2 cups vinegar
2-1/2 cups sugar
1 tablespoon salt
1 (3-inch) stick cinnamon
2 tablespoons mustard seed
8 whole cloves
2 cups chopped and peeled tomatoes
2 cups chopped tart apples
1 cup chopped onion
1 cup chopped green pepper
1 cup chopped celery
2 tablespoons chopped red pepper
Cornstarch

Combine vinegar, sugar, salt, cinnamon, mustard seed and cloves in a Dutch oven or stockpot; bring to rapid boil. Add rest of ingredients and simmer for 30-40 minutes; thicken with cornstarch. Pour into hot sterilized jars. (Makes 2 pints)

JEAN WIETING

Walnut-Cilantro Chutney

3 bunches cilantro, fresh
3/4 cup chopped walnuts
1/2 to 3/4 cup white vinegar
1/2 cup sugar
1/2 teaspoon garlic powder
1/2 teaspoon cayenne pepper
Salt to taste

Place all ingredients in a food processor and process. Cover and chill in refrigerator for at least 3 hours to blend flavors. *"Keeps in refrigerator for months. Excellent served with chicken or pork, or with steamed fresh green beans or cauliflower."*

JANET GILSDORF

Sausage Stuffing for Turkey

2 (7-ounce) packages sage-seasoned croutons
1 pound mild Italian sausage, browned and drained of fat
3 tablespoons butter, melted
1 cup onion, chopped
1-1/2 cups celery, diced
1/2 cup green pepper, chopped
1-1/2 teaspoons salt
1 teaspoon tarragon
2-1/2 to 3 cups chicken broth

Combine all ingredients in a very large mixing bowl. Stuff turkey and bake. (Enough stuffing for a 12-14 pound turkey)

LORRIS BETZ

Wild Rice and Hazelnut Stuffing for Turkey

2 (8-ounce) cans sliced water chestnuts, drained
1 medium onion, coarsely chopped
1-1/2 tablespoons butter
1-1/2 tablespoons hazelnut oil*
1/2 cup toasted hazelnuts, chopped
4 tablespoons chopped parsley, fresh
Salt and pepper to taste
1 teaspoon summer savory, dried
3 cups cooked wild rice

In a small skillet saute water chestnuts and onion in butter and oil until onion is soft. Mix with remaining ingredients in a large bowl. Stuff the turkey and bake. (Enough for a 12-pound turkey)

*COOK'S TIP: Can substitute 3 tablespoons butter rather than butter and hazelnut oil.

JANET GILSDORF

Ann Arbor Restaurant Recipes

From: Afternoon Delight, Ann Arbor, MI

Clam Chowder

2 tablespoons margarine
2/3 cup celery, finely diced
3/4 cup onion, finely diced
2 cups diced soup potatoes, well-scrubbed
2-1/2 cups hot water
1 ounce clam base
Pinch of thyme
Pinch of garlic base or granulated garlic
1/2 teaspoon salt
Pinch of white pepper
2-3 cups hot water
7 ounces chopped clams with juice
1 carrot, peeled and grated
1-1/4 cups milk
1/2 cup half-and-half cream
Roux of 1/2 cup butter and 1/2 cup flour

Saute celery and onion in the margarine. Add potatoes and water. Simmer for half an hour and add clam base, thyme, garlic, salt, pepper and hot water. Simmer for 15 minutes and add clams and carrot. Simmer 15 minutes and add milk and water. Heat through until simmering point. Thicken chowder with the roux.

From: Afternoon Delight, Ann Arbor, MI

Peanut Butter Pie

2 ounces cream cheese
1 cup sifted confectioners' sugar
1/3 cup half-and-half cream
1 teaspoon vanilla
1 cup peanut butter
1-1/2 cups whipping cream
Chocolate cookie or graham cracker crust

Using electric mixer combine cream cheese, sugar, cream, vanilla and peanut butter. Chill a small bowl and beaters in freezer. Whip the cream until very stiff. Add one-third of the whipped cream to the peanut butter mixture and fold into remaining whipped cream. Spoon into chocolate cookie or graham cracker crust and chill at least 2 hours. *(We use the chocolate crusts and serve the pie with hot fudge and whipping cream. Chopped Spanish peanuts are also a nice garnish.)* (Makes 1 pie)

RACHEL C. SAFFER,
KITCHEN MANAGER

From: Angelo's Lunch, Ann Arbor, MI

Raisin Bread

3 pounds flour
3 eggs
1/4 pound sugar
2 tablespoons Crisco shortening
2 tablespoons salt
1/4 pound cake yeast
3 cups water
1-1/2 pounds raisins

Combine the above ingredients in a bowl and mix together. Transfer batter to tabletop and knead by hand for 20 minutes. Let rise for 20 minutes. Cut and shape into loaves, let rise for another 20 minutes. Place the loaves on a greased pan (cookie sheet is fine) and bake at 350 degrees for 1 hour 20 minutes. *Angelo recommends changing the position of the bread in the oven every 20 minutes. You may want to vary the amount of water in the recipe to keep the batter dense and heavy.* (This recipe is for 4 healthy sized loaves.)

From: Argiero's Italian Restaurant, Ann Arbor, MI

Fettuccine Al Burro

3 ounces melted butter
7 ounces grated Parmesan and Romano cheeses, mixed
Dash of salt
1/2 teaspoon garlic powder
1/4 to 1/2 teaspoon nutmeg
Chopped parsley
12 ounces fettuccine noodles
Parmesan cheese

Boil pasta for 10-12 minutes (or al dente). Measure remaining ingredients into a large bowl. Drain pasta but leave moist (keep a few tablespoons of hot water for the sauce). Stir wet pasta into sauce ingredients. Add extra hot water if you like a thinner sauce. Serve hot with added Parmesan cheese on top. (Serves 2-3)

ROSE ARGIERO

From: Barton Hills Country Club, Ann Arbor, MI

Sherry Black Bean Soup

4 cups rough garnish (mixture of carrots, onions, celery, leeks)
2 tablespoons bacon grease
2-1/2 pounds black beans
1-1/2 teaspoons sage
3/4 teaspoon black pepper
2 tablespoons beef base
1-1/2 teaspoons garlic
3/4 teaspoon marjoram
2 bay leaves
2 tablespoons ham base
1 gallon ham stock
1-1/2 cups sherry
3/4 teaspoon sugar
1-1/2 teaspoons M.S.G.

Saute rough garnish with bacon grease and add all ingredients. Simmer 45 minutes or until beans are soft. Strain with food mill and adjust taste. (Yields 5 quarts)

From: Barton Hills Country Club, Ann Arbor, MI

Manhattan Clam Chowder

1 cup leeks
1 cup onions
1 cup celery
1 cup green peppers
1 (28-ounce) can diced tomatoes
2 (6-1/2 ounce) cans chopped clams
1 quart diced potatoes
6 ounces salt pork
1 tablespoon clam base
3 quarts fish stock
3/4 teaspoon thyme (spice bag)
3/4 teaspoon savory (spice bag)
2 bay leaves (spice bag)
3/4 teaspoon garlic
2 tablespoons sugar
3/4 teaspoon Worcestershire sauce
1-1/2 teaspoons M.S.G.
Arrowroot
1/2 cup sweet butter

Saute vegetables with salt pork. Dust with flour and add rest of ingredients. Simmer 20 to 25 minutes and bind with arrowroot. Finish off with sweet butter. (Yields 6 quarts)   CHEF LUNDY

277

From: Cottage Inn Cafe, Ypsilanti, MI

Pelagos Pizza

BASIC DOUGH:
2 cups (2/3 ounce) compressed fresh yeast or 2 packages dry yeast
1/2 cup lukewarm water
7 cups bread flour (all-purpose flour, optional)
1-1/2 cups water
2 teaspoons salt
2 tablespoons clover honey
4 tablespoons olive oil

Dissolve yeast in water and let rest for 10 minutes. Add 1 cup of flour to form a soft starter dough. Cover with a cloth and allow to work for about an hour. Add 1-1/2 cups water and the salt, honey and olive oil; blend well. Begin adding the flour, one cup at a time, until the dough becomes too stiff to stir. Knead in the remaining flour for 10 minutes or more till a smooth and elastic dough is achieved. Divide the dough into six portions, cover with a cloth to rise again. Allow to double in size. Now punch them down and knead each into a circle. Press the circle into a flat (1/8 inch thick) pizza with a raised rim about 8 inches in diameter. (Yields approximately six 8-inch pizzas)

PESTO SAUCE:
1 cup fresh basil leaves (compacted)
6 cloves garlic
Kosher salt
3/4 cup olive oil
3 tablespoons Peccorino Romano
3 tablespoons Parmesan
3 tablespoons pine nuts

Crush basil leaves and garlic in a food processor with a pinch of kosher salt (to preserve green color of basil). Add oil in small amounts to puree and finally add cheese and pine nuts. Process until smooth and consistent.

TOPPINGS:
6 ounces Italian Fontina cheese, shredded
6 ounces whole milk Mozzarella (buffalo) shredded
6 fresh (or 2 cans) pear tomatoes
1 pound or 36 bay prawns (peeled and deveined, split, cooked)
6 ounces Bucheron (goat's milk) cheese, whipped
Sprigs of fresh tarragon (optional)

Brush the pizza circles with olive oil and garlic and bake half-way in a 400 degree oven. Top with pesto sauce, Fontina and Mozzarella cheese, tomatoes, prawns, and piped goat's cheese. Bake until done and garnish with sprigs of tarragon.

PATRICK PIERSON, CHEF

From: Cousins Heritage Inn, Dexter, MI

"These recipes are designed for the average American family who watch the price of the meat they are buying. They are tested and proven recipes that have delighted some of Detroit's elite epicureans."

Braised Short Ribs With Mushrooms

6 (12-ounce) short ribs, rough chop
2 tablespoons bacon fat (or oil of preference)
Salt and black pepper, crushed or ground
2 white or Spanish onions, rough chop
2 carrots, rough chop
2 celery stalks
1 cup Burgundy wine (or chicken stock, meat broth or water)
1 teaspoon thyme
2 tablespoons butter
1/4 pound mushrooms, quartered

Preheat oven to 400 degrees. In smoking hot pan or on grill outdoors to avoid smoke indoors, sear (brown) meat with salt and pepper in fat. This is a very important step. You must brown the meat well (almost char) to get that steak flavor and seal in juices. Cook 3 pieces at a time if pan is not large or the volume of meat will cool the pan down and you will get a boil instead of a sear. After browning remove meat and set into roasting pan. Immediately add vegetables and more fat into pan. Stir till brown or glazed, meaning the sugars in the onions are carmelized. If they start to turn black, add more fat and reduce flame a bit. Add browned veggies to roasting pan. If you have a nice brown glaze on your pan, put into it a cup of Burgundy wine or chicken stock, or water, or a cup of any meat/ham broth. Over heat the liquid will lift the glaze off the pan. This is a great concentration of flavor. Pour this liquid over the beef. Sprinkle with thyme. Cover and set roasting pan in oven for 1/2 hour, then reduce to 300 degrees. In 3 hours reduce heat to 275 degrees. If you braise meat over 300 degrees, you will cut into a dry pulpy boring meat. Meat is done when fork easily breaks it apart just by a twist. Once again, deglaze the roasting pan saving all the savory juices. Set meat aside and pull out bones. Put bones and juices into a small pot. Simmer 5-10 minutes. Strain stock into a saucepan. Take grease off of strained stock by skimming top. Bring stock to a boil. Add mushrooms. Whisk in some butter and adjust salt and pepper. You should have just enough sauce to cover the meat. Too much means a weak body sauce; too little calls for a little water or other stock. Set meat on plate and pour over sauce with mushrooms. The work is worth it if you live to eat.

GREG UPSHUR, CHEF

From: Cousins Heritage Inn, Dexter, MI

Red Bean Dip for Mexican Chips

1 cup cooked red beans
1 onion, chopped
1 green pepper, chopped
Butter
Cayenne
1 tablespoon lemon juice
1 teaspoon Tabasco
4 ounces bleu cheese
2 tablespoons olive oil
1 teaspoon cumin

Saute cooked beans with onions and green pepper in butter till brown. Put into food processor with all other ingredients. Puree. Adjust seasoning to taste. Serve with Mexican chips.

GREG UPSHUR, CHEF

From: Cousins Heritage Inn, Dexter, MI

Apple Pancakes

4 apples
3 eggs
1/2 cup wheat flour
Salt
Cinnamon
Pinch of baking powder
Sugar or syrup for top

Grate or chop apples in a food processor. Squeeze out excess juice. Put apples into a mixing bowl. Mix with eggs. Combine flour, salt, cinnamon and baking powder. Add to apples. Stir all ingredients together. Beat lightly with spoon. If mixture is still developing pools of juice, add more flour. Melt 2 tablespoons of vegetable shortening in hot pan so that melted shortening is one inch deep. Drop 1 heaping tablespoon of batter at a time and press in pan. (Thinner the better.) After they are cooked, sprinkle with sugar. (Enough for 3) *"Easy and fast. For a lazy morning."*

GREG UPSHUR, CHEF

From: Cousins Heritage Inn, Dexter, MI

Mashed Potatoes

5 medium-size potatoes, washed and quartered
1 teaspoon salt (or to taste)
1 tablespoon butter (more or less according to diet and taste)
Chives
Parsley

Set potatoes into just enough water to cover. Bring to a boil, then simmer, almost steeping, till very tender. (I don't cook with salt in water. Salt will toughen the skin. Boiling will make a gluey potato.) Strain water off. Whip potatoes with butter and salt. Addition of garden herbs (chives, parsley) will enhance the flavor. *"When cooking at home for the family, I am more concerned with utilization than with cosmetics of the food. The skin of the potato contains most of the vitamins and minerals. The fiber is best for growing children."*

GREG UPSHUR, CHEF

From: Dominick's Restaurant, Ann Arbor, MI

Italian Fried Rice

2 eggs
1/2 pound Italian sausage
3 large garlic cloves, chopped
2 celery stalks, chopped
6 medium mushrooms, sliced
2 scallions, cut into 1/4-inch pieces
1 teaspoon red crushed pepper
4 tablespoons pimentos, chopped
8 ounces frozen peas
4 tablespoons Progresso olive oil
4 cups cooked cold rice
Salt and pepper to taste

In an 8-inch fry pan, prepare 2 one-egg omelets, cut into thin strips 1 inch long. Set aside. Remove sausage from casing or use bulk. Saute and set aside. Add garlic and celery. Saute until transparent. Add mushrooms, scallions and red crushed pepper. Saute 3 minutes; add pimentos and peas, cook 2 minutes. Remove from pan, set aside. In same pan, add oil, fry cold rice until golden; add sausage to rice; stir until blended. Add vegetables, stir while cooking until blended. Serve on large platter and decorate outside rim of dish. (Serves 4-6)

MARY LABREQUE

From: Dough Boys Bakery, Ann Arbor, MI

Chocolate Madeleines

Marcel Proust immortalized these plain French sweets in Swann's Way when he wrote of them evocatively in a poetic passage that begins: "...my Mother, seeing that I was cold, offered me some tea... She sent out for one of these short, plump little cakes called 'petit madeleines', which look as though they had been molded in the fluted scallop of a pilgrim's shell. And soon... I raised to my lips a spoonful of the tea in which I had soaked a morsel of the cake."

2 eggs, separated
1/2 cup sugar
1/2 cup Dutch cocoa
1/2 cup sifted all-purpose flour
1 teaspoon baking powder
1 pinch salt
4 ounces sweet butter, melted
1 tablespoon rum (or rum flavoring)

Beat egg yolks, sugar and cocoa together. Fold in flour, baking powder, salt, then incorporate butter and rum. Whisk egg whites until stiff and fold in. Brush molds with butter and fill each shell two-thirds full. Bake in 425 degree oven for about 10-15 minutes until risen and firm. (Yields 22-24).

Note: Plain madeleines can be made by using 1 cup sifted all-purpose flour and 1 teaspoon vanilla or 1 teaspoon grated lemon rind in addition to the rum (or rum flavoring); sugar should be increased to 1 cup and butter to 3/4 cup.

Granita di Caffe
(Coffee Ice)

1 cup water
1/2 cup sugar
2 cups strong espresso coffee

In a 2-quart saucepan, bring the water and sugar to a boil over moderate heat, stirring only until the sugar dissolves. Timing from the moment the sugar and water begin to boil, cook for exactly 5 minutes. Immediately remove the pan from the heat and let the syrup cool to room temperature. Stir in the espresso coffee. Pour the mixture into an ice-cube tray from which the divider has been removed. Freeze the granita for 3-4 hours, stirring it every 30 minutes and scraping into it the ice particles that form around the edges of the tray. The finished granita should have a fine, snowy texture. For a coarser texture that is more to the Italian taste, leave the ice-cube divider in the tray and freeze the granita solid. Then remove the cubes and crush them in an ice crusher. (Makes about 1-1/2 pints)   DONI LYSTRA, OWNER/PARTNER

From: Dough Boys Bakery, Ann Arbor, MI

Ladyfingers

2 tablespoons butter, softened
1/4 cup flour
2 eggs
5 egg yolks
1/2 cup sugar
1 cup all-purpose flour, sifted before measuring
1 teaspoon double-acting baking powder
1 teaspoon vanilla extract
1/4 teaspoon finely grated lemon peel
1/2 cup confectioners' sugar, sifted

Preheat oven to 450 degrees. With a pastry brush or paper towel, coat the bottom and sides of two 12-mold ladyfinger tins or 2 large baking sheets with the softened butter. Sprinkle the 1/4 cup of flour into the pans and tip them from side to side to spread evenly. Then invert the pans and rap them sharply on a table to remove the excess flour. Warm a large mixing bowl in hot water and dry quickly but thoroughly. Drop in the eggs and egg yolks, add the sugar and beat with a whisk or a rotary or electric beater until the mixture is thick, pale yellow and has almost tripled in volume. (With an electric mixer, this will take 10-15 minutes; with a whisk or rotary beater, it may take as long as 25-30 minutes.) Sift the flour and baking powder over the eggs a little at a time, gently but thoroughly folding them together with a rubber spatula as you proceed. When all the flour has been absorbed, fold in the vanilla and lemon peel. Scoop the batter into a large pastry bag fitted with a 1/2-inch plain tip and pipe it into the molds or onto the baking sheets in strips about 3-1/2 inches long and 2 inches apart. Sprinkle the ladyfingers evenly with the 1/2 cup of confectioners' sugar and bake in the middle and upper third of the oven for about 5 minutes, or until the ladyfingers are a delicate gold color and slightly crusty on top. With a spatula, gently transfer the ladyfingers to cake racks to cool. (Makes about 24 four-inch-long ladyfingers)

DONI LYSTRA,
OWNER/PARTNER

From: The Earle, Ann Arbor, MI

Smoked Salmon Mousse

**Oiled and parchment lined 5-cup loaf pan
3/4 ounce gelatin
1/4 cup water
12 ounces smoked salmon (skinned and boned)
1/4 cup lemon juice
2-1/2 cups whipping cream
1/2 cup scallions, sliced
2 teaspoons Kosher salt
1/4 teaspoon white pepper
1/2 teaspoon Tabasco sauce
3 bunches watercress leaves**

Sprinkle gelatin over cold water. Allow to soften. Heat gently to dissolve. Cut salmon in 1/2-inch cubes; puree till smooth with lemon juice, push through fine sieve. Whip cream to soft peaks. Add gelatin; fold into salmon mixture, with other ingredients. Pack into mold, smooth top. Refrigerate at least 5 hours before unmolding. To unmold, rub warm towel around the outside of pan. Invert and shake loose. (12 servings)

CHEF SHELLEY CAUGHEY

From: The Earle, Ann Arbor, MI

Gateau De Mousse au Chocolat

**10 ounces Baker's chocolate
10 ounces butter, unsalted
8 egg whites
Pinch of cream of tartar
10 egg yolks
1-1/2 cups granulated sugar**

Preheat oven to 350 degrees. Melt chocolate and butter gently over hot water; stir frequently. Remove when almost melted. Beat egg whites and cream of tartar to form stiff peaks. Set aside. Beat egg yolks and sugar to ribbon stage. Blend chocolate into yolk mixture. Fold in egg whites in three parts. Pour two-thirds of mixture into buttered and sugared 6-inch springform pan. Bake till just set. Frost cake when cool with remaining one-third of batter.

CHEF SHELLEY CAUGHEY

From: Escoffier, Ann Arbor, MI

Caesar Salad

2 cloves garlic
6-9 anchovy fillets
1/2 lemon
1/4 teaspoon dry mustard
1 egg yolk
1/2 cup olive oil
2 tablespoons red wine vinegar
4 drops Tabasco sauce
2 drops Worcestershire sauce
2 heads Romaine lettuce
Grated Parmesan cheese
Freshly grated pepper to taste

Mash the garlic in a wooden salad bowl with two forks. Using a wooden salad spoon rub the crushed garlic around the bowl, scrape out the garlic pieces. Mash the anchovies with two forks until there is a paste. Squeeze the lemon and add the mustard. Mash all together with the salad spoon. Add the egg yolk and blend. Pour in the oil and vinegar and the rest of the seasonings and mix. Break the lettuce into the bowl and add the grated cheese and mix. Serve with fresh bread croutons.

PETER RASMUSSEN, CHEF

From: Escoffier, Ann Arbor, MI

Creme Caramel

8 eggs (6 yolks and 2 whole eggs)
1 pint whipping cream
1 pint half-and-half cream
1/2 teaspoon vanilla
1 tablespoon sugar
Additional 1/2 cup sugar
4-5 tablespoons water

Mix the eggs, whipping cream, half and half, vanilla and sugar together. Set aside. Put 1/2 cup of sugar in a saucepan and carmelize it over a medium flat. Take off of the stove and add water and blend. Pour into a mold and chill. Add the first mixture and place in a water bath in the oven and bake for 60 minutes at 300 degrees. Chill and serve.

PETER RASMUSSEN, CHEF

From: Escoffier, Ann Arbor, MI

White Chocolate Mousse

4 eggs
1 cup sugar
1 pint whipping cream
1/2 pound white chocolate

Separate the eggs. Whip the egg whites with 1/2 cup of sugar until stiff and place them in a large bowl. Whip the egg yolks with 1/2 cup of sugar for 5-6 minutes and add them to the egg whites. Whip the cream until stiff and add them to the eggs. Chop the chocolate in small chunks and add. Fold everything together and serve topped with Raspberry Sauce.

RASPBERRY SAUCE:
2 pints fresh raspberries
1/2 cup sugar
2 tablespoons cornstarch
1/2 cup water

Bring all ingredients to a boil. Chill and serve. (Serves 8)

PETER RASMUSSEN, CHEF

From: Gandy Dancer, Ann Arbor, MI

Charley's Chowder Soup

3 ounces olive oil
3 medium cloves garlic, smashed
4 ounces onions, chopped fine
"Titch" each of oregano, basil and thyme
3 ounces celery, chopped fine
6 ounces stewed tomatoes, chopped fine
1 gallon water
2 pounds boneless fish (pollack or turbo)
3 ounces clam base (may substitute clam juice)
1 ounce parsley, chopped fine
Salt to taste

Place olive oil in a large pot, heat until very hot. Drop in the smashed garlic cloves. Cook the cloves until golden. Important that you do not burn the garlic as this will ruin the taste. Remove the cloves from the oil. Add the onions and cook for a minute or two. Add the basil, oregano and thyme and cook for another minute. Add the celery and cook until translucent. Add the tomatoes and cook for about 45 minutes or until oil appears above tomatoes. Add water, fish, clam base and cook for 1/2 hour uncovered at full heat. Reason for this is to remove moisture and concentrated fish bacteria and to extract oils for flavoring the chowder. Add salt, cover the pot and keep cooking for another 1 hour at low heat. Stir often to break up fish and blend flavor. Garnish with parsley. When chowder is finished, remove any excess oils that may come to the surface.

From: The Gourmet's Goose, Ann Arbor, MI

American Curried Shrimp

30 jumbo shrimp (devein and break off shell leaving the tail shell on)
24 large Thompson seedless grapes
3 oranges (peeled, seeded and quartered to total 24 pieces)
12 (6-inch) skewers*

MARINADE:
3 tablespoons Silver Palate American Curried Mustard**
1 cup walnut oil (Silver Palate preferred)**
1/2 cups Oriental soy sauce**
Juice and zest of 1 orange
Juice and zest of 1 lemon
1-1/2 tablespoons honey
1 teaspoon chopped dried red pepper**
2-3 cloves garlic (peeled and chopped)
1 teaspoon top quality Indian curry powder**

Combine the ingredients for the marinade and add the shrimp to this mixture.
Let the shrimp soak at room temperature for 3 hours or overnight in the
refrigerator turning frequently. Slide 1 grape onto one of the skewers. Slide a
shrimp, then an orange section onto the skewer. Add another orange section
and finish with a grape. Repeat process on remaining skewers. Brush kebobs,
including fruit, with the marinade. Broil over coals or in an oven. If broiling in
the oven, cook 3 minutes on each side, 5 inches from the heating element, and
baste with marinade when you turn them over. If cooking over coals, make
sure the coals are red hot and covered with grey ashes. Depending on your fire,
the kebobs take approximately 12 minutes to cook. Turn them and baste
frequently. Do not overcook! Delicious served on a bed of long grain white
rice seasoned with fresh chopped ginger and parsley, Oriental soy sauce and
butter. (Serves 6)

*Disposable wooden skewers are available in most Oriental groceries and are
fine for cooking over coals. I've found, however, the exposed ends blacken
under the broiler so I use metal skewers in my oven. Soaking wooden skewers
in water before "stringing" reduces chances of blackening.

**Ingredients available at "The Gourmet's Goose".

PEGGY DE PARRY

From: The Gourmet's Goose, Ann Arbor, MI

Artichoke and Green Peppercorn Sauce for Pasta

1 cup olive oil, divided
1 egg
1 tablespoon Pommery or Dijon mustard
2 teaspoons raw green peppercorns, rinsed
1-2 cloves garlic
Juice of 1/2 lemon
2-3 drops hot red pepper sauce
Pinch cayenne pepper
Pinch sea salt or regular salt
1 cup quartered canned or fresh cooked artichoke hearts

In blender container, combine one-fourth cup of the olive oil, egg, mustard, peppercorns, garlic, lemon juice, hot pepper sauce, cayenne and salt. Blend or process until smooth. With blender or processor going, pour in remaining olive oil slowly, in a steady stream, until mixture is emulsified. Add artichokes, and blend or process, with on and off turns, until artichoke is coarsely chopped but not pureed. Serve over hot pasta, as a sauce for steak or as a vegetable dip. (Makes about 2 cups of sauce, enough for one pound of pasta)

"This is a sauce I came up with before opening the shop and it's been a big hit at the store for the four years we've been open."
PEGGY DE PARRY

From: The Gourmet's Goose, Ann Arbor, MI

Rotini With Pumate and Peas

1 pound rotini pasta*
1 medium onion
2 tablespoons butter plus 2 tablespoons olive oil
1 cup frozen peas
1/3 cup sun-dried tomatoes* (Pumate)
1/3 cup extra virgin olive oil*
1/3 cup balsamic vinegar*
Salt and pepper to taste

Cook pasta 5-7 minutes, drain well and set aside. Saute onions in 2 tablespoons olive oil and 2 tablespoons butter until very tender and translucent (about 15-20 minutes). Add peas and tomatoes to saute pan and heat all ingredients 1 minute longer. Turn off heat, toss pasta, oil, vinegar and salt and pepper to taste. Transfer to serving dish.

*Available at "The Gourmet's Goose".
PEGGY DE PARRY

289

RESTAURANT RECIPES

From: The Gourmet's Goose, Ann Arbor, MI

Tabbouleh

3/4 cup cracked wheat
1 cup parsley, firmly packed
1/2 cup fresh mint, loosely packed or 1 tablespoon dried
2 stalks celery, strings removed
8 green onions
3 medium tomatoes, peeled, seeded, quartered
1/2 cup sunflower seeds, dry roasted
3 tablespoons oil
2 tablespoons fresh lemon juice
1 teaspoon cumin
1 teaspoon coriander
1-1/2 teaspoons salt
Freshly ground pepper
Spinach leaves
Cherry tomatoes (garnish)

Place wheat in a small bowl, cover with hot water and let stand for 30 minutes; drain and set aside. Place parsley and mint in dry work bowl and mince with on/off turns. Transfer to mixing bowl. Place celery in work bowl and mince using on/off turns. Add to parsley. Place onions in compact grouping in feed tube and slice using light pressure. Add to parsley mixture. Place tomatoes in work bowl and chop coarsely using on/off turns. Add to mixing bowl with cracked wheat, sunflower seeds, oil, lemon juice and seasonings. Taste and adjust seasonings. Serve mounded on spinach leaves and garnish with cherry tomatoes. (Makes 5 cups)

"One of the many variations of Tabbouleh we make at the shop in the summer."

PEGGY DE PARRY

From: Haab's Restaurant, Ypsilanti, MI

Prime Steak London Broil Marinade

6 ounces prime top sirloin steaks (10 ounces each, cut 1-inch thick)
1 cup red wine
1/3 cup vinegar
1/2 cup salad oil
1/4 teaspoon sweet basil
1/4 teaspoon oregano
1/4 teaspoon black pepper
2 teaspoons salt
1 small garlic clove, crushed
2 teaspoons chopped onion
1 bay leaf, broken

Combine wine, vinegar, oil, basil, oregano, pepper, salt, garlic, onion and bay leaf. Pour over steaks, cover and let stand in refrigerator 8 hours. Broil to preferred degree of doneness. (Serves 6) *"This is our largest selling entree."*

MIKE KABAT, OWNER

From: Hudson's (Briarwood Mall), Ann Arbor, MI

Quiche Lorraine

1 (8-inch) unbaked pie shell
1/4 cup crisp fried bacon, chopped coarsely
1/4 cup diced onion
6 ounces julienne ham
6 ounces julienne Swiss cheese
2 whole fresh eggs
4 ounces half-and-half cream
1/4 teaspoon dry mustard
Nutmeg

Perforate raw pie shell with a table fork. Pie should be room temperature. Bake empty shell at 350 degrees for 12 minutes. Fry chopped onions until soft; drain. Add fried chopped bacon to onions. Sprinkle onion-bacon mixture over bottom of baked pie shell. Combine ham and cheese and add to pie shell. Combine eggs, cream and mustard. Pour egg-cream-mustard mixture over meat mixture. Let rest for 10 minutes. Sprinkle small amount of ground nutmeg over top of pie. Bake at 350 degrees until set, approximately 25-30 minutes. (Makes one 8-inch pie)

From: Le Dog, Ann Arbor, MI

Turkey in Avocado With Cranberries

4 medium-sized ripe but firm avocados
2 cups cooked turkey cut into 1/2-inch cubes or julienne
1/2 teaspoon chef's salt
1 cup cranberry-orange relish
1/2 cup mayonnaise
1 can cranberry sauce
8 lettuce leaves
8 sprigs parsley
Additional mayonnaise for garnish (optional)

Split avocados in half. Remove pits. Cut pits in half and return a half pit to each avocado half. Chill. In a bowl, mix turkey, chef's salt, cranberry-orange relish and mayonnaise. Chill. From a can of cranberry sauce cut four slices approximately 1/3-inch thick, and cut each slice in half. Chill. Remove pits from avocado halves. Divide turkey-cranberry mixture among avocado halves. Place each half on a lettuce leaf. Cover half the filling with a half slice of cranberry sauce. Decorate with a sprig of parsley and serve with additional mayonnaise. (8 servings)

CHEF'S SECRET: Splitting the avocado pits and placing them back in the avocado prevents the avocado from turning brown. The easiest way to split an avocado seed is first score the brown outer skin with a sharp nail and then cut along the scoring.

From: Le Dog, Ann Arbor, MI

Swedish Fruit Soup

1 pound mixed dried fruit or dried apricots
11 cups water
4 tablespoons sugar
3 tablespoons cornstarch
5 tablespoons cold water

Wash the fruit and if possible soak it in the water for several hours. Add the sugar to the fruit and boil until tender. Mix the cornstarch with the cold water and pour into the fruit, stirring constantly. Bring to a boil again. Serve the soup lukewarm or cold as a first or last course. (8 servings)

From: Minerva Street Chocolate, Inc., Ann Arbor, MI

Basic Truffle Recipe

2 pounds semisweet chocolate, preferably imported
2 cups heavy cream
4 ounces unsalted butter
Sifted Dutch processed cocoa powder

Sift Dutch processed cocoa powder into a bowl for later use in decoration for truffles. To make chocolate ganache, place chocolate, cream, and butter in top of double boiler; heat over simmering water, stirring often with wooden spoon, until chocolate melts. When chocolate has melted, beat with spatula until smooth. Remove from heat. Refrigerate, covered with foil, overnight until ganache has time to harden. Working with a small amount of ganache at a time, form into balls about 1 inch in diameter. Place on baking sheets with wax paper. Have cocoa powder ready for use. Coat truffles as follows: Drop a truffle into the chocolate coating. Gently lift truffle out and hold above bowl for a few seconds to let excess chocolate drip back into bowl. Gently scrape finger against edge of dish to remove more of the excess chocolate; this prevents chocolate from forming platforms under pieces as they set. Lift truffle off of finger and gently slide truffle onto waxed paper-lined baking sheets. Immediately dust top of truffle with cocoa powder. Repeat procedure for remaining truffles. When truffles are coated, set in chocolate papers. Place candies in a flat box with a protective candy pad or Saran Wrap directly over candies to prevent scratching. Wrap the box in Saran Wrap tightly and store in refrigerator. Truffles will keep up to 3 weeks.

JUDY WEINBLATT

From: Minerva Street Chocolate, Inc., Ann Arbor, MI

Basic Procedures for Tempered Chocolate

"Tempering is the process of alternating heating and cooling of chocolate to specific temperatures to strengthen it and make it easier to use for dipping, molding or painting. An instant registering thermometer (not a candy thermometer) is required."

1. Do not attempt to temper chocolate on a humid day. Nor should dipping, molding or painting be done on a warm day, or in a kitchen where the temperature exceeds 70 degrees F (21 C). Do not temper chocolate on a surface where any moisture is present.

2. Use a good semisweet or milk chocolate couveture.

3. You may melt the chocolate over a water bath, or my favorite method is to heat the chocolate over a heating plate. Be sure to cut the chocolate into smallish pieces to begin the melting process.

4. Heat the chocolate to 100 degrees. Remove from heat and add a handful of "chocolate seeds" (pieces of chocolate which have been cut or grated into tiny pieces). Stir down the chocolate using a rubber spatula in the container.

5. If using milk chocolate do not heat above 93 degrees at first, cool the chocolate, and reheat to 85 degrees.

6. Bring your chocolate down to 80 degrees, then up to between 84-86 degrees. Keep the temperature constant and do not let it fall below 84 degrees or the entire process will have to be repeated.

JUDY WEINBLATT

From: Minerva Street Chocolate, Inc., Ann Arbor, MI

Chocolate Truffles With Walnuts

2 pounds semisweet chocolate, preferably imported
2 cups heavy cream
4 ounces unsalted butter
4 tablespoons Armagnac or Cognac
60 walnut halves, unsalted

Select the best of the walnut halves. Store in tightly covered container in freezer or refrigerator for later use as decoration for truffles. To make chocolate ganache, place chocolate, cream and butter in top of double boiler; heat over simmering water, stirring often with wooden spoon until chocolate melts. When chocolate has melted, beat with spatula until smooth. Remove from heat. Stir in Armagnac until well combined and transfer to medium bowl. Refrigerate, covered with foil, overnight until ganache has time to harden. Working with a small amount of the ganache at a time, form into balls about 1 inch in diameter. Place on baking sheet with wax paper. Have walnut halves ready. Gently push truffle on one walnut half, then dip the truffle into coating. Gently lift truffle out and hold above bowl for a few seconds to let excess chocolate drip back into the bowl. Gently scrape finger against edge of dish to remove more of the excess chocolate (this prevents chocolate from forming platforms under pieces as they set). Then place other walnut half on top of truffle. Lift truffle off of finger and gently slide truffle onto waxed paper lined baking sheets. When truffles are coated, set in chocolate papers. Place candies in a flat box with a protective candy paper or Saran Wrap directly over candies to prevent scratching. Wrap the box in Saran Wrap tightly and place in refrigerator for storage. Truffles will keep up to 3 weeks.

JUDY WEINBLATT

From: Minerva Street Chocolate, Inc., Ann Arbor, MI

Chocolate Hazelnut Truffles

1/2 cup filberts
34 ounces semisweet chocolate, preferably imported, broken into small pieces
3 cups heavy cream
4 ounces unsalted butter
3 tablespoons Frangelico liqueur

Select 48 nuts of uniform size; store in tightly covered container in freezer or refrigerator, for later use as decoration for truffles. Chop remaining filberts coarsely; you should have about 1/4 cup. To make chocolate ganache, place chocolate, cream and butter in top of double boiler; heat over simmering water, stirring often with wooden spoon until chocolate melts. When chocolate has melted, beat with spatula until smooth. Remove from heat. Stir in Frangelico and chopped hazelnuts until well combined and transfer to medium bowl. Refrigerate, covered with foil, overnight until ganache has time to harden. Working with a small amount of the ganache at a time, form into balls about 1 inch in diameter. Place on baking sheet with wax paper. Have the 48 reserved filberts ready. Coat truffles as follows: Drop a truffle into the chocolate coating. Gently lift truffle out and hold above bowl for a few seconds to let excess chocolate drip back into the bowl. Gently scrape finger against edge of dish to remove more of the excess; this prevents chocolate from forming platforms under pieces as they set. Lift truffle off of finger and gently slide truffle onto waxed paper lined baking sheets. Immediately dip a filbert in chocolate, immerse completely for a solid coating, partway for a white topped effect. Place nut on chocolate coated truffle. Repeat procedure with remaining truffles and filberts. When truffles are coated and set, place in chocolate papers. Place candies in a flat box with a protective candy paper or Saran Wrap over candies to prevent scratching. Wrap the box in Saran Wrap tightly and place in refrigerator for storage. Truffles will keep up to 3 weeks.

JUDY WEINBLATT

From: Minerva Street Chocolate, Inc., Ann Arbor, MI

Golden Nugget Truffles

7 tablespoons unsalted butter, at room temperature
1-1/2 cups sifted confectioners' sugar
3 tablespoons grated orange zest
3 tablespoons kirsch
1 teaspoon fresh lemon juice
2 pounds semisweet chocolate, preferably imported
1-1/2 cups heavy cream
1 tablespoon Cointreau

To make orange centers for truffles, beat 3 tablespoons of the butter till creamy. Gradually beat in sugar, then orange zest, kirsch and lemon juice. Beat until mixture is stiff and very smooth, about 5 minutes. Put in air-tight container; refrigerate at least overnight. To make chocolate ganache, place cream in pot to boil. After cream comes to a full boil, add the rest of the butter and bring to a boil again. Meanwhile place the 2 pounds of semisweet chocolate in Cuisinart. Add cream and butter mixture to the chocolate, with the motor running. The chocolate, cream, butter mixture should be very thick and creamy. Add the Cointreau and make sure that it is well combined with chocolate mixture. Transfer to air-tight container; refrigerate at least overnight. Working with a small amount of the orange filling at a time, form into balls, a scant 1 inch in diameter. Use all of the mixture to form small centers. Working with chocolate mixture, form centers into balls, poke a small hole in the center after it has been well rounded and place the butter/orange mixture inside, then quickly roll the whole ball. Gently lift truffle out and hold above bowl for a few seconds to avoid excess chocolate from forming platforms under pieces as they set. Lift truffle off of finger and gently slide truffle onto waxed paper-lined baking sheets. Repeat procedure with remaining truffles. When truffles are coated, set in chocolate papers. Place candies in a flat box with a protective candy pad or Saran Wrap directly over candies to prevent scratching. Wrap box in Saran Wrap and store in refrigerator. Truffles will keep up to 3 weeks.

JUDY WEINBLATT

RESTAURANT RECIPES

From: Monahan's Fish Market, Ann Arbor, MI

Marinated Fish for the Grill

1 pound halibut steaks (or tuna steaks or striped bass steaks)
MARINADE:
3 tablespoons soy sauce
3 cloves crushed garlic
1 tablespoon white wine (or sherry or Sake)
1 tablespoon peanut oil (or vegetable oil)
1/4 teaspoon black pepper
Salt to taste

Marinate steaks for 1-2 hours and grill halibut about 7 minutes (tuna about 5 minutes, striped bass up to 10 minutes) each side, if 1-1/2 inch thick.

JOELLE MCFARLAND

From: Monahan's Fish Market, Ann Arbor, MI

Skewered, Barbequed Large Shrimps

1 pound large shrimp (deveined, partially butterflied with shell still on)
2 tablespoons Herbes de Provence
1/4 cup extra virgin olive oil
5 cloves crushed garlic
1/2 teaspoon black pepper
1/2 teaspoon salt
1 tablespoon Balsamic vinegar

Mix last 6 ingredients in glass bowl. Coat inner part of shrimp with mixture. Let stand in marinade a minimum of 1 hour and up to 24 hours. Put about 5 or 6 shrimp per skewer and barbeque on medium-hot grill until done and pink, about 5-6 minutes. *Can be used as an appetizer.*

JOELLE MCFARLAND

From: The Moveable Feast, Ann Arbor, MI

Fish Pate

1-1/2 cups water
1-1/2 cups milk
1/8 stick unsalted butter
1/4 teaspoon salt
3 cups flour
4 whole eggs
Dash of freshly ground nutmeg
1-1/2 pounds filets of sole or other firm-fleshed pale fish
4 egg whites
3 packages frozen chopped spinach, cooked and drained
1 tablespoon olive oil
Salt and pepper
2 or more cloves garlic, pressed
6-8 thin strips of smoked salmon, uncooked (or fresh)

Bring water, milk, butter and salt to a slow simmer. Remove from heat, add three cups of flour. Add whole eggs, one by one, stirring constantly. Return to heat and over low flame, continue to stir until bottom of pan is dry looking, and the mass of dough sticks together. Add freshly ground nutmeg and spread out on a flat pan to cool. This is called a "panade". In a food processor puree the filets until smooth. Add egg whites and process only to incorporate. Set aside. Puree drained, cooked spinach in the food processor with the olive oil. Add salt, pepper and garlic. Combine chopped fish with the panade mixture and re-puree if necessary to obtain a homogeneous consistency. Oil pan and add a layer of this fish-panade mixture about one-fourth the way up the pan. Now add a layer of the strips of smoked salmon (or fresh salmon) spread evenly over the white mixture. Add a layer of the pureed spinach and then the panade until all the fillings are used. Oil a piece of aluminum foil and cover the pate tightly. Submerge the filled pate pan in another pan with boiling water about half way up the sides and bake in a 350 degree oven for 1-1/2 hours. Remove from water and weight with a brick or a heavy rectangular object and cool for at least six hours. Slice thinly.

RICKY AGRANOFF

From: The Moveable Feast, Ann Arbor, MI

Saute of Leeks Julienne

2 bunches leeks, trimmed and cleaned
2 tablespoons butter
2 tablespoons olive oil
Salt and pepper

Cut leeks into 2-inch julienne strips, and saute in butter and olive oil. Season with salt and pepper, cooking uncovered until tender.

KATIE HILBOLDT CURTIS

From: The Moveable Feast, Ann Arbor, MI

Veal Provencal

8 tomatoes, fresh, peeled and seeded
2 pounds veal
Salt and pepper to taste
3 tablespoons tomato paste
4 cloves garlic, crushed
3 lemons, juiced
Spinach pasta
Chives

Drop tomatoes in boiling water for 2 minutes. Remove and place into bowl of cold water. Peel and seed. Chop pulp in small pieces and set aside. Trim veal and cut into chunks. Season well with salt and pepper. Oil casserole and heat, then add veal cubes. Cook until juices have evaporated and remove. Add tomato pulp, paste, garlic, lemon juice, salt and pepper to casserole. Cook uncovered 30 minutes or until reduced. Add veal to sauce and simmer 15 minutes. Taste for seasoning. Serve on heated platter over spinach pasta and top with freshly chopped chives. May be accompanied with a saute of leeks julienne. (6-8 servings)

KATIE HILBOLDT CURTIS

From: The Moveable Feast, Ann Arbor, MI

Pissaladiere
(The French Cousin of Italian Pizza)

CRUST:
2-2/3 cups flour
2/3 cup lukewarm water
1 package dry yeast
2 whole eggs
1-1/2 teaspoons salt
1 tablespoon basil
Freshly ground pepper

Prepare the yeast dough: Sift the flour into a bowl and make a well in the center. Pour the warm water into the well and crumble the yeast over it. Allow to stand a few minutes until completely dissolved. Add the eggs, salt, basil and pepper to the well and mix the center ingredients. Gradually draw in the flour to form a soft dough. Turn it out onto a floured board and knead for five minutes, working in more flour if necessary. Transfer to an oiled bowl and turn the dough over so that the top is oiled. Cover with a damp cloth and allow to rise one hour in a warm place.

TOPPING:
1/2 cup olive oil
3 pounds onions, thinly sliced
1 tablespoon fresh rosemary
1 tablespoon basil
4 cloves fresh garlic, chopped
2 tablespoons red wine vinegar
Salt and pepper
Dash of Tabasco
4 pounds tomatoes, peeled and sliced
4 ounces anchovy fillets, drained and rinsed and cut in half
    lengthwise
1 cup Nicoise olives (black)

Heat the oil in a saute pan and add the onions, herbs and garlic. Cook over a very low flame, stirring occasionally until the onions are very soft. Add the vinegar, salt and pepper. Season with a dash of Tabasco. When the dough has risen, knead it lightly. Grease a baking sheet and pat the dough into the pan. Spread the onion mixture on top and arrange the tomatoes over the onions. Make a lattice of anchovy fillets, filling the spaces with olives. Bake in a preheated oven (375 degrees) until browned. Serve hot or at room temperature.

KATIE HILBOLDT CURTIS

From: The Moveable Feast, Ann Arbor, MI

Shrimp and Avocado Remoulade

4-6 shrimp per person, depending on the size
4-5 avocados, ripe and peeled, dipped in lemon juice and cut into
  slices as a garnish
COURT BOUILLON:
1 large onion, sliced
1 carrot, peeled and sliced
1 rib celery, diced
5 sprigs parsley
2 bay leaves
6 cups cold water
2 cups dry white wine
5-6 peppercorns

Peel and devein shrimp. Prepare court bouillon. Combine all ingredients in a large pan and bring to a boil. Cover and simmer 20 minutes to one-half hour and strain through a sieve before using. Bring court bouillon to a boil and add shrimp in small batches. When shrimp comes to a boil (approximately 2 minutes) remove and spread on a sheet tray to cool. Prepare Remoulade Sauce. (This will serve approximately 10 people)

REMOULADE SAUCE:
6 eggs
2 tablespoons Dijon mustard
2 cups olive oil
3 tablespoons lemon juice, fresh
1 tablespoon tarragon vinegar
1 tablespoon capers and juice
2 tablespoons finely chopped sour cornichons
1 tablespoon chopped parsley
1 teaspoon tarragon
Salt and pepper

Hard cook four of the eggs. Separate the yolks from the whites. Cut the whites into julienne and set aside. Combine the hard-cooked yolks with two raw yolks and add mustard. Mash and make a paste. Add the oil to this paste in a slow steady steam, whisking while you pour. Stir in the remaining ingredients and reserve julienned egg whites to garnish the shrimp. Toss the cooked shrimp with the Remoulade Sauce. Arrange on a serving platter or individual plates and garnish with avocado slices. Sprinkle with julienned egg whites.

KATIE HILBOLDT CURTIS

From: Raja Rani, Ann Arbor, MI

Chappati
(Bread)

1 cup whole wheat flour
1/2 tablespoon vegetable oil
1/2 cup water

Mix all of the above into dough. Cover and let set for an hour. Knead the
dough for 3 minutes and divide in small balls. Roll into a round shape and
cook on top of a hot griddle and butter.   LOVELEEN BAJWA

From: Raja Rani, Ann Arbor, MI

Raieta
(Cold Cucumber Salad)

2 cups yogurt
1 cucumber, grated
1 tablespoon roasted ground cumin
1/2 tablespoon fresh ground black pepper

Mix all of the above together and keep refrigerated.
                                LOVELEEN BAJWA

From: Raja Rani, Ann Arbor, MI

Garam Masala
(Spice Mixture)

6 black cardamom seeds
2 cinnamon sticks
6 cloves
3 tablespoons black cumin
1/4 tablespoon each nutmeg and mace
6 curry patas (leaves)*

Cook black cumin seeds in a pan stirring constantly until they start to become
fragrant. Add the rest of the ingredients and let cool for 10 minutes. Grind the
ingredients in a coffee grinder, pass through a fine sieve and store in airtight
container. (This spice may be added to meat dishes the last 10 minutes of
cooking.)

*Available at A and M Food Store in Ann Arbor.
                                LOVELEEN BAJWA

303

RESTAURANT RECIPES

From: Raja Rani, Ann Arbor, MI

Panir
(Dessert Ingredient)

1 gallon milk
3/4 cup fresh lemon juice

Bring the milk to a boil in a large saucepan. When the milk boils, add lemon juice stirring constantly until the milk has curdled completely. Strain through a muslin cloth, squeezing well to extract all the whey. The loose curd is called Chenna which is used in making many sweets. When the Chenna is put under weight and made into a slab, it is cut into cubes which is called Panir.

LOVELEEN BAJWA

From: Raja Rani, Ann Arbor, MI

Mattar Panir
(Vegetable Side Dish)

1 cup chopped onions
1/4 cup garlic
1/4 cup chopped gingerroot
1/2 cup safflower oil (or Ghee if you prefer)
2 tablespoons turmeric
2 tablespoons paprika
2 tablespoons coriander powder
2 tablespoons cumin powder
2 tablespoons garam masala
1/2 teaspoon black cumin, ground
1 teaspoon poppy seeds
1/2 cup chopped tomatoes
2 cups whey or vegetarian stock
1 gallon milk's cubed deep fat fried Panir
1 cup frozen peas
1/2 cup chopped coriander leaves
1/4 cup chopped pistachios

Add onions, garlic and ginger to the cooking oil and brown. Add turmeric, paprika and rest of the spices. Stir constantly over medium heat. Add tomatoes and cook a few more minutes. Add whey or vegetarian stock and bring to a boil. Add cheese or panir and peas and bring to another boil. Sprinkle with coriander leaves and pistachios and serve.

LOVELEEN BAJWA

From: Raja Rani, Ann Arbor, MI

Massor Dal
(Pink-Washed Lentil)

5 cups water
1 cup dal
1/8 teaspoon turmeric
1 teaspoon salt

TARKA:
3 tablespoons vegetable oil
1/2 cup onions, chopped
1/2 teaspoon garlic, chopped
1/2 teaspoon gingerroot, chopped
1/2 teaspoon whole cumin
1/2 cup fresh tomatoes
1/4 teaspoon paprika
1 tablespoon fenugreeck leaves*
Sprinkle of fresh coriander

Boil water and add massor dal, turmeric and salt. Cook for 20 minutes on medium heat. In another pan heat oil and brown onions, add garlic, gingerroot, whole cumin and tomatoes and cook for 5 minutes. Add paprika and fenugreeck leaves (mathi leaves). Mix this together with the dal. Transfer to serving dish and garnish with fresh coriander.

*Available at A and M Food Store in Ann Arbor.

LOVELEEN BAJWA

From: Raja Rani, Ann Arbor, MI

Sabbaji
(Fried Vegetable Dish)

1/4 cup safflower oil or Ghee
1/2 cup chopped onions
1 tablespoon chopped gingerroot
2 cups cut-up cauliflower
1 cup chopped potatoes
1 teaspoon turmeric powder
1 teaspoon cumin powder
1 teaspoon salt

Fry onions and gingerroot in oil until they turn pink. Add the rest of the ingredients. Cook on low heat for 15 minutes.

LOVELEEN BAJWA

305

From: The Real Seafood Company, Ann Arbor, MI

Chocolate Mousse

10 ounces semisweet chocolate
2 tablespoons sweet unsalted butter
4 egg yolks
6 tablespoons sugar
1/4 cup brandy
4 egg whites, beaten stiff
1 cup whipping cream, whipped
2 ounces whipped cream
1 teaspoon shredded chocolate, for sprinkling
1 cigarette russe

In a stainless steel bowl place chocolate and butter. Place bowl in the top of a double boiler, set over simmering water to melt chocolate. In a separate bowl, mix egg yolks and sugar until lemon color. Add brandy and mix well. Add chocolate mixture. Mix well until smooth. Place in freezer stirring often until cool or temperature becomes 75-80 degrees. Fold in egg whites. Place in refrigerator for approximately 30 minutes or until it gets cool and stiff. Fold in whipped cream and refrigerate for at least 6 hours or until stiff. Place 6 ounces of mousse in glass using a pastry bag. Squirt about 1 ounce of whipped cream over top. Sprinkle with shredded chocolate and place cigarette russe 1/3 into whipped cream. Serve immediately.

From: The Real Seafood Company, Ann Arbor, MI

Blackened Fish

SEASONING MIX:
2 cloves garlic, chopped very fine
2 tablespoons thyme leaves
2 tablespoons basil leaves
2 tablespoons parsley leaves, chopped fine
2 tablespoons white pepper, ground fine
1 tablespoon salt
1 tablespoon cayenne pepper

2 ounces olive oil (for each fillet)
4-5 fish fillets (skinless, 1/2 to 3/4-inch thick)
1 teaspoon clarified butter (for each fillet)
Additional 1 teaspoon melted butter (for each fillet)
1 sprig parsley (for each fillet)

Combine all ingredients for seasoning mix and mix very well. In a large cast-iron skillet place enough olive oil to cover pan, 2 ounces or more if needed. Heat until smoking. Just before cooking sprinkle seasoning mix, about 1/2 teaspoon, evenly on both sides of fillets patting it in by hand. Place in the hot skillet flesh side down first and cook uncovered over same high heat until fish flakes easily when tested with fork and underside looks charred, about 2 minutes (time will vary according to the fillet's thickness and the heat of the skillet). Turn the fish over and pour 1 teaspoon butter (clarified) on top and cook until fish is done, about 2 minutes more. Remove from skillet and place on platter. Pour 1 teaspoon of melted butter over the fillet and serve while piping hot. Garnish with sprig of parsley.

Note: Red fish and pompano are ideal for this method of cooking. If tile fish is used, you may have to split the fillets in half horizonally to have the proper thickness. If you cannot get any of these fish, salmon, red snapper, lake trout, swordfish or black fish fillets can be substituted. In any case, the fillets or steaks must not be more than 3/4-inch thick.

From: The Real Seafood Company, Ann Arbor, MI

New England Clam Chowder

3 ounces green pepper, fresh
6 ounces bacon, diced fine while cold, 1/2 inch
16 ounces onions, diced fine, 1/2 inch
1/4 teaspoon oregano leaves
1 teaspoon thyme leaves
1/4 teaspoon basil leaves
8 ounces celery, diced fine, 1/2 inch
2 quarts water
16 ounces potatoes, raw and diced fine
5 ounces clam base (Minors)
2 (16-ounce) cans clams, chopped
1/4 teaspoon ground white pepper
3/4 cup homogenized milk
3/4 cup whipping cream
2 tablespoons parsley, chopped fine

ROUX:
4 ounces butter
3 ounces all-purpose flour

Cut peppers in half lengthwise. Clean out center and cut in strips 1/2-inch wide. Cut strips diagonally into Chinese cut pieces about 1/4-inch size. Place bacon in large pan and render down completely. Add onions, oregano, thyme and basil, mix well and saute until translucent. Add celery and saute until translucent. (Cover pan while sauteing celery, to help cooking process by steaming.) Add green peppers to garniture and cook al dente. While vegetables are cooking, place water in soup pot and bring to boil. Add potatoes and boil for 8 minutes. Add garniture, clam base and clams to soup pot except for roux and bring to boil. To make roux, melt butter in pan. Mix in flour with a whip. Do not allow to burn. Cook slowly for about 6 minutes or until dry in appearance. Mix roux and 1/2 quart soup pot broth together for a better thickening agent. Mix these over the stove so it will cook well. If saute pan is not large enough, place roux into round bowl and mix in the broth from the soup pot. Add white pepper, mix well, bring to boil. Add milk, whipping cream and parsley. Bring to boil and serve.

From: The Red Bull Restaurant, Ann Arbor, MI

Beef Brochette

3 ounces tenderloin tips (cut in 1 ounce pieces)
2 pieces tomato quarters
2 pieces onions, large dice
2 pieces green pepper, 1-inch dice
2 pieces mushroom caps, blanched
Red Wine Marinade (see recipe, page 310)
1-1/2 ounces rice, cooked
Parsley garnish

Assemble the brochette in the following order: tenderloin, tomato, onion, green pepper, mushroom, tenderloin, mushroom, green pepper, onion, tomato, tenderloin. Place brochette in marinade. Let marinate 24 hours minimum. At service, charbroil. Do not over-cook, medium rare, unless specified otherwise. Plate on bed of rice. Garnish with parsley. (1 serving)

WILLIAM BROWN

From: The Red Bull Restaurant, Ann Arbor, MI

Chicken Skewer Florentine

3 ounces chicken breast meat (cut in 1 ounce cubes)
2 pieces onion
2 pieces red peppers
2 pieces mushrooms
2 ounces white wine marinade (see recipe, page 310)
1-1/2 ounces rice, cooked
1/2 ounce spinach, sauteed
Parsley for garnish

Prepare the skewer in the following order: chicken, onion, red pepper, mushroom, chicken, mushroom, red pepper, onion, chicken. Place skewer in white wine marinade. Allow to marinate 24 hours minimum. At service, charbroil skewer and plate on a bed of rice lightly topped with spinach. Garnish with parsley. Note: If skewer is sticking, season grill with salt water and lightly brush with oil. (1 serving)

WILLIAM BROWN

From: The Red Bull Restaurant, Ann Arbor, MI

Linguine With Red Clam Sauce

5 ounces linguine
3 ounces chopped clams
Olive oil to saute
2 teaspoons garlic, minced
1 ounce white wine
4 ounces marinara sauce

Cook linguine. At the same time saute chopped clams in olive oil. Add garlic, add wine, add cooked linguine and marinara sauce. Toss and serve.
(1 serving)   WILLIAM BROWN

From: The Red Bull Restaurant, Ann Arbor, MI

Linguine With White Clam Sauce

5 ounces linguine
3 ounces chopped clams
Olive oil to saute
2 teaspoons garlic, minced
1 ounce white wine
2 teaspoons oregano
2 teaspoons basil
3 ounces clam juice
3/4 ounce heavy cream

Cook linguine. At the same time saute chopped clams in olive oil. Add garlic, add wine, add all other ingredients. Add cooked linguine; toss and serve.
(1 serving)   WILLIAM BROWN

From: The Red Bull Restaurant, Ann Arbor, MI

White or Red Wine Marinade

1 gallon dry white wine (or medium dry red wine and no dill)
8 ounces garlic, minced
2 ounces rosemary
2 ounces basil
1 ounce dill leaf
1/4 ounce white pepper
8 ounces Dijon mustard

Blend all ingredients together. Add 8 ounces Dijon mustard last.
WILLIAM BROWN

310

From: Seva, Ann Arbor, MI

Coconut Muffins

1/2 cup butter, melted
3/4 cup honey
1 cup buttermilk
3 eggs
3 cups whole wheat pastry flour ("soft" whole wheat)
1-1/2 teaspoons baking powder
3/4 teaspoon baking soda
1-1/2 cups shredded coconut

Whisk together the butter, honey, buttermilk and eggs. Sift together the flour, baking powder and soda. Toss coconut into dry ingredients. Add wet ingredients to dry ingredients and mix together just enough to thoroughly combine. Spoon batter out into greased or paper-lined muffin cups and bake for 25-30 minutes in a 375 degree oven. (Yields 1 dozen muffins)

MAREN PETERSON
HEAD CHEF

From: Seva, Ann Arbor, MI

Gingerbread Muffins

6 tablespoons butter
2 tablespoons freshly-grated ginger
1/2 cup sorghum molasses
1/4 cup honey
1 cup buttermilk
3 eggs
1 cup raisins
3 cups whole wheat pastry flour ("soft" whole wheat)
1-1/2 teaspoons baking powder
3/4 teaspoon baking soda
1 teaspoon mustard powder
3/4 teaspoon ground cloves
3/4 teaspoon ground cinnamon
1/2 teaspoon ground nutmeg

Simmer the butter and ginger together over low heat for 30 minutes. Whisk together the butter/ginger mixture, molasses, honey, buttermilk, eggs and raisins. Sift together the flour, baking powder, baking soda, mustard powder, cloves, cinnamon and nutmeg. Add wet ingredients to dry ingredients and mix together just enough to thoroughly combine. Spoon batter into greased or paper-lined muffin cups and bake for 25-30 minutes in a 375 degree oven. (Yields 1 dozen muffins)

MAREN PETERSON
HEAD CHEF

From: Seva, Ann Arbor, MI

Creamy Sweet Potato Soup

2 pounds sweet potatoes (should yield about 5 cups)
4 cups soup stock or water
1/2 cup butter (1/4 pound)
2 cups diced onion
1 cup diced carrot
1/2 cup cream
1/4 teaspoon ground black pepper
3/4 teaspoon salt

Peel sweet potatoes and cut into small dice size. Put sweet potatoes into a 3-quart saucepan with the soup stock. Cook, covered, over medium heat until very tender (45 minutes to 1 hour). Puree until very smooth in food processor fitted with a steel blade, or mash and press through a fine sieve. Return puree to saucepan and set aside. In a medium-sized frying pan, saute until tender the butter, onion and carrot. Add sauteed vegetables to puree in saucepan with the cream, black pepper and salt. Simmer 1/2 hour. (Yields about 8 cups)

MAREN PETERSON
HEAD CHEF

From: Seva, Ann Arbor, MI

Wild Rice Soup

1/2 cup wild rice (about 1/4 pound)
5 cups rich soup stock (enhance flavor with bouillon if necessary)
1 cup diced carrots
1 cup diced celery
1 cup diced onion
1 cup diced tomato
1/2 teaspoon salt
1/4 teaspoon pepper
3/4 teaspoon basil
1/4 teaspoon garlic powder

Rince the wild rice well. In a 3-quart saucepan, bring to a boil the soup stock. Add wild rice to saucepan, lower heat and simmer uncovered for 30 minutes. Add carrots, celery and onion and cook until tender over medium heat. Add tomato, salt, pepper, basil and garlic powder and simmer 15 minutes. (Yields about 8 cups)

MAREN PETERSON
HEAD CHEF

From: Victors Restaurant, Ann Arbor, MI

Chicken Picatta With Fettuccine Noodles

20 ounces boneless and skinless chicken breasts, pounded slightly
Salt and pepper
2 eggs
1 teaspoon chopped parsley
1/4 teaspoon sweet basil
2 teaspoons grated Parmesan cheese
3 ounces butter
6 ounces Fettuccine noodles
1 ounce butter
Salt, pepper, nutmeg
1 cup heavy cream
1 ounce romano cheese

Season chicken breasts with salt and pepper and dip into flour. Mix whole eggs with parsley, sweet basil and Parmesan cheese; whip lightly. Marinate chicken breasts in egg mixture for 15-20 minutes. Heat saute pan with 3 ounces of butter. Do not permit butter to brown at this point. Insert into pan the pieces of chicken and pour the remaining egg mixture over the chickens. Saute to golden brown on both sides; reduce the heat somewhat when turning the Picattas for the first time. The meat is done most of the time when it is brown on each side. Cook fettuccine noodles in plenty of water to al dente (drain immediately). Melt remaining butter in shallow pan, add noodles, salt, pepper and nutmeg. Add cup of cream and simmer until cream forms a sauce, then add romano cheese, and mix well and serve. (4 servings)

From: Victors Restaurant, Ann Arbor, MI

Kodiak
(Crab Cakes)

20 ounces Snow crabmeat, well drained and shredded
2 eggs
2 packages instant oatmeal
1 cup French bread, diced without rind
2 tablespoons flour
1 teaspoon chopped parsley
1/4 teaspoon dill weed
Salt, pepper, Worcestershire sauce to taste
2-3 tablespoons butter
1/2 cup butter

Put all ingredients in a bowl except butter and mix well, also knead with your hands. Mixture should be bound to make patties of it. Make 3-4 ounce patties and fry on both sides to a golden brown in a saute pan with butter under moderate heat. Top with Bernaise Sauce and glaze under the Salamander.

BERNAISE SAUCE:
1/4 teaspoon tarragon leaves, finely chopped
1 teaspoon onion, finely chopped
2 tablespoons vinegar
3 egg yolks
1 teaspoon water
6 ounces clarified butter (at body temperature)
1/4 teaspoon chopped parsley
Salt, pepper, Tabasco
Lemon juice (optional)

Put tarragon leaves, onions and vinegar in a shallow pan and simmer until liquid has all vaporized, remove from heat and let cool. Put egg yolks in a bowl with one teaspoon of water. Whip with hand whip over steam (double boiler) until eggs start thickening. Do not overheat, this would yield scrambled eggs. When eggs are thick and foamy, whip in warm butter very little at a time. If too much butter is added the emulsion breaks. When all the butter has been mixed with the yolks, add tarragon mixture, parsley and seasoning. If a more tangy flavor is desired, add lemon juice. This sauce should be thick enough to coat crab patties without running off. If too thick, just add lukewarm water.
(4 servings)

From: Weber's Inn, Ann Arbor, MI

Carrot Cake

2 cups sugar
2 cups flour
2 teaspoons baking soda
2 teaspoons cinnamon
1 teaspoon salt
1-1/2 cups vegetable oil
4 eggs
3 cups grated carrots

Mix dry ingredients first, then add remaining ingredients. Bake at 350 degrees for 30 minutes.

ICING:
1 (1-pound) box confectioners' sugar
1 (8-ounce) package cream cheese
1/2 cup butter
1 teaspoon vanilla

Combine all icing ingredients until smooth and spread on cooled cake.

NOTE: May add nuts to cake mixture or spinkle on top after icing.

STEPHANIE MARSHALL
PASTRY CHEF

From: Weber's Inn, Ann Arbor, MI

Jambalaya

SEASONING MIX:
1/2 bay leaf
White pepper to taste
1/4 teaspoon gumbo file powder (optional)
Black pepper to taste
1/4 teaspoon basil
1/4 teaspoon salt
Cayenne pepper to taste
1/4 teaspoon dried thyme
1/4 teaspoon oregano

Combine seasoning mix ingredients in a bowl and set aside.

1-1/4 tablespoons margarine
2 ounces bay scallops
2 ounces smoked ham, cut in 1-inch strips
3 ounces shrimp
1 cup tomato paste
3/4 cup clam or chicken broth
4 ounces dry sherry
1/3 cup chopped celery
1/2 cup chopped tomatoes
1/3 teaspoon minced garlic
1/3 cup chopped onions
1/4 cup chopped green pepper

In a large heavy skillet melt the margarine over high heat. Add the seasoning mix; cook 3 minutes. Add scallops, shrimp and ham. Stir well and continue cooking until done. Do not overcook. Add tomato paste, stock and sherry stirring well. Bring mixture to a boil; reduce heat and simmer about 10-12 minutes. Saute vegetables and add to mixture. Remove bay leaf. Adjust seasoning. Serve over steamed white rice. (Serves 3-4 people)

CHEF CURTIS JOHNSON

From: **The Whiffletree, Ann Arbor, MI**

White Chocolate Mousse

CRUST:
3 cups vanilla wafers, chopped
1/2 cup butter, melted
FILLING:
1 pound white chocolate
10 egg whites
4 cups whipping cream
2 whole eggs
4 egg yolks
3 ounces white creme de cacao
TOPPING:
1 (16-ounce) package frozen raspberries, sieved

Blend wafers and butter together and press in bottom of an 8-inch springform pan. Melt the chocolate over a double boiler. Remove from heat and let chocolate reach 95 degrees. Whip egg whites until stiff. Whip cream until stiff. In another bowl whip chocolate and add whole eggs, egg yolks and creme de cacao until smooth. Add some whites and some cream and continue to whip 15 seconds longer. Fold egg whites, whipped cream and chocolate mix together. Pour chocolate mixture into pan. Cover with plastic wrap and freeze. Serve topped with raspberries.

From: **The Whiffletree, Ann Arbor, MI**

Chilled Gazpacho Soup

4 ounces onion, chopped fine
8 ounces cucumber, peeled and chopped fine
6 ounces green pepper, chopped fine
1/2 clove garlic, chopped fine
1 teaspoon basil
1 teaspoon oregano
1/2 teaspoon thyme
2 ounces olive oil
2 ounces wine vinegar
Juice of 1 whole lemon
1 teaspoon salt
1/2 teaspoon ground cumin
8 ounces diced black olives
1 (#303) can whole tomato/1 plum tomato
1 (46-ounce) can tomato juice

Run all ingredients except tomato and tomato juice through a blender and let sit 1 hour. Add tomatoes and tomato juice. Garnish with a spear of cucumber, slice of avocado, seasoned croutons and topped with a dab of sour cream.

From: Zingerman's Delicatessen, Ann Arbor, MI

Fondue

Fondue was invented by Swiss mountain herdsmen. It was an easy-to-make, nourishing meal. Traditionally, it was made in a special flat bottomed pot called a "caquelot" which rests on a small burner to keep the fondue hot while it is being eaten. Also traditionally, the wine used in the fondue should be drunk with dinner. (The cook is entitled, of course, to sample the wine while cooking but must not forget to keep stirring!)

1 clove garlic
2 cups dry white wine (Swiss Neuchatel)
1 tablespoon fresh lemon juice
1/2 pound Swiss Gruyere cut into 1/2-inch cubes
1/2 pound Swiss Emmenthal cut into 1/2-inch cubes
3 tablespoons flour
Kirsch
Finely ground pepper
1 loaf sour dough French bread cut into 1-inch cubes

Rub fondue pot with garlic. Add wine and heat until bubbles begin to form. Add lemon juice. Dredge cheese cubes in flour to evenly coat. Begin adding cheese to pot, stirring constantly. Continue stirring until all cheese is in pot and fondue is thick and smooth. Add kirsch and pepper to taste. Skewer bread cube with fork and dip.

Variations: For a milder fondue, use only Emmenthal. For a stronger fondue, use only Gruyere or a mixture of Gruyere and Appenzeller. Substitute brandy for Kirsch. Substitute boiled potatoes for bread cubes.

From: Zingerman's Delicatessen, Ann Arbor, MI

Tea

A pot of tea is as good as the tea leaves and the way it is brewed.

1. Use approximately 1 teaspoon tea per cup. (The better the tea, the less you will need.)

2. Bring fresh cold tap water (or spring water) to a boil. Do not overboil. (Cold tap water has less impurities than hot, and overboiling causes water to become flat tasting.)

3. Preheat your pot with hot water before brewing. A warm pot makes a taste difference.

4. Allow tea to brew for approximately 5 minutes. Personal taste and type of tea leaf will determine length of brewing time; small, flat leaves infuse more quickly than long, tightly twisted ones. Underbrewing produces a thin tea, lacking body and the pungency of fine tea. Overbrewing produces a bitterness which can overshadow the complexity of a fine tea.

5. Keeping tea as hot as possible while brewing and serving will maximize your enjoyment of its flavor.

6. Serve tea plain or with milk and sugar (or honey). Savor fine tea like fine wine, appreciating its intricate flavor, pungency and aroma.

From: Zingerman's Delicatessen, Ann Arbor, MI

Balsamic Tomato Sauce

The added zip of balsamic vinegar makes this tomato sauce refreshingly good.

4 cloves garlic, crushed
1/4 cup extra virgin olive oil*
1 medium onion, diced
1 tablespoon each oregano, thyme, basil
1 teaspoon ground black pepper
2 (14-ounce) cans peeled Pagani Italian plum tomatoes
2 fresh tomatoes, coarsely chopped
1/2 cup fresh parsley, chopped
1/4 cup Pagani tomato paste (it comes in a tube!)
1/2 cup balsamic vinegar

In a large saucepan, fry garlic in hot oil until brown. Remove cloves, discard. In remaining oil, saute onions until soft with oregano, thyme, basil and pepper. Add remaining ingredients and simmer slowly for 1 to 1-1/2 hours. Serve warmed Italian fini tortellini sprinkled with freshly grated Parmesan Reggiano, over any fresh pasta; for that matter, as part of a pizza feast, over your favorite stuffed filet or rolled chicken breast.

*Zingerman's carries a variety of extra virgin olive oils. Colavita or Bel Canto are moderately priced choices with a nice but not overwhelming olive flavor.

CHEF KITTY

From: Zingerman's Delicatessen, Ann Arbor, MI

Vinaigrette

Vinaigrette is a real "French Dressing". It blends two of France's finest culinary ingredients - olive oil and vinegar. It is perfect for green salads, for marinades, or as a dipping sauce for fresh vegetables or seafood. The secret to success is the use of quality ingredients. In your basic vinaigrette, sequence is also important.

1 tablespoon mustard
2 tablespoons vinegar
6 tablespoons oil
Salt and pepper to taste

Begin by whisking together the mustard and vinegar. Add the oil slowly until thickened. Salt and pepper to taste.

Variations: Try an herb mustard or herb vinegar; add chopped fresh herbs or minced garlic; Roquefort for Bleu cheese dressing.

320

Kids Recipes

KIDS RECIPES

Acknowledgement . . .

Many of the recipes you will find on the following pages were donated by Valerie Indenbaum and Marcia Shapiro. These are included in their own book, "The Everything Book", a publication for teachers of young children. This book is a wonderful collection of fingerplays, poems, songs and many ideas for children's activities. "The Everything Book" may be obtained from Gryphon House, 3706 Otis Street, Mt. Rainier, Maryland 20822.

Thanks, Valerie and Marcia, for this noteworthy contribution to our cookbook.

Cooked Playdough

1 cup all-purpose flour
1/2 cup salt
2 teaspoons cream of tartar
1 cup water
2 tablespoons oil
1 teaspoon desired food coloring

Cook all ingredients over medium heat stirring constantly until it forms a ball. Remove and knead. Store in tightly-covered container.

KAY MOLER

Crazy Goop

2 cups liquid glue
1 cup liquid starch

Mix both ingredients together. Add more starch, if necessary, until it forms a non-sticky, pliable mass. You can stretch it, break it, snap it and have fun. Note: This cannot be colored.

KAY MOLER

Fingerpaint

1 cup laundry soap
1 cup cold water
4 cups hot water
1 cup laundry soap
1 cup cornstarch
Food coloring

Cook laundry soap, cold and hot water together in a large pot until clear. Add the additional laundry soap, cornstarch and food coloring and cook until thick, stirring constantly.

KAY MOLER

No-Cook Playdough

3 cups all-purpose flour
1 cup salt
1 cup water (more if necessary)
Few drops food coloring

Mix together all ingredients and store in tightly-covered container.

KAY MOLER

Whipped Soap Paint

1 cup Ivory Snow powder
1/2 cup warm water
Food coloring (optional)

Mix soap powder with warm water in a bowl. Have children beat with egg beater until mixture is frothy but not stiff. Apply mixture to construction paper with brushes to create a design. Can add food coloring to whipped flakes.

THE EVERYTHING BOOK

Bread Dough Recipe for Ornaments

8 cups all-purpose flour
2 cups salt
3 cups water

Mix flour and salt in a large mixing bowl; add water, mix and knead. Form into ball. Roll out dough and make into shape (wreath, candy cane, star, Santa, etc.). Make hole for string. Place on wax paper and dry overnight or bake 1 hour on ungreased cookie sheet at 300 degrees. When dry, paint. For thick shapes, bake 1 hour; thin shapes 1/2 hour. To preserve, paint on shellac.

THE EVERYTHING BOOK

Soap Crayons

1 cup powdered laundry soap
30-40 drops food coloring
Water

Mix soap and food coloring with enough water until liquid.
Stir well. Pack soap into ice cube trays. Set in sunny, dry
place for two days. Crayons will become hard and great for
writing in the sink or tub.

THE EVERYTHING BOOK

Bubble Solution

1 cup water
1/3 cup liquid soap
1 tablespoon sugar

Combine bubble ingredients. Make a wand by bending the
end of an 8-inch pipe cleaner to form a hook. Dip into
solution and blow gently.

THE EVERYTHING BOOK

Sand Paint

White cornmeal
Food coloring

Pour some cornmeal into several small bowls. Sprinkle a
few drops of food coloring over meal, using a different color
for each dish and mash the mixtures around with a spoon
until meal is all colored. Draw a design on a piece of heavy
paper. Spread glue on the lines of the design. Sprinkle
different colors of cornmeal mixture over glue. Let dry and
gently shake off loose cornmeal.

THE EVERYTHING BOOK

KIDS RECIPES

Easter Egg Dye

1 teaspoon food coloring
1 tablespoon vinegar
1 cup hot water

Mix all ingredients together. Use a different color for each container. Spoon-dip a hard-boiled egg into the dye to color it any way you want.   THE EVERYTHING BOOK

Marbled Easter Eggs

1 teaspoon food coloring
1 tablespoon vinegar
1 cup hot water
1 tablespoon salad oil

Mix food coloring, vinegar, water and salad oil together. Eggs dyed in this solution will have a marbled coloring.
                                        THE EVERYTHING BOOK

Tie Dyes

Make your own dyes using natural materials:
For yellow use saffron, crocuses, daffodils or onionskins;
For green use young grass, broccoli, spinach or escarole;
For blue use blueberries;
For red use beets;
For brown use coffee, tea or walnut shells

Place in an enamel pot and cover with water. Boil 5 minutes (longer to make colors darker). Strain through colander. Cool. Cut or tear pieces of white cotton. Dip cloth in colors.
                                        THE EVERYTHING BOOK

Modeling Dough Ornaments

2 cups salt
1 cup cornstarch
1-1/2 cups water

Mix salt and cornstarch together. Bring water to a boil; remove from heat. Add salt and cornstarch slowly while stirring. Continue to cook over low heat until the dough is hard to stir. Remove from pan. Let cool. Knead. Store in an air-tight container. Then, model ornaments and paint. *Makes a wonderful present.*

THE EVERYTHING BOOK

Orange Brew

1 (6-ounce) can concentrated orange juice
1 cup milk
1/2 cup water
10-12 ice cubes
1 teaspoon vanilla

Whip in blender until frothy.

THE EVERYTHING BOOK

Easy Punch

1 (.2-ounce) package Kool Aid (any flavor)
1 (6-ounce) can frozen orange juice concentrate
1 quart gingerale

Mix Kool Aid according to package directions. Add orange juice concentrate and Kool Aid. Add gingerale and decorate with ice ring when in punch bowl. (Makes 16, 6-ounce servings) *"Can be made well in advance. Add gingerale just before serving."*

PEG GRIFFIN

KIDS RECIPES

Punch

1 (.2-ounce) package cherry Kool Aid
1-1/2 cups sugar
1 (6-ounce) can each frozen lemonade, orange
   juice and pineapple juice
1-1/2 quarts water
2 quarts gingerale

Combine all ingredients and chill.

STEPHANIE MINERATH

Halloween Witch's Brew

2/3 cup instant tea
14 ounces orange Tang
2 packages dry lemonade mix
2 cups sugar
2 teaspoons cinnamon
2 teaspoons powdered cloves

Mix together. To brew, add 1-1/2 to 2 reaspoons mix to 1
cup boiling water.   THE EVERYTHING BOOK

Fudge

3 (6-ounce) packages semisweet chocolate chips
1 (14-ounce) can sweetened condensed milk
1-1/2 teaspoons vanilla extract
1/2 cup chopped nuts (optional)
1 small package M & M's (optional)

Over low heat, melt the chips. Remove from heat, add
remaining ingredients. Spread into a well-greased 8-inch
square pan and decorate with M & M's, if desired. Chill.

SHEILA HAUSBECK

Church Window Candy

1 (6-ounce) package semisweet chocolate pieces
1/4 cup butter or margarine
3 cups multicolored tiny marshmallows
3/4 cup chopped nuts

In a large saucepan over low heat, melt chocolate pieces and butter. Remove from heat and cool. Stir in the marshmallows and 1/4 cup nuts. Divide mixture in half. Shape each half into a log about 1-1/2 inches in diameter and 6 inches long. Roll logs in remaining 1/2 cup nuts. Chill. Cut into 1/2-inch slices. (Makes 2 dozen pieces)

THE EVERYTHING BOOK

Oven Caramel Corn

2 cups brown sugar
1 cup butter or margarine
1/2 cup light corn syrup
1 teaspoon salt
7-1/2 quarts popped popcorn
1 teaspoon baking soda
Peanuts (optional)

Cook brown sugar, margarine, syrup and salt in a saucepan for 5 minutes after bringing it to a boil. Remove from stove. Add soda. Add to popcorn and mix well. Spread on cookie sheets and place in a 200 degree oven for 1 hour, stirring at 15-minute intervals. Peanuts may be added before putting in oven.

ANN BETZ

KIDS RECIPES

Suckers

3 cups sugar
1 cup corn syrup
2 cups water
Food coloring
Flavoring: Anise, peppermint, etc. (optional)

Cook all ingredients to 300 degrees on a candy thermometer. Pour a small amount over popsicle sticks on greased pan. (Regular recipe without flavoring tastes like butterscotch).

ANN BETZ

Graham Cracker House

Royal frosting (3 egg whites, 1 pound confectioners'
  sugar)
1/2-pint and 1-pint paper milk containers
1 package graham crackers
Trims (raisins, nuts, candies)

Make royal frosting by beating egg whites to a frothy foam and then beating in confectioners' sugar. Use milk cartons as the base, royal frosting as glue and graham crackers as the walls, stuck to cartons. Place two graham crackers on top for roof. Frost crackers and decorate with trims.

THE EVERYTHING BOOK

Cloud Sandwich

2 tablespoons marshmallow cream
2 squares graham crackers

Spread marshmallow cream between two graham crackers. *Fast and easy snack.*

THE EVERYTHING BOOK

Apple Santa

1 large, polished red apple
5 marshmallows
5 cranberries
5 toothpicks
2 cotton balls
Cloves

Place apple stem side down. Insert toothpicks; one at each side for arms and two in front for feet (Santa is sitting). Push a marshmallow on arm toothpick, followed by cranberry for hand. Do same for other arm and legs. Push a toothpick in on top for head. Then push into toothpick in this order: flattened cotton ball for beard, marshmallow for head, flattened cotton ball for hat, cranberries for top. Stick cloves in for eyes and use clove buttons for trim on apple. (Makes 1 Santa)

THE EVERYTHING BOOK

A Holiday Tree

1/4 cup margarine
2 cups confectioners' sugar
2 tablespoons milk
Green food color
Cone-shaped ice cream cone
Trims (red hots, marshmallows, chocolate chips, raisins)

Combine margarine, confectioners' sugar, milk and food color in a bowl. Cover upside down cone with frosting. Use trims to decorate.

THE EVERYTHING BOOK

KIDS RECIPES

Candy Cane Cookies

1/2 cup butter or margarine, softened
1/2 cup shortening
1 cup confectioners' sugar
1 egg
1-1/2 teaspoons almond extract
1 teaspoon vanilla
2-1/2 cups all-purpose flour
1 teaspoon salt
1/2 teaspoon red food coloring
1/2 cup crushed peppermint candy
1/2 cup sugar

Preheat oven to 375 degrees. In a large bowl mix thoroughly the butter, shortening, confectioners' sugar, egg and flavors. Blend in flour and salt. Divide dough into two parts. Blend red food coloring into one part. Shape 1 teaspoon dough from each half into 4-inch rope by rolling back and forth on lightly floured board. Place ropes side by side, press together lightly and twist. Place on ungreased baking sheet. Curve top down to form handle of cane. Bake about 9 minutes or until set and very light brown. Mix candy and sugar. Immediately sprinkle cookies with candy mixture. Remove from baking sheet. (Makes 4 dozen cookies)

GRACE BACON

Banana Snowmen

2 bananas
2 cups raisins
Shredded coconut

Place bananas and raisins in blender. Mix at high speed until chopped. Scrape into bowl. Chill until mixture can be handled. Shape into 1-inch balls and roll in shredded coconut. Stack three balls and secure with a toothpick.

THE EVERYTHING BOOK

332

KIDS RECIPES

Cereal Christmas Tree

3 tablespoons margarine
32 large or 3 cups miniature marshmallows
1/2 teaspoon vanilla
1/2 teaspoon green food coloring
4 cups Cheerios or Rice Krispies
Gumdrops, red hots, etc. for decorating

Place margarine and marshmallows in a saucepan over low heat stirring constantly until melted. Remove from heat. Stir in vanilla and coloring. Fold in cereal until evenly coated. Quickly shape warm mixture on wax paper with buttered hands. Use 1/2 cup mixture per tree. Gumdrops, red hots or other edible items can be used for decorating trees.

THE EVERYTHING BOOK

Holiday Wreaths

1/2 cup butter
1/2 teaspoon salt
30 large marshmallows
1 teaspoon vanilla
3 drops green food coloring
4-1/2 cups cornflakes
Cinnamon candies

In a large saucepan melt the butter, salt and marshmallows over low heat. Add vanilla and food coloring. Stir in cornflakes carefully so they do not crush. Shape into balls with your hands. Place on waxed paper. Press thumb into center forming a wreath. Decorate with red cinnamon candies. (Makes 2 dozen cookies)

GRACE BACON
SHELLY ROBBINS

Gingerbread Men

3/4 cup melted butter or margarine
1 cup molasses
1/2 cup honey
1 cup thick sour milk (or buttermilk)
6-1/2 cups sifted, unbleached enriched all-purpose
  flour
1/2 teaspoon salt
2 teaspoons ginger
4 teaspoons baking powder
3/4 teaspoon baking soda
1 tablespoon lemon or orange extract
Decorations: Raisins, red hot candies, almond
  slivers

In a large bowl mix the melted butter or margarine,
molasses and honey until smooth. Add milk, then the flour
sifted with salt, ginger, baking powder and soda. Add lemon
or orange extract. Mix to a smooth, stiff dough. Chill.
Preheat oven to 350 degrees. Roll out on a lightly floured
surface to 1/3-inch thick. Cut into shapes and place on
ungreased baking sheet. Decorate with raisins, red hot
candies and almond slivers. Bake for 8-10 minutes. Cool.
(Makes 50 large gingerbread men) *"This makes a soft
bread-like cookie, the kind children like."*

GRACE BACON

Peanut Butter Bugs

4 tablespoons peanut butter
1 tablespoon honey
1 tablespoon wheat germ
2-1/2 tablespoons powdered milk

Mix together to form an easy to handle playdough. Form
into oval shapes. Add eyes, legs, wings, etc. using raisins,
chocolate chips or use your imagination.

THE EVERYTHING BOOK

Good Cut-Out Cookies

1-1/2 cups confectioners' sugar
1 cup butter
1 egg
1-1/2 teaspoons vanilla
2-1/2 cups all-purpose flour
1 teaspoon baking soda
1 teaspoon cream of tartar

Mix sugar and butter in a bowl. Add egg and vanilla. Mix well. Mix dry ingredients and blend in. Refrigerate 2-3 hours. Preheat oven to 375 degrees. Roll 1/8-inch thick or thicker and cut in desired shapes. Bake 7-8 minutes.

SHELLY ROBBINS

Snow Balls

2 cups crunchy peanut butter
3/4 cup marshmallow creme
3-1/2 ounces semisweet chocolate chips
Shredded coconut

Blend first 3 ingredients in a bowl. Form into small balls. Roll balls in shredded coconut. Refrigerate if too soft to handle.

THE EVERYTHING BOOK

Toasted Pumpkin Seeds

Carve pumpkin and remove seeds. Clean seeds and let dry on paper towel. Place dry seeds in shallow baking pan, dot with **butter**, sprinkle with **salt**. Bake at 350 degrees for 20-30 minutes until brown. Stir occasionally. If an oven is not available, seeds may be fried in an electric fry pan, using oil or oil and butter, add salt. Drain.

THE EVERYTHING BOOK

KIDS RECIPES

Skidoos

1 cup butter
1 cup sugar
1 egg
1 cup chopped walnuts
1/4 teaspoon salt
2 cups sifted all-purpose flour

Preheat oven to 350 degrees. Cream butter in a mixing
bowl; add sugar gradually creaming till well mixed. Add egg,
beating well. Combine nutmeats, salt and flour. Add to
butter mixture, blending until smooth. Drop 1 teaspoon of
dough onto ungreased cookie sheet. Bake for 12-15
minutes. (Makes 3 dozen 2-inch cookies)

CATHY MAZZOLINI

S'Mores

First you take some **marshmallows**. You have to have a
stick and you put marshmallows on a stick and then you
cook them over a fire and when they're done you take some
graham crackers and some **Hersey's chocolate candy
bars** and you put them all together and you have S'Mores.

MICHELLE TASCH
AGE 9

Peanut Butter Playdough

1 cup peanut butter
1 cup honey
1 cup confectioners' sugar
1 cup oatmeal

Combine all ingredients and mix thoroughly. *Make
something beautiful and then eat it!*

THE EVERYTHING BOOK

336

Creme Doodles

1 (7-ounce) jar marshmallow creme
1 cup peanut butter
1/2 cup honey
2 (1-1/2 ounce) chocolate bars, crumbled
1-1/2 cups raisins
1 cup chopped walnuts
2 cups grated coconut

Combine marshmallow creme, peanut butter and honey in a bowl, mixing with electric mixer or wire whisk until well-blended. Add chocolate, raisins and nuts; mix well. Shape rounded teaspoonfuls of mixture into 1-inch balls; roll in coconut. Chill or freeze. (Makes 6 dozen) *"An easy, no-cook candy kids love and can make in a snap."*

ANN BETZ

Chocolate-Covered Worms

Melt **chocolate chips** and get **chow mein noodles**. Put them in the bowl and mix it up and put them on a tray, like you're going to make little cookies. Then put them in the refrigerator and let them freeze and then eat them.

BRIDGET O'DONNELL

Popcorn Balls

6 tablespoons butter
3 cups miniature marshmallows
3 tablespoons orange gelatin
Popcorn

Melt butter in a saucepan. Add marshmallows and stir until melted. Blend in gelatin. Pour over popcorn and mix well. Butter hands and form into balls.

THE EVERYTHING BOOK

Snuffles Truffles

1 (8-ounce) package cream cheese
1 tablespoon honey
1/3 cup chopped raisins
2 tablespoons chopped nuts
Graham cracker crumbs

Combine all ingredients except cracker crumbs. Roll into balls. Then roll into crumbs and chill.

THE EVERYTHING BOOK

No-Cook Mint Patties

1/3 cup light corn syrup
1/4 cup butter
1 teaspoon peppermint extract
1/2 teaspoon salt
1 pound confectioners' sugar
1 drop each red and green food coloring

Blend corn syrup, butter and peppermint. Add salt and sugar. Divide mixture into three parts. Make one part red, one part green and leave one part white. Shape into balls and flatten with fork on waxed paper. Let dry.

THE EVERYTHING BOOK

Banana Bobs

Bananas, cut into chunks
Honey
Wheat germ

Dip bananas in the honey and wheat germ. Use toothpicks for serving.

THE EVERYTHING BOOK

Toffee

1 cup sugar
1 cup butter
3 tablespoons water
1 teaspoon vanilla
3 milk chocolate bars (1.2 ounces)
1/2 cup sliced almonds

Boil sugar, butter and water until mixture browns and pulls away from side of pan (about 10 minutes). Add vanilla. Pour into buttered cookie sheet. Place chocolate bars on top of hot sugar mixture. Spread chocolate evenly as it melts. Sprinkle nuts over chocolate. Cool. Break into pieces.

THE EVERYTHING BOOK

Popsicles

1 cup hot water
2 cups lemonade
1 package flavored gelatin

Mix and pour into popsicle mold or ice cube tray. Freeze.

THE EVERYTHING BOOK

KIDS RECIPES

White Chocolate Pretzels

1 pound white chocolate
1-3/4 cups Spanish peanuts, chopped
1-3/4 cups thin pretzel sticks

Melt chocolate and add peanuts and pretzels. Drop onto waxed paper. (Makes about 50)

THE EVERYTHING BOOK

Popcorn Ball Snowman

Mix some popped **popcorn** with melted **butter** and miniature **marshmallows** to make popcorn balls. Make large, medium and small. While balls are still warm, stick the large, medium and small balls on top of each other to form snowmen. Use toothpicks or popsicle sticks for arms, and **gumdrops** for buttons.

THE EVERYTHING BOOK

Bird's Nest Salad

1 carrot, grated
1/2 cup Chinese noodles
1 tablespoon mayonnaise, to moisten
1/4 cup cooked peas or grapes

Combine carrots, noodles and mayonnaise. Place a mound on a salad plate. Press the mound in the middle with a spoon to form a nest. Add a few peas or grapes to the nest for "eggs" and serve.

THE EVERYTHING BOOK

340

Crisp Pastel Cookies

3/4 cup butter
1/2 cup sugar
1 (3-ounce) package gelatin, any flavor
2 eggs
1 teaspoon vanilla
2-1/2 cups all-purpose flour
1 teaspoon baking powder
1 teaspoon salt
Sugar

Preheat oven to 400 degrees. Combine butter, sugar and gelatin in a large mixing bowl. Beat until light and fluffy. Add eggs and vanilla. In another bowl sift together flour, baking powder and salt. Add to creamed mixture. Roll dough to 3/4-inch balls. Place 3 inches apart on ungreased cookie sheet. Flatten each with bottom of glass dipped in sugar. (Also can be used in cookie press.) Bake for 6-8 minutes. Watch because they burn easily.

KAY SHAW

"Cow Pie" No-Bake Cookies

1-3/4 cups sugar
1/4 cup margarine
1/2 cup milk
3 tablespoons cocoa
1/2 cup peanut butter
1 teaspoon vanilla
3 cups rolled oats

Combine sugar, margarine, milk and cocoa in a saucepan and boil for 1-2 minutes. Add peanut butter, vanilla and oats. Mix thoroughly. Drop by spoonful on wax or foil paper. (Makes 2 dozen cookies) *"These are Angie's favorite cookies."*

LORRI MIHELICH

Ice Cream Cone Cupcakes

Flat-bottomed ice cream cones
Cupcake Mix
Frosting
Colored sprinkles

Preheat oven to 350 degrees. Make batter for cupcakes as directed on cake mix package. Place the cones on a cookie sheet and fill 1/2 full (about 1/4 cup of batter). If you put in too much or too little, the cones will not have a nice rounded top. Bake 15-18 minutes. Cool. Give each child their own spreading knives and container of frosting and sprinkles. Let them frost and decorate their own cones.

THE EVERYTHING BOOK

Fruit Leather

2 cups fruit pulp (apple, peach, pear, strawberries, apricots, etc.)
1/2 cup sugar

When using fresh fruit, cook and put through a food mill to remove stems and seeds. Or remove seeds and stems, chop and cook, then puree in a blender or food processor, one cup at a time. Mix fruit and sugar. Spread on plastic wrap attached to a cookie sheet with tape. Mixture should be very thin, perhaps only 1/8 to 1/16 of an inch thick. Bake in 150 degree oven until fruit looks like leather. Leave door ajar slightly for moisture to escape. When no longer sticky, cool slightly, remove plastic wrap and roll up in a log.

ANN BETZ

Rocky Road Cake

1/2 cup butter
1/2 cup vegetable oil
1 cup water
2 cups all-purpose flour, sifted
1-3/4 cups sugar
1 teaspoon salt
1/4 cup unsweetened cocoa
2 eggs
1/2 cup buttermilk mixed with 1 teaspoon baking
    soda
1-1/2 teaspoons vanilla

Preheat oven to 350 degrees. In a small saucepan, bring butter, oil and water to a boil. Remove from heat and cool 10 minutes. Combine flour, sugar, salt and cocoa, pressing out all the lumps. Pour in butter-oil mixture and beat just until smooth. Beat in eggs, then stir in buttermilk-soda solution and vanilla. Pour batter into 13 x 9-inch pan (greased well) and bake 30-35 minutes or until cake begins to pull from sides of pan. Let cool at least 45 minutes before frosting.

FROSTING:
1/4 cup unsweetened cocoa
1/3 cup buttermilk
1/2 cup butter
3-1/2 cups confectioners' sugar
2/3 cup miniature marshmallows
1/2 cup chopped walnuts (optional)
1 teaspoon vanilla

Heat and stir cocoa, buttermilk and butter over low heat until mixture is smooth. Transfer mixture to mixing bowl. Beat in sugar until mixture is of good spreading consistency. Stir in marshmallows, nuts and vanilla. *"Everybody loves this cake, but kids go crazy over it and love to help mix the batter, frosting and help spread frosting on cake."*

SUSAN HURWITZ

343

KIDS RECIPES

Butter

1 carton whipping cream
Baby food jars
Salt (optional)

Divide one carton of whipping cream between a few jars and shake, shake, shake and shake. Separate the butter from the buttermilk. Sample each. You may want to salt the butter. Serve with crackers.

THE EVERYTHING BOOK

Dry Apple Rings

Apples, cut into rings
Salted water

Peel, core and cut apples into rings. Dip into salted water for 15 minutes. Dry for two weeks. Can make raisins from grapes the same way.

THE EVERYTHING BOOK

Special Fruit Salad

1/2 peach or pear (canned or fresh)
Decorations: Cloves, raisins, cheese, olives,
**   pimento, celery, carrot strips**
Lettuce

Use the peach or pear half for a face. Make eyes, nose and mouth with cloves, raisins, small cheese cut-outs or pieces of olive or pimento. A lettuce leaf can be a skirt and celelry or carrot strips make arms and legs.

THE EVERYTHING BOOK

Latkes
(Potato Pancakes)

12 large potatoes, washed and peeled
9 tablespoons all-purpose flour
1-1/2 teaspoons baking powder
3 teaspoons salt
3 beaten eggs
Vegetable oil for frying
Applesauce, sour cream or jam

Cut potatoes in half and grate. Put potatoes, flour, baking powder, salt and eggs in bowl. Mix until smooth. Mom or Dad should drop the mixture by spoonfuls into a frying pan with about 1/4 inch of hot oil. Turn when brown. Dry on paper towels. Serve plain or with applesauce, sour cream or jam.*(Onion, a traditional ingredient has been left out; kids do not seem to like it!)*

THE EVERYTHING BOOK

Bunny Salad

2 large carrots (peeled and grated)
2 apples (washed and diced)
1/2 cup diced celery
1/2 cup raisins
1/4 teaspoon salt
1/4 cup mayonnaise
1/4 cup sour cream
1/4 teaspoon vinegar or lemon juice

Have children peel and grate carrots. Dice apples and celery and help measure rest of ingredients. Refrigerate until served.

THE EVERYTHING BOOK

Red Jello Hearts

4 envelopes unflavored gelatin
9 ounces cherry gelatin
4 cups boiling water

Dissolve gelatin in boiling water and pour into shallow baking pan. Chill. When gelatin is set, cut with metal heart-shaped cookie cutter. Hearts are eaten with hands.

THE EVERYTHING BOOK

Applesauce Jello Mold

1 (3-ounce) package raspberry gelatin
1 cup boiling water
1 (15-ounce) jar applesauce

In a mixing bowl dissolve gelatin in water. Add applesauce and stir to mix. Pour into mold and refrigerate until solid. (6 servings) *"Children and adults love this and it is hard to find something that children and adults both love. Especially when you have picky eaters like I do."*

MATTHEW RADER'S MOTHER

Pretzels

1 package dry yeast, dissolved in cold water
3 cups flour
1 teaspoon sugar
1 teaspoon kosher salt

Mix yeast mixture to flour and sugar. Add about one more cup of flour until it can be kneaded. Knead on floured countertop. Shape. Sprinkle with kosher salt. Bake at 350 degrees for about 20 minutes. (Makes 20 pretzels)

THE EVERYTHING BOOK

Pumpkin Bread
(A Halloween Favorite!)

2 cups sugar
2-1/2 cups all-purpose flour
1 teaspoon cinnamon
1 teaspoon salt
2 teaspoons baking soda
1 cup oil
2 eggs
2 cups canned pumpkin
1 teaspoon vanilla
1 cup raisins
1 cup chopped nuts

Sift all dry ingredients in a large bowl. Add rest of ingredients. Add raisins and nuts. Mix. Bake at 350 degrees for 1 hour and 15 minutes. Bake in greased loaf pans. (Makes 2 loaves)

THE EVERYTHING BOOK

Pink Bread

1/4 cup warm water (115-120 degrees F)
1 package dry yeast
7-1/2 to 8-1/2 cups unbleached all-purpose flour
1 teaspoon salt
1/4 cup oil
2 tablespoons sugar
2 cups tomato juice
1/4 cup ketchup

Combine water and yeast. Put 4 cups flour, salt, oil and sugar into a bowl. Add tomato juice, ketchup and yeast mixture and beat well. Add enough flour to make a dough that is not sticky. Knead 10 minutes. Bake at 350 degrees for 1 hour.

THE EVERYTHING BOOK

KIDS RECIPES

Chocolate Fondue

1 (6-ounce) package chocolate chips
1/2 cup sugar
1/2 cup milk
1/2 cup chunky peanut butter
Condiments for dipping

Melt the chocolate chips, sugar and milk in a fondue pot; then add peanut butter. Serve with pineapple chunks, bananas, apples, marshmallows, pecans, maraschino cherries, angel food cake pieces. *"A fun but messy party idea."*

CAROL MESZAROS

Elephant Stew

1 elephant
2 rabbits (optional)
Salt and pepper to taste

Cut elephant into bite-size pieces (takes about 2 months). Cook about 4 weeks at 465 degrees. For larger groups add 2 rabbits, but only if necessary as most people don't like to find hare in their stew. Season to taste. (3,800 servings)

ANONYMOUS

Peanut Butter and Jelly Sandwiches

You put **jelly** on some **bread** and **peanut butter**. You put two pieces of bread together and eat.

TINA ARMES

Green Eggs and Ham

Green food coloring
Scrambled eggs
Ham

First read the book "Green Eggs and Ham" by Dr. Seuss.
Using food color, make green scrambled eggs and green
ham.

THE EVERYTHING BOOK

Quick Homemade Pizzas

2 pounds ground beef
2 (8-ounce) cans refrigerated biscuits (20)
Pizza sauce
Pepperoni
Grated mozzarella

Brown beef in a skillet. Roll biscuits into circles of 4-5 inches.
Place on greased cookie sheet. Top each biscuit with pizza
sauce, beef or pepperoni sliced thin. Sprinkle with cheese.
Bake at 400 degrees for 10-12 minutes. (Makes 20 small
pizzas)

THE EVERYTHING BOOK

Dog Kabobs

Cut up some cooked **hot dogs** into bite-sized pieces. Also
cut up some **cheese** and **pineapple** into bite-sized chunks.
Spear all the pieces with sandwich toothpicks.

THE EVERYTHING BOOK

349

KIDS RECIPES

Index

INDEX

ANN ARBOR'S COOKIN'!
c/o Ronald McDonald House®
1600 Washington Heights
Ann Arbor, MI 48104

Please send me _____ copies of Ann Arbor's Cookin' @ $12.00 each   _____
Postage and handling in Continental U.S. @ $ 2.00 each   _____
TOTAL ENCLOSED   _____

Please make checks payable to Arbor House
Name _____
Street _____
City _____ State _____ Zip _____

- -

ANN ARBOR'S COOKIN'!
c/o Ronald McDonald House®
1600 Washington Heights
Ann Arbor, MI 48104

Please send me _____ copies of Ann Arbor's Cookin' @ $12.00 each   _____
Postage and handling in Continental U.S. @ $ 2.00 each   _____
TOTAL ENCLOSED   _____

Please make checks payable to Arbor House
Name _____
Street _____
City _____ State _____ Zip _____

- -

ANN ARBOR'S COOKIN'!
c/o Ronald McDonald House®
1600 Washington Heights
Ann Arbor, MI 48104

Please send me _____ copies of Ann Arbor's Cookin' @ $12.00 each   _____
Postage and handling in Continental U.S. @ $ 2.00 each   _____
TOTAL ENCLOSED   _____

Please make checks payable to Arbor House
Name _____
Street _____
City _____ State _____ Zip _____

NOTES